深圳市华大基因学院指定教材

English for Genomics and Its Application

基因组学及应用专业英语

主　编◎孙　颖
副主编◎黄　玉　石　琼

中山大学出版社
·广州·

版权所有　翻印必究

图书在版编目（CIP）数据

基因组学及应用专业英语/孙颖主编；黄玉，石琼副主编. —广州：中山大学出版社，2015.9

ISBN 978 - 7 - 306 - 05394 - 7

Ⅰ. ①基… Ⅱ. ①孙… ②黄… ③石… Ⅲ. ①基因组学—英语—高等学校—教材 Ⅳ. ①H31

中国版本图书馆 CIP 数据核字（2015）第 185915 号

出版人：	徐　劲
策划编辑：	周建华
责任编辑：	周建华
封面设计：	曾　斌
责任校对：	江克清
责任技编：	何雅涛
出版发行：	中山大学出版社
电　　话：	编辑部 020 - 84111996，84113349，84111997，84110779
	发行部 020 - 84111998，84111981，84111160
地　　址：	广州市新港西路 135 号
邮　　编：	510275　　　　　传　真：020 - 84036565
网　　址：	http://www.zsup.com.cn　　E-mail:zdcbs@ mail.sysu.edu.cn
印　刷　者：	佛山市浩文彩色印刷有限公司
规　　格：	787mm×1092mm　1/16　14.25 印张　321 千字
版次印次：	2015 年 9 月第 1 版　2015 年 9 月第 1 次印刷
定　　价：	38.00 元

如发现本书因印装质量影响阅读，请与出版社发行部联系调换

本书编委会

主　编：孙　颖
副主编：黄　玉　石　琼
编　委：孙　颖　黄　玉　石　琼
　　　　赵晓萌　陈洁明　徐军民

前　言

基因组学在生命科学各个领域中发挥着越来越重要的作用，成为当今生命科学、医学等重要研究领域强有力的工具。基因组学及其研究涉及的相关方法和技术，如基因组学样本的规范化收集、测序技术、大数据的产生、存贮以及数据的分析和应用等，已成为目前生物医学领域关注的焦点。同时，近年来，随着第二代测序技术的迅速发展，数以亿计的原始测序数据正源源不断地从测序仪上产生，这些海量的数据给生物信息学、基因组学及应用等带来了全新的挑战。

为了帮助在校高年级大学生以及研究生学习、了解基因组和在生命科学各领域的研究进展及其应用，我们编写了《基因组学及应用专业英语》一书，系统地介绍在大数据背景下，新一代测序技术、基因组学及其在医学、农业、环境、生物多样性等方面的应用进展，为生命科学及医学等领域的学生、学者和研究人员提供专业英语教材及辅助阅读材料。本书既适用于研究生的专业阅读和参考材料，也可以作为教师和从事生物医学研究相关人员的专业英语学习资料。

本教材以内容精炼、知识新颖、难易适中作为选材的主要标准，以英文原版教材为参考，精选来自 Nature、Science 等顶级期刊中有关基因组及其应用的文献，确保使用最纯正的英文表达，讲述最核心的技术路线，涵盖最前沿的研究进展，使学生在学习过程中既能学到前沿的基因组学及应用专业知识，又能提高学术英语能力。

本教材内容覆盖广泛，包括基础的高通量测序技术（二代测序技术）的原理和应用，测序产出的大数据及其在个性化医疗、动物和植物基因组及环境基因组研究、生物多样性保护上的应用，以及基于基因组学的生物样本库建设和资源收集现状和展望。教材总共分为 8 章，每章分成 3 课，各围绕一个主题，选取 1～2 篇高质量综述或数篇文章的精华段落作为主要内容，由浅入深，涉及内容范围由大到小，让读者对基因组及其应用有一个广泛而深入的了解和把握。

教材每课课后均编排词汇表（Glossary），以帮助学生掌握基因组学核心词汇。此外，除常规的音标标注外，还加入了专业英语常用词根、词缀、构词法的标注和说明，常用短语和专有名词缩写也一一在列，使记单词变得事半功倍。同时，在每篇文章中以黑体突出显示专业词汇，使学生在学习时能更快找到它们在文中的位置，更好地理解其含义及使用方法。词汇表后设有难句解释（Notes to Difficult Sentences）模块，对难句进行翻译并对涉及的专业知识重点进行详细解释，从而进一步拓展专业知识，在提升学生的专业英语阅读能力的同时，帮助学生读懂、读通、读透，进而完全掌握课程内容，扩宽知识面。本教材每章节后编排了丰富的课后阅读材料（Reading Material），材料内容新颖有趣，简单易读，贴近生活，让学生充分消化吸收所学内容，进一步强化知识，做到活学活用。

本教材的撰写与出版得到深圳市科技计划深港创新圈项目"DNA条形码系统支撑的深港水产食品安全体系建设"（SGLH20131010105856414）和江苏省镇江市高层次创新创业人才引进计划项目"长江流域经济鱼类的基因组学研究及育种应用"的资助，还得到深圳华大基因研究院与华大（镇江）水产科技产业有限公司的大力支持。此外，本书参考和使用了国内外一些专业文献资料和图表以及国外生物领域的杂志和网站内容，在此一并表示衷心的感谢！

本书已在华大基因研究院创新班和中国科学院大学华大教育研究中心研究生班试用，获得一致好评，并在此基础上，进一步修订。由于编者能力有限，错误、缺点在所难免。书中如有不妥之处，敬请同行与读者批评指正。

孙　颖

2015年6月8日

Contents

Chapter 1 Next-generation Sequencing (NGS) ⋯ 1
  Lesson 1   From Convention to Second-generation Sequencing ⋯ 2
  Lesson 2   Application of Next-generation Sequencing ⋯ 8
  Lesson 3   First Baby Born after Full Genetic Screening of Embryos ⋯ 12

Chapter 2 Big Data ⋯ 25
  Lesson 1   Too Much Information: Better Health from Big Data ⋯ 26
  Lesson 2   Life Sciences in Big Data Era ⋯ 31
  Lesson 3   Big Data Meets Public Health ⋯ 36

Chapter 3 Personal Genomics & Personalized Medicine ⋯ 48
  Lesson 1   The Advent of Personal Genome Sequencing ⋯ 49
  Lesson 2   The Future of Personal Genomics ⋯ 55
  Lesson 3   Obstacles to the Translation of Personalized Medicine into the Clinic ⋯ 59

Chapter 4 Animal & Plant Genome Research and Its Agricultural Applications ⋯ 72
  Lesson 1   Plant and Animal Sequencing ⋯ 73
  Lesson 2   Animal Code: Our Favorite Genomes ⋯ 79
  Lesson 3   Sequencing of Animal/Plant Genomes and Its Application ⋯ 87

Chapter 5 Metagenomics ⋯ 102
  Lesson 1   Metagenomics: The Science of Biological Diversity ⋯ 103
  Lesson 2   How Gut Bacteria Help Make Us Fat and Thin ⋯ 109
  Lesson 3   Next-generation Sequencing Propels Environmental Genomics to the Front
             Line of Research ⋯ 115

Chapter 6 Genomes and Biodiversity ⋯ 128
  Lesson 1   Genome 10K: a Proposal to Obtain Whole-Genome Sequence for 10 000
             Vertebrate Species ⋯ 129
  Lesson 2   Biodiversity, Genomes, and DNA Sequence Databases ⋯ 135

Lesson 3　　Examples of Genome & Transcriptome Projects ················ 141

Chapter 7　Biobanking ·· 154
　　Lesson 1　　Current Status, Challenges, Policies & Bioethics of Biobanks ············ 155
　　Lesson 2　　Building Better Biobank ·· 160
　　Lesson 3　　Biobank Promises to Pinpoint the Cause of Disease ···················· 166

Chapter 8　Big Resources in Biobanks ·· 178
　　Lesson 1　　Specimen Types for DNA Net Earth ·· 179
　　Lesson 2　　Specimen Collections in U. S. Biobanks: Results from a National Survey ······ 184
　　Lesson 3　　Examples of Aquatic Biobanks Worldwide ·· 190

Glossary ·· 202

References ·· 215

Chapter 1   Next-generation Sequencing (NGS)

Over the past several years, next-generation DNA sequencing technologies have catapulted to prominence, with increasingly widespread adoption of several platforms that individually implement different flavors of massively parallel cyclic-array sequencing. Common characteristics extend beyond the technologies themselves, to the quantity and quality of data that are generated, such that all raise a similar set of new challenges for experimental design, data analysis and interpretation. The reduction in the costs of DNA sequencing by several orders of magnitude is democratizing the extent to which individual investigators can pursue projects at a scale previously accessible only to major genome centers. The dramatic increase in interest in this area is also evident in the number of groups that are now working on sequencing methods to supplant even the new technologies discussed here. Given the current state of flux, it is difficult to peer even a few years into the future, but we anticipate that next-generation sequencing technologies will become as widespread, commoditized and routine as microarray technology has become over the past decade. Also analogous to microarrays, we expect that the challenges will quickly shift from mastering of the technologies themselves to the question of how best to go about extracting biologically meaningful or clinically useful insights from a very large amount of data.

Lesson 1
From Convention to Second-generation Sequencing

DNA sequence represents a single format onto which a broad range of biological phenomena can be projected for high-throughput data collection. Over the past three years, massively parallel DNA sequencing platforms have become widely available, reducing the cost of DNA sequencing by over two orders of magnitude, and democratizing the field by putting the sequencing capacity of a major genome center in the hands of individual investigators. These new technologies are rapidly evolving, and near-term challenges include the development of robust protocols for generating sequencing **libraries**, building effective new approaches to data-analysis, and often a rethinking of experimental design. Next-generation DNA sequencing has the potential to dramatically accelerate biological and biomedical research, by enabling the comprehensive analysis of genomes, transcriptomes and interactomes to become inexpensive, routine and widespread, rather than requiring significant production-scale efforts.

The field of DNA sequencing technology development has a rich and diverse history. However, the overwhelming majority of DNA sequence production to date has relied on some version of the Sanger biochemistry. Over the past five years, the incentive for developing entirely new strategies for DNA sequencing has emerged on at least four levels, undeniably reinvigorating this field. First, in the wake of the Human Genome Project, there are few remaining avenues of optimization through which significant reductions in the cost of conventional DNA sequencing can be achieved. Second, the potential utility of short-read sequencing has been tremendously strengthened by the availability of whole genome assemblies for *Homo sapiens* and all major model organisms, as these effectively provide a reference against which short reads can be mapped. Third, a growing variety of molecular methods have been developed, whereby a broad range of biological phenomena can be assessed by high-throughput DNA sequencing (e.g., genetic variation, RNA expression, protein-DNA interactions and **chromosome** conformation). And fourth, general progress in technology across disparate fields, including microscopy, surface chemistry, nucleotide biochemistry, **polymerase** engineering, computation, data storage and others, have made alternative strategies for DNA sequencing increasingly practical to realize.

1. Sanger sequencing

Since the early 1990s, DNA sequence production has almost exclusively been carried out with **capillary**-based, semi-automated implementations of the Sanger biochemistry (Fig. 1.1a). In high-throughput production pipelines, DNA to be sequenced is prepared by one of two approaches: first, for shotgun *de novo* sequencing, randomly fragmented DNA is cloned into a high-copy-number plasmid, which is then used to transform *Escherichia coli*; or second, for targeted **resequencing**, PCR amplification is carried out with primers that flank the target. The output of both approaches is an amplified template, either as many "**clonal**" copies of a single plasmid insert present within a spatially isolated bacterial colony that can be picked, or as many PCR **amplicons** present within a single reaction volume. The sequencing biochemistry takes place in a "cycle sequencing" reaction, in which cycles of template denaturation, primer annealing and primer extension are performed. The primer is complementary to known sequence immediately flanking the region of interest. Each round of primer extension is stochastically terminated by the incorporation of **fluorescently labeled** dideoxynucleotides (ddNTPs). In the resulting mixture of end-labeled extension products, the label on the terminating ddNTP of any given fragment corresponds to the nucleotide identity of its terminal position. Sequence is determined by high-resolution electrophoretic separation of the single-stranded, end-labeled extension products in a capillary based polymer gel. Laser excitation of fluorescent labels as fragments of discreet lengths exit the capillary, coupled to four-color detection of **emission spectra**, provides the readout that is represented in a Sanger sequencing "trace". Software translates these traces into DNA sequence, while also generating error probabilities for each **base-call**. The approach that is taken for subsequent analysis—for example, genome assembly or variant identification—depends on precisely what is being sequenced and why. Simultaneous electrophoresis in 96 or 384 independent capillaries provides a limited level of parallelization. After three decades of gradual improvement, the Sanger biochemistry can be applied to achieve read-lengths of up to 1000 bp, and per-base "raw" accuracies as high as 99.999%. In the context of high throughput shotgun genomic sequencing, Sanger sequencing costs on the order of $0.50 per kilobase.

2. Second-generation DNA sequencing

Alternative strategies for DNA sequencing can be grouped into several categories. These include (I) microelectrophoretic methods; (II) sequencing by **hybridization**; (III) real-time observation of single molecules; (IV) cyclic-array sequencing. Here, we use "second generation" in reference to the various implementations of cyclic-array sequencing that have recently been realized in a commercial product (Fig. 1.1b). The concept of cyclic-array sequencing can be summarized as the sequencing of a dense array of DNA features by iterative cycles of enzymatic manipulation and imaging-based data collection. Two reports in 2005 described the first integrated implementations of cyclic-array strategies that were both practical and cost-competitive with conventional sequencing, and other groups have quickly followed.

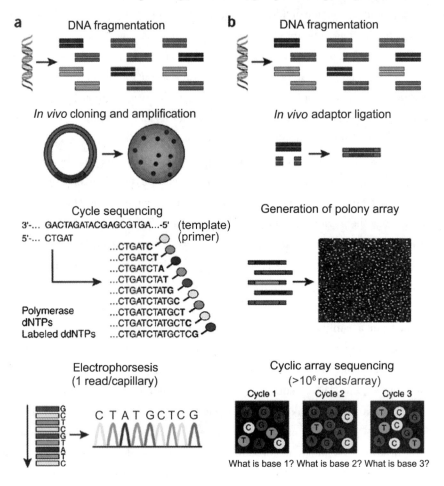

Figure 1.1 Work flow of conventional(a)versus second-generation(b)sequencing

Although these platforms are quite diverse in sequencing biochemistry as well as in how the array is generated, their workflows are conceptually similar (Fig. 1.1b). Library preparation is accomplished by random fragmentation of DNA, followed by **in vitro ligation** of common **adaptor** sequences. Alternative protocols can be used to generate **jumping libraries** of mate-paired tags with controllable distance distributions. The generation of clonally clustered amplicons to serve as sequencing features can be achieved by several approaches, including **in situ** polonies, emulsion PCR or bridge PCR. What is common to these methods is that PCR amplicons derived from any given single library molecule end up spatially clustered, either to a single location on a planar substrate (in situ polonies, bridge PCR), or to the surface of micron-scale beads, which can be recovered and arrayed (emulsion PCR). The sequencing process itself consists of alternating cycles of **enzyme**-driven biochemistry and imaging-based data acquisition. The platforms that are discussed here all rely on sequencing by synthesis, that is, serial extension of primed templates, but the enzyme driving the synthesis can be either a polymerase or a **ligase**. Data are acquired by imaging of the full array at each cycle (e.g., of fluorescently labeled nucleotides incorporated by a polymerase). Global advantages of second-generation or cyclic-array strategies, relative to Sanger sequencing, include the following:

(1) *in vitro* construction of a sequencing library, followed by *in vitro* clonal amplification to generate sequencing features, circumvents several bottlenecks that restrict the parallelism of conventional sequencing (that is, transformation of *E. coli* and colony picking).

(2) Array-based sequencing enables a much higher degree of parallelism than conventional capillary-based sequencing. As the effective size of sequencing features can be on the order of 1 μm, hundreds of millions of sequencing reads can potentially be obtained in parallel by rastered imaging of a reasonably sized surface area.

(3) Because array features are immobilized to a planar surface, they can be **enzymatically** manipulated by a single reagent volume. Although **microliter**-scale reagent volumes are used in practice, these are essentially amortized over the full set of sequencing features on the array, dropping the effective reagent volume per feature to the scale of **picoliters** or **femtoliters**.

Collectively, these differences translate into dramatically lower costs for DNA sequence production.

Glossary

library /ˈlaɪbreri/
文库
A collection of DNA fragments that is stored and propagated in a population of micro-organisms through the process of molecular cloning.

Homo sapiens /ˌhoʊmoʊ ˈseɪpienz/
人；智人
Homo sapiens is the binomial nomenclature (also known as the scientific name) for the human species.

chromosome /ˈkroʊməsoʊm/
染色体
A chromosome is a packaged and organized structure containing most of the DNA of a living organism.

polymerase /ˈpɒləməˌreɪs/
聚合酶
An enzyme that synthesizes long chains or polymers of nucleic acids. DNA or RNA polymerases are used to assemble DNA or RNA molecules, respectively, by copying a DNA or RNA template strand using base-pairing interactions.

capillary /ˈkæpəleri/
毛细管；毛细管的
Capillaries are the smallest of a body's blood vessels that make up the microcirculation. These microvessels, measuring around 5 to 10 μm in diameter, connect

arterioles and venules, and they help to enable the exchange of water, oxygen, carbon dioxide, and many other nutrients and waste substances between the blood and the tissues surrounding them.

resequencing /reˈzekwənsɪŋ/

重测序

re + sequence + ing

The purpose of the sequencing of part of an individual (whose reference genome is already known) genome is to detect sequence differences between the individual and the standard genome of the species.

clonal /ˈklounəl/

无性（繁殖）系的；无性（繁殖）系般的

clone—clonal, clonally, cloner, cloning, monoclone, polyclone

amplicon /ˈæmplɪkɒn/

扩增子

An amplicon is a piece of DNA or RNA that is source and/or product of natural or artificial amplification or replication events.

fluorescently labeled

荧光标记的

fluorescent—fluorescently

emission spectra

发射光谱

base-call

碱基识别

Base calling is the process of assigning bases (nucleo-bases) to chromatogram peaks.

hybridization /ˌhaɪbrɪdaɪˈzeʃn/

杂交；配种

hybrid—hybridize; hybridization; hybridoma

(1) The process of combining different varieties of organisms to create a hybrid.

(2) The process of joining two complementary strands of nucleic acids (DNA, RNA or oligonucleotides).

in vitro /ɪnˈvitrou/

体外；离体

In vitro studies are performed with cells or biological molecules studied outside their normal biological context.

ligation /laɪˈgeɪʃn/

（核酸分子末端）连接

The covalent linking of two ends of DNA or RNA molecules, most commonly done using DNA ligase, RNA ligase (ATP) or other enzymes.

adaptor /əˈdæptə/

接头

An adapter is a short, chemically synthesized, double stranded DNA molecule which is used to link the ends of two other DNA molecules. It may be used to add sticky ends to cDNA allowing it to be ligated into the plasmid much more efficiently.

jumping library

跨步文库

A collection of genomic DNA fragments generated by chromosome jumping.

in situ /ɪnˈsaɪtuː/

原位；在原地

To examine the phenomenon exactly in place where it occurs (e.g. without moving it to special medium).

enzyme /ˈenzaɪm/

酶

ligase /ˈlaɪˌgeɪs/

连接酶

Ligase is a specific type of enzyme that facilitates the joining of DNA/RNA strands together by catalyzing the formation of a phosphodiester bond.

enzymatically /enzaɪˈmætɪklɪ/

酶促地

Enzymes are molecules that accelerate, or catalyze the chemical reactions.

microliter /ˈmaɪkroʊlitə/

微升（μL） $1\mu L = 1 mm^3$

picoliter /pɪkəˈlaɪtə/

皮升（pL） $1 pL = 10^3 \mu m^3$

femtoliter /ˈfemtoʊlitə/

飞升（fL） $1 fL = 1 \mu m^3$

Notes to Difficult Sentences

(1) Second, the potential utility of short-read sequencing has been tremendously strengthened by the availability of whole genome assemblies for *Homo sapiens* and all major model organisms, as these effectively provide a reference against which short reads can be mapped.

　　第二，人类及其他主要模式生物的全基因组组装项目有效地为短序列的匹配提供参考序列，从而极大提高了短序列测序的潜在效用。

　　拓展：自 1985 年美国科学家率先发起人类基因组计划以来，随着测序技术的不断发展，越来越多的基因组计划不断被推出和实施，例如，经济作物如水稻、棉花、番茄、花生的基因组计划，重要动物如大熊猫、鲤鱼、牛、蜜蜂的基因组计划，等等。现在，涵盖数以千万个体或物种的大规模基因组计划不断被提出，如 i5k（5000 种昆虫基因组计划）、G10K（万种脊椎动物基因组计划）、100 000 Genomes Project（英国 10 万基因组计划）等，生命科学领域全面迈入基因组和后基因组时代。

(2) What is common to these methods is that PCR amplicons derived from any given single library molecule end up spatially clustered, either to a single location on a planar substrate (*in situ* polonies, bridge PCR), or to the surface of micron-scale beads, which can be recovered and arrayed (emulsion PCR).

　　这些技术的共同点是，通过任何给定的单个文库得到的 PCR 扩增子最后都会在一定空间上聚集成群，要么聚集到平面上的某一点（原位克隆阵列，桥式 PCR），要么聚集到微米级的小磁珠上，可再次重新获取和排序（乳液 PCR）。

　　拓展：乳液 PCR 主要用于基因组测序。把用作 DNA 扩增模板的 DNA 片段分散在油液的小水滴内，逐一对小水滴内的 DNA 模板进行 PCR 扩增。理想状态下，一个小水滴只含有一个 DNA 模板和一个磁珠，由于小水滴内的 DNA 模板数目极少，可以减少当大量长短不一的模板一起扩增时所产生的短片段易被扩增的偏差，也可降低模板之间通过同源重组而扩增产生非天然连接的 DNA 片段的机会。

Lesson 2
Application of Next-generation Sequencing

The past several years have seen an accelerating flurry of publications in which next-generation sequencing is applied for a variety of goals. Important applications include: (I) full-genome resequencing or more targeted discovery of **mutations** or **polymorphisms**; (II) mapping of structural rearrangements, which may include copy number variation, balanced translocation breakpoints and chromosomal inversions; (III) "RNA-Seq", analogous to **expressed sequence tags** (**EST**) or **serial analysis of gene expression** (**SAGE**), where shotgun libraries derived from mRNA or small RNAs are deeply sequenced; the counts corresponding to individual species can be used for quantification over a broad dynamic range, and the sequences themselves can be used for **annotation** (e.g., splice junctions and transcript boundaries); (IV) large-scale analysis of DNA **methylation**, by deep sequencing of bisulfite-treated DNA; (V) "ChIP-Seq", or genome-wide mapping of DNA-protein interactions, by deep sequencing of DNA fragments pulled down by chromatin **immunoprecipitation**. Over the next few years, the list of applications will undoubtedly grow, as will the sophistication weth which existing applications are carried out.

The applications of NGS seem almost endless, allowing for rapid advances in many fields related to the biological sciences. Resequencing of the human genomes is being performed to identify genes and regulatory elements involved in pathological processes. NGS has also provided a wealth of knowledge for comparative biology studies through whole-genome sequencing of a wide variety of organisms. NGS is applied in the fields of public health and **epidemiology** through the sequencing of bacterial and viral species to facilitate the identification of novel virulence factors.

Additionally, gene expression studies using RNA-Seq (NGS of RNA) have begun to replace the use of microarray analysis, providing researchers and clinicians with the ability to visualize RNA expression in sequence form. These are simply some of the broad applications that begin to skim the surface of what NGS can offer the researcher and the clinician. As NGS continues to grow in popularity, it is inevitable that there will be additional innovative applications.

Chapter 1 Next-generation Sequencing (NGS)

1. Whole-exome sequencing

Mutation events that occur in gene-coding or control regions can give rise to indistinguishable clinical presentations, leaving the **diagnosing** clinician with many possible causes for a given condition or disease. With NGS, clinicians are provided a fast, affordable, and thorough way to determine the genetic cause of a disease. Although high-throughput sequencing of the entire human genome is possible, researchers and clinicians are typically interested in only the protein-coding regions of the genome, referred to as the exome. The exome comprises just over 1% of the genome and is therefore much more cost-effective to sequence than the entire genome, while providing sequence information for protein-coding regions (Fig. 1.2).

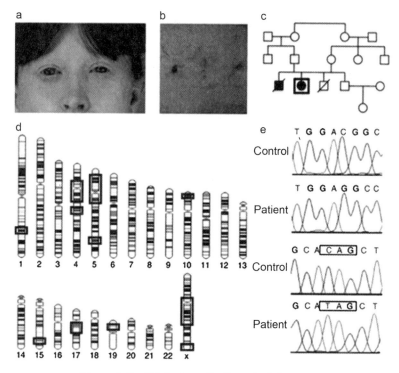

Figure 1.2 Clinical application of whole-exome sequencing in the detection of two disease-causing mutations

Figure 1.2 demonstrates the direct effect that NGS can have on the correct diagnoses of a patient. It summarizes the use of homozygosity mapping followed by whole-exome sequencing to identify two disease-causing mutations in a patient with **oculocutaneous albinism** and congenital neutropenia. **a** and **b** display the phenotypic traits common to oculocutaneous albinism type 4 and neutropenia observed in this patient. **c** is a pedigree of the patient's family, both the affected and unaffected individuals. The idiogram (graphic chromosome map) in **d** highlights the areas of genetic homozygosity. These regions were identified by single-nucleotide-polymorphism array analysis and were considered possible locations for the disease-causing mutation (s). **e** and **f** display chromatograms for the two disease-causing mutations identified by whole-exome sequencing. **e** depicts the mutation in SLC45A2, and **f** depicts the mutation in G6PC3. This case portrays the valuable role that NGS can play in the correct diagnosis of an individual patient who displays disparate symptoms with an unidentified genetic cause.

Exome sequencing has been used extensively in the past several years in gene discovery research. Several gene discovery studies have resulted in the identification of genes that are relevant to inherited skin disease. Exome sequencing can also facilitate the identification of disease-causing mutations in **pathogenic** presentations where the exact genetic cause is not known.

2. Targeted sequencing

Although whole-genome and whole-exome sequencing are possible, in many cases where a suspected disease or condition has been identified, targeted sequencing of specific genes or genomic regions is preferred. Targeted sequencing is more affordable, yields much higher coverage of genomic regions of interest, and reduces sequencing cost and time. Researchers have begun to develop sequencing panels that target hundreds of genomic regions that are hotspots for disease-causing mutations. These panels target only desired regions of the genome for sequencing, eliminating the majority of the genome from analysis. Targeted sequencing panels can be developed by researchers or clinicians to include specific genomic regions of interest. In addition, sequencing panels that target common regions of interest can be purchased for clinical application; these include panels that target hotspots for cancer-causing mutations. Targeted sequencing—whether of individual genes or whole panels of genomic regions—aids in the rapid diagnosis of many genetic diseases. The results of disease-targeted sequencing can aid in therapeutic decision making in many diseases, including many cancers for which the treatments can be cancer-type specific.

Glossary

mutation /mjuːˈteɪʃn/
突变
A mutation is a permanent change of the nucleotide sequence of the genome of an organism, virus, or extrachromosomal DNA or other genetic elements.

polymorphism /ˌpɒlɪˈmɪfzəm/
多态性
poly + morph + ism
morph—polymorph; polymorphism; polymorphic;
Polymorphism occurs when two or more clearly different phenotypes exist in the same population of a species, in other words, the occurrence of more than one form or morph.

expressed sequence tags (EST)
表达序列标签
EST is a short sub-sequence of a cDNA sequence. They may be used to identify gene transcripts, and are instrumental in gene discovery and gene sequence determination.

serial analysis of gene expression (SAGE)
基因表达序列分析
SAGE is a technique used by molecular biologists to produce a snapshot of the messenger RNA population in a sample of interest in the form of small tags that correspond to fragments of those transcripts.

annotation /ˌænəˈteɪʃn/

注释

Annotation is the process of identifying the locations of genes and all of the coding regions in a genome and determining what those genes do.

methylation /meθɪˈleɪʃn/

甲基化；甲基化作用

methyl—methylate; methylation; methylase

The addition of a methyl group to a substrate or the substitution of an atom or group by a methyl group.

immunoprecipitation /ˌɪmjʊnoʊprɪsɪpɪˈteɪʃən/

（IP）免疫沉淀反应

immuno + precipitate + ion

IP is the technique of precipitating a protein antigen out of solution using an antibody that specifically binds to that particular protein. This process can be used to isolate/concentrate a particular protein from a sample containing many thousands of different proteins.

epidemiology /ˌepɪˌdiːmiˈɑːlədʒi/

流行病学；传染病学

Epidemiology is the science that studies the patterns, causes, and effects of health and disease conditions in defined populations.

diagnose /ˌdaɪəɡˈnoʊs/

诊断

Diagnosis is the identification of the nature and cause of a certain phenomenon, usually short for medical diagnosis (often abbreviated dx or Dx), which means the process of determining which disease or condition explains a person's symptoms and signs.

pathogenic /ˈpæθəˈdʒenɪk/

致病的；病原的；发病的

patho-（病理）—pathogen, pathogeny, pathogenic, pathogenesis, pathology, pathologic, pathological, pathologist

Pathogenic means the capable of producing disease. A pathogen is anything that can produce disease. Typically the term is used to describe an infectious agent such as a virus, bacterium, prion, fungus, viroid, or parasite that causes disease in its host.

oculocutaneous albinism

/ˌɒkjʊlɒkʌˈteɪniəs ˈælbɪnɪzəm/

眼皮肤白化病

Oculocutaneous albinism (OCA) is a form of albinism involving the eyes (oculo-), skin (-cutaneous) and the hair as well. It is caused by mutations in several genes that control the synthesis of melanin within the melanocytes.

Notes to Difficult Sentences

Although whole-genome and whole-exome sequencing are possible, in many cases where a suspected disease or condition has been identified, targeted sequencing of specific genes or genomic regions is preferred.

虽然全基因组或全外显子组测序已经成为可能，但在很多情况下某种疾病或情况已经得到确认，那么对某些特定基因或基因组区域进行靶向测序则显得更有优势。

拓展：相对于全基因组和全外显子组测序，靶向测序价格便宜，对目标区域的覆盖度更高、耗时更短，目前市面上的绝大部分基因检测产品都是利用靶向测序，例如BGI出的一款专门针对新生儿的基因检测产品——安馨可™，能为新出生的宝宝提供50种常见遗传病和20种药物敏感基因的检测，涵盖遗传代谢病、遗传性耳聋、先天性免疫缺陷病，部分早期发现可改善预后的单基因病以及药物基因组。

Lesson 3
First Baby Born after Full Genetic Screening of Embryos

Connor, a healthy baby boy, has made history (Fig. 1.3). He is the first child to be born after his parents had the entire genomes of a batch of their **IVF** (*in vitro* fertilization) **embryos** screened for **abnormalities**, with intention of picking the healthiest for **implantation**.

The technique could increase the number of successful **pregnancies** from IVF. And although the researchers stopped short of actually sequencing the boy's genome, the advance is proof that this could be done— potentially ushering in an era of designer babies.

IVF accounts for between 1 and 5 per cent of all births in developed countries, but it is very inefficient. An estimated 80 per cent of embryos either don't implant or **miscarry**,

Figure 1.3　Connor Levy, the first IVF baby

while only a third of IVF cycles result in a successful pregnancy, largely due to abnormalities in the number of chromosomes an embryo possesses.

"If you take a woman in her early 30's, around a quarter of her embryos will be abnormal. For a woman in her early 40's, it's around three-quarters," says Dagan Wells at the University of Oxford, who pioneered the new technique. The problem is that many abnormal embryos look normal under a microscope. "We need better ways of working out which embryo is the one that we should implant," says Wells.

To do this, he first took cells from seven 5-day-old embryos and **extracted** their DNA. He then used a technique called next-generation sequencing (NGS) to assess the number of chromosomes in each cell. This involves breaking the DNA into fragments that a computer then reads and predicts where on the chromosome each fragment came from. The sequence of an entire genome can be read in this way—although Wells's team didn't do this. They were merely interested in the proportion of DNA coming from each chromosome.

1. DNA library

In earlier studies, the team had compared the DNA fragments produced using NGS from healthy cells, those taken from abnormal embryos and those taken from cells with known chromosomal abnormalities. These were used as a library against which the DNA from the seven embryos could be compared.

Of the seven embryos, three were found to be normal, and one was implanted into the mother, resulting in the birth of Connor in Pennsylvania last month. A second woman is also expecting a baby after undergoing the same process. Neither woman has a history of **inherited disease**; they merely wanted to maximise their chances of having a baby through IVF.

The hope is that by selecting only healthy embryos for implantation, more women will become pregnant and fewer will experience miscarriages. Recent clinical trials of a related technique called pre-implantation genetic screening have suggested that the method could boost the implantation rate by around a third, while the miscarriage rate could be halved. The big advantage of using NGS is that multiple embryos could be screened simultaneously, significantly reducing the cost.

"This isn't going to solve the problem of reproductive ageing, as a couple in their early 40's may find they have no healthy embryos from which to choose," says Wells. However, it should boost the success rate for IVF in younger women, and also avoid the storage of embryos that have no chance of growing into a healthy baby.

The technique can also be tweaked to allow mutations in any gene of interest to be examined, such as those that cause **cystic fibrosis**. "This potentially gives us the opportunity to look at multiple genes and chromosomal copies," says Stuart Lavery, director of IVF Hammersmith, one of the UK's largest IVF units. "It gives us a very powerful tool for pre-implantation genetic diagnosis."

2. Misuse potential

However, the fact that NGS can be done on a single cell from human embryos also raises the potential for misuse. Last year, researchers in the US sequenced the entire genome of an 18-week-old **fetus** using fragments of fetal DNA in the mother's blood along with DNA samples from both parents. Wells's technique shows that it's possible to do this far earlier—before an embryo has even implanted in the **uterus**.

"It shows that there is the potential for getting an unprecedented amount of information about an embryo before it's transferred to the **womb**," says Wells, who presented his technique at the annual meeting of the European Society of Human Reproduction and Embryology in London today. "We need to be very careful that this isn't used for trivial, non-medical reasons."

Earlier this year, Dutch researchers published a paper suggesting that eye and hair colour can be predicted from a DNA sample, and they are now using such tests to help police identify suspects or victims of crime. The same group is also developing tests to predict the shape of facial features, such as prominent cheekbones or a large nose, and **complexion**.

"For now, eye and hair colour are the only appearance traits that can be predicted from DNA with any practically useful accuracy," says Manfred Kayser of Erasmus Medical Centre in Rotterdam, the Netherlands, who led the research. "Some of the available tests are very sensitive and work from a small number of cells provided that the DNA is not heavily degraded. However, the fact that something is scientifically and technically possible doesn't necessarily mean that it should be done."

3. Designer babies

In the UK, genetic testing of embryos is strictly regulated, but this isn't the case in other countries such as the US.

"At some points in the not too distant future, prospective parents will have the technical ability to look at the genome of their embryos and select embryos based on the traits they see, whether those are disease traits, cosmetic traits, behavioural traits, or boy or a girl," says Hank Greely, director of the Center for Law and the Biosciences at Stanford University in California.

What's more, enforcing a worldwide ban on such genetic selection might be unworkable, says Greely. "There are roughly 200 countries in the world. If 199 ban it, that's a great commercial opportunity for the 200th," he says.

Even so, Wells thinks there are several reasons why using this technology to create designer babies is unlikely to catch on. The first is that couples only tend to produce a limited number of embryos, and all of them carry their own genetic characteristics.

"Two people who are both 5 foot 2 tall are unlikely to produce a basketball player," he says. And the more traits a couple tried to select, the more embryos would be eliminated. Pick more than one or two traits, and there may be no more embryos left to choose from. "To go through all the difficulties, expense and uncertainty of an IVF cycle to choose something trivial, I can't see many people doing it," Wells says.

4. Making a baby the scientific way

Marybeth Scheidts and David Levy didn't know they would be making medical history when Marybeth went into labor on 18 May. But their son, Connor, born at 11.23pm and weighing 3.6 kilograms, is the first child to be born following a new genetic screening technique that could dramatically boost the success rate of IVF.

Incredibly, the test was performed before the embryo from which Connor grew had been implanted in Marybeth's uterus.

Marybeth, aged 36, and David, aged 41, have been together for almost 17 years, and had always wanted children. But after five years of trying to conceive without success, they visited a fertility clinic for tests. At first, it seemed the problem was David's low **sperm** count, but then it emerged that Marybeth's **ovulation** was erratic as well. "It was a real blow," says David. "Seeing other people with children, and not having any issues, it was heart breaking."

After three failed attempts at **intrauterine insemination**, the couple finally opted for IVF, which worked, resulting in the creation of 13 embryos. Seven of them looked normal, and usually one would be randomly selected for implantation. However, the family had enrolled on a clinical trial of a new embryo screening technique, which revealed that just three of their embryos carried the correct number of chromosomes. Two were frozen, and one was implanted.

Two weeks later, David had just started a new job as a nurse at a hospital in Philadelphia, when Marybeth called and asked if she could meet him for lunch. It was then she announced that she was pregnant. "It was overwhelming," says David.

Nearly two months after Connor was born, the couple say they are adjusting well to life as a three. "Connor only wakes up when he needs changing or feeding; he's been smiling for the last two weeks and doing a lot of cooing," says David.

Should they decide to have another child in the future, they say they feel reassured knowing that their two remaining embryos are genetically normal. They also have a choice of gender—

one is male, the other is female.

Glossary

IVF /ˌaɪviːˈef/
试管受精
IVF (*in-vitro* fertilization) is a process by which an egg is fertilised by sperm outside the body.
embryo /ˈembrioʊ/
胚胎
An embryo is a multicellular diploid (二倍体) eukaryote in its earliest stage of development, from the time of fertilization until birth, hatching (孵化), or germination.
abnormality /ˌæbnɔːrˈmæləti/
畸形
ab (不) + normal (正常) + ity (名词形式)
Abnormality refers to the condition which is present in a human body resulting in disorders of any part of the body and certain kind of disease.
implantation /ˌɪmplɑːnˈteɪʃn/
移植
im (向内,入) + plant (种植) + ation (名词后缀)
Implantation is the very early stage of pregnancy at which the conceptus (胚体) adheres to the wall of the uterus. It is by this adhesion that the foetus receives oxygen and nutrients from the mother to be able to grow.
pregnancy /ˈpreɡnənsi/
怀孕
Pregnancy is the time during which one or more offspring develops inside a woman.
miscarry /ˌmɪsˈkæri/
流产
Miscarry is the (natural) death of an embryo or fetus before it can survive independently.
extract /ˈekstrækt/
(DNA/RNA/蛋白) 提取
To extract is the process of isolating targeted compounds from mixture.

inherited disease /ɪnˈherɪtɪd dɪˈziːz/
遗传疾病
An inherited disease is a genetic problem caused by one or more abnormalities in the genome, especially a condition that is present from birth (congenital, 先天的).
cystic fibrosis /ˈsɪstɪk faɪˈbroʊsɪs/
囊泡性纤维症
Cystic fibrosis (CF) is a genetic disorder that affects mostly the lungs but also the pancreas, liver, kidneys and intestine
fetus /ˈfiːtəs/
胎儿
fetus—fetal (胎的,胎儿的)
A fetus is the term used to refer to a prenatal mammal or other viviparous (胎生的) vertebrate between its embryonic state (胚胎期) and its birth.
uterus /ˈjuːtərəs/
子宫
womb /wuːm/
子宫
The uterus (or womb) is a major female hormone-responsive reproductive sex organ of most mammals, including humans.
complexion /kəmˈplekʃn/
肤色
Complexion refers to the color of human skin. It is a biological trait.
sperm /spɜːrm/
精子
Sperm is the male reproductive cell.
ovulation /ˌɒvjuˈleɪʃn/
排卵
Ovulation is the phase of a female's menstrual cycle when an egg is released from ovaries.

intrauterine insemination
/ˌɪntrəˈjuːtəraɪn ɪnˌsemɪˈneʃn/
子宫内受精；人工授精
Intrauterine insemination is the deliberate introduction of sperm into a female's uterus or cervix（子宫颈）for the purpose of achieving a pregnancy through *in vivo* fertilization.

Notes to Difficult Sentences

Recent clinical trials of a related technique called pre-implantation genetic screening have suggested that the method could boost the implantation rate by around a third, while the miscarriage rate could be halved.

最近，一项叫做胚胎植入前基因筛查的相关技术的临床研究显示，该技术能使着床率提高大约1/3，使流产率降低一半。

拓展：基因筛查是利用基因技术对未生婴儿或新生婴儿进行基因测试，达到最佳效果，以确保其不会患上重大遗传性疾病的新技术。目前，比较成熟的基因筛查技术有唐氏综合症筛查、苯丙酮尿症筛查、耳聋基因筛查，等等。华大基因无创产前基因检测能够全面分析23对染色体的数目异常和染色体的部分结构异常，21、18和13三条染色体的准确率高达99%，同时可对其他高风险染色体异常进行分析。

Reading Material 1

Comparison of Next-Generation Sequencing Systems

With fast development and wide applications of next-generation sequencing (NGS) technologies, genomic sequence information is within reach to aid the achievement of goals to decode life mysteries, make better crops, detect pathogens, and improve life qualities. NGS systems are typically represented by SOLiD/Ion Torrent PGM from Life Sciences, Genome Analyzer/HiSeq 2000/MiSeq from Illumina, and GS FLX Titanium/GS Junior from Roche (Table 1.1).

1. Roche 454 system

Roche 454 was the first commercially successful next generation system. This sequencer uses pyrosequencing technology. Instead of using dideoxynucleotides to terminate the chain amplification, pyrosequencing technology relies on the detection of pyrophosphate released during nucleotide incorporation. The library DNAs with 454-specific adaptors are denatured into single strand and captured by amplification beads followed by emulsion PCR. Then on a picotiter plate, one of dNTP (dATP, dGTP, dCTP, dTTP) will complement to the bases of the template strand with the help of ATP sulfurylase, luciferase, luciferin, DNA polymerase, and adenosine 5'-phosphosulfate (APS) and release pyrophosphate (PPi) which equals the amount of incorporated nucleotide. The ATP transformed from PPi drives the luciferin into oxyluciferin and generates visible light. At the same time, the unmatched bases are degraded by apyrase. Then another dNTP is added into the reaction system and the pyrosequencing reaction is repeated.

The read length of Roche 454 was initially 100~150 bp in 2005, 200 000 + reads, and could output 20 Mb per run. In 2008, 454 GS FLX Titanium system was launched; through upgrading, its read length could reach 700 bp with accuracy 99.9% after filter and output 0.7 G data per run within 24 hours. In late 2009, Roche combined the GS Junior a bench top system into the 454 sequencing system which simplified the library preparation and data processing, and output was also upgraded to 14 G per run. The most outstanding advantage of Roche is its speed: it takes only 10 hours from sequencing start till completion. The read length is also a distinguished character compared with other NGS systems. But the high cost of reagents remains a challenge for Roche 454. It is about 12.56×10^{-6} per base (counting reagent use only). One of the shortcomings is that it has relatively high error rate in terms of poly-bases longer than 6 bp. But its library construction can be automated, and the emulsion PCR can be semiautomated which could reduce the manpower in a great extent.

2. AB SOLiD system

Sequencing by Oligo Ligation Detection (SOLiD) was purchased by Applied Biosystems in 2006. The sequencer adopts the technology of two-base sequencing based on ligation sequencing. On a SOLiD flowcell, the libraries can be sequenced by 8 base-probe ligation which contains ligation site (the first base), cleavage site (the fifth base), and 4 different fluorescent dyes (linked to the last base). The fluorescent signal will be recorded during the probes complementary to the template strand and vanished by the cleavage of probes' last 3 bases. And the sequence of the fragment can be deduced after 5 round of sequencing using ladder primer sets.

The read length of SOLiD was initially 35 bp reads and the output was 3 G data per run. Owing to two-base sequencing method, SOLiD could reach a high accuracy of 99.85% after filtering. At the end of 2007, ABI released the first SOLiD system. In late 2010, the SOLiD 5500xl sequencing system was released. From SOLiD to SOLiD 5500xl, five upgrades were released by ABI in just three years. The SOLiD 5500xl realized improved read length, accuracy, and data output of 85 bp, 99.99%, and 30 G per run, respectively. A complete run could be finished within 7 days. The sequencing cost is about 40×10^{-9} per base estimated from reagent use only by BGI users. But the short read length and resequencing only in applications is still its major shortcoming. Application of SOLiD includes whole genome resequencing, targeted resequencing, transcriptome research (including gene expression profiling, small RNA analysis, and whole transcriptome analysis), and epigenome (like ChIP-Seq and methylation). Like other NGS systems, SOLiD's computational infrastructure is expensive and not trivial to use; it requires an air-conditioned data center, computing cluster, skilled personnel in computing, distributed memory cluster, fast networks, and batch queue system. Operating system used by most researchers is GNU/LINUX. Each solid sequencer run takes 7 days and generates around 4 TB of raw data. More data will be generated after bioinformatics analysis. Automation can be used in library preparations, for example, Tecan system which integrated a Covaris A and Roche 454 REM e system.

Table 1.1 Advantage and mechanism of sequencers

Sequencer	454 GS FLX	HiSeq 2000	SOLiDv4	Sanger 3730xl
Sequencing mechanism	Pyrosequencing	Sequencing by synthesis	Ligation and two-base coding	Dideoxy chain termination
Read length	700 bp	50 SE, 50 PE, 101 PE	50 + 35 bp or 50 + 50 bp	400 ~ 900 bp
Accuracy	99.9%	98%, (100PE)	99.94% raw data	99.999%
Reads	1 M	3 G	1200 ~ 1400 M	—
Output data/run	0.7 Gb	600 Gb	120 Gb	1.9 ~ 84 kb
Time/run	24 h	3 ~ 10 d	7 d for SE 14 d for PE	20 min ~ 3 h
Advantage	Read length, fast	High throughput	Accuracy	High quality, long read length
Disadvantage	Error rate with polybase more than 6, high cost, low throughput	Short read assembly	Short read assembly	High cost low throughput

3. Illumina GA/HiSeq system

In 2006, Solexa released the Genome Analyzer (GA), and the company was purchased by Illumina in 2007. The sequencer adopts the technology of sequencing by synthesis (SBS). The library with fixed adaptors is denatured to single strands and grafted to the flowcell, followed by bridge amplification to form clusters which contains clonal DNA fragments. Before sequencing, the library splices into single strands with the help of linearization enzyme, and then four kinds of nucleotides (ddATP, ddGTP, ddCTP, ddTTP) which contain different cleavable fluorescent dye and a removable blocking group would complement the template one base at a time, and the signal could be captured by a (charge-coupled device) CCD.

At first, solexa GA output was 1 G/run. Through improvements in polymerase, buffer, flowcell, and software, in 2009, the output of GA increased to 20 G/run in August (75 PE), 30 G/run in October (100 PE), and 50 G/run in December (Truseq V3, 150 PE), and the latest GAIIx series can attain 85 G/run. In early 2010, Illumina launched HiSeq 2000, which adopts the same sequencing strategy with GA, and BGI was among the first globally to adopt the HiSeq system. Its output was 200 G per run initially, improved to 600 G per run currently which could be finished in 8 days. In the foreseeable future, it could reach 1 T/run when a personal genome cost could drop below $1K. The error rate of 100 PE could be below 2% in average after filtering (BGI's data). Compared with 454 and SOLiD, HiSeq 2000 is the cheapest in sequencing with $0.02/million bases (reagent counted only by BGI). With multiplexing incorporated in P5/P7 primers and adapters, it could handle thousands of samples simultaneously. HiSeq 2000 needs (HiSeq control software) HCS for program control, (real-time analyzer software) RTA to do on-instrument base-calling, and CASAVA for secondary analysis. There is a 3 TB hard disk in HiSeq 2000. With the aid of Truseq V3 reagents and associated softwares, HiSeq 2000 has improved much on high GC sequencing. MiSeq, a bench top sequencer launched in 2011 which shared most technologies with HiSeq, is especially convenient for amplicon and bacterial sample sequencing. It could sequence 150 PE and generate 1.5 G/run in about 10 hours including sample and library preparation time. Library preparation and their concentration measurement can both be automated with compatible systems like Agilent Bravo, Hamilton Banadu, Tecan, and Apricot Designs.

Reading Material 2

New Challenges of Next-Gen Sequencing

I first started MassGenomics in the early days of next-gen sequencing, when Illumina was called "Solexa" and came in fragment-end, 35 bp reads. Even so, the unprecedented throughput of NGS and the nature of the sequencing technology brought a whole host of difficulties to overcome, notably:

(1) Bioinformatics algorithms developed for capillary-based sequencing didn't scale.
(2) Sequencing reads were shorter and more error-prone.
(3) The instruments were expensive, limiting access to the technology.
(4) Most of the genetics/genomics/clinical community had no experience with NGS.

All of these are essentially solved problems: new bioinformatics tools and algorithms were developed, the reads became longer and more accurate, benchtop sequencers and sequencing-service-providers hit the market, and NGS was widely adopted by the research community. Mission accomplished!

Yet these victories were short-lived, because we find ourselves facing new challenges, harder challenges. Here are a few of them.

1. Data storage

You've probably seen the plot of Moore's Law compared to sequencing throughput. In short, the cost of DNA sequencing has plummeted much faster than the cost of disk storage and CPU. A run on the Illumina HiSeq 2000 provides enough capacity for about 48 human exomes. Even if you don't keep the images, each exome requires about 10 gigabytes of disk space to store the bases, qualities, and alignments in compressed (BAM) format. At three runs a month, each instrument is generating 1.4 terabytes of data files. It adds up quickly.

Analysis of sequencing data—variant calling, annotation, expression analysis, genetic analysis—also requires disk space. Most non-BGI research budgets are finite, so investigators must choose between (I) deleting data, (II) spending money, or (III) holding up data production/analysis. None of those sound very appealing, do they?

2. Achieving statistical significance

NGS is no longer an exploratory tool, and descriptive studies reporting a dozen or a couple hundred genomes/exomes are harder and harder to publish. This is particularly true for common diseases, in which large numbers of samples are typically required to achieve statistical significance. The number 10 000 has been discussed as an appropriate number. Even if that many samples could be found, the cost of sequencing so many is substantial. If you had an Illumina X Ten system and could do whole genomes for $1000 each (that only covers reagents, by the way), it's still ten million dollars. That's probably over budget for most groups, so they'll have to take another tack:
(1) Sequencing fewer samples, which will make the work harder to fund/publish.
(2) Combining some sequencing with follow-up genotyping, which limits the discovery power.
(3) Collaborating with other labs/consortia, whose sample populations, phenotypes, or study designs may vary.
How many of your project planning meetings have ended with someone saying, "Well, maybe we'll get lucky."?

3. Finding samples

Getting access to large sample cohorts is another challenge. As I've previously written about, given the widespread availability of exome and genome sequencing, samples are the new commodity. High-quality DNA samples from informative sources—tumor tissue, diabetes patients, families with rare disorders, even healthy members of minority populations—are increasingly valuable. Why should an investigator collaborate with you, when they might send the samples off for sequencing on their own?

Sequencing samples with public funds (i. e., NIH grants) adds another layer of difficulty: all sequencing data must be submitted to public repositories. This means that the volunteer must have given informed consent not just for study but for data sharing. Local IRBs even need to sign off. The net result is that many of the samples that come to us for sequencing don't meet the criteria, and must be returned.

4. Privacy

Even if you have an outstanding, comprehensive informed consent document, it might be difficult to get volunteers to sign it. There's a growing public concern about the privacy of genetic information. As Yaniv Erich demonstrated by hacking the identities of CEPH sample contributors, genetic profiles obtained from SNP arrays, exome, or genome sequencing can be used to identify individual people. They also contain some very private details—like ancestry and disease risk alleles—that might be exploited, made public, or used for discrimination.

How long is it before genetic profiling replaces Google-stalking as a screening tool for job candidates or romantic interests? Thanks for coming in, Mr. Johnson. All we need now is your Facebook password and a cheek swab.

5. Functional validation of genomic findings

Numerous research groups have demonstrated the immense discovery power of NGS. The mere fact that dbSNP—the NCBI database of human sequencing variation—has swelled to more than 50 million distinct variants tells us something about what pervasive genome sequencing capabilities might uncover. And yet, the variants implicated in sequencing-based studies of human disease are increasingly difficult to "sell" to peer reviewers on genetic information alone. Our inability to predict the phenotypic impact of genetic variants lurks beneath the veneer of genetic discoveries like a shark following a deep-sea trawler.

Referees of most high-impact journals want to see some form of functional validation of genomic discoveries. That's a daunting challenge for many of us accustomed to the rapid turnaround, high-throughput nature of NGS. Most functional validation experiments are slow and laborious by comparison.

6. Translation of NGS to the clinic

We all know that NGS is destined for the clinic. Targeted sequencing panels are already in routine use at many cancer centers; in time, this will likely become exome/genome sequencing. Possibly transcriptome (RNA-Seq) and methylome (Methyl-Seq) as well. Undiagnosed inherited diseases, and rare genetic disorders whose genetic cause is unknown, are two other common-sense applications. There are many hurdles to overcome in order to apply a new technology to patient care. CLIA/CAP certification is a complex, expensive, and time-consuming process.

The reporting is more difficult, too. Unlike the research setting in which most NGS results have arisen, a clinical setting requires very high confidence in order to report anything back to the patient or treating physician. This is a good thing, since patient care decisions might be made based on genomic findings. Yet it means that we have a considerable amount of work ahead to ensure that genomic discoveries are followed up, replicated, and otherwise vetted to the point where they can be of clinical use.

Chapter 2 Big Data

In the life sciences, data can come in many forms, including information about genomic sequences, molecular pathways, and different populations of people. Those data create a potential bonanza, if scientists can overcome one stumbling block: how to handle the complexity of information. Tools and techniques for analyzing big data promise to mold massive mounds of information into a better understanding of the basic biological mechanisms and how the results can be applied in, for example, the health care.

Lesson 1
Too Much Information: Better Health from Big Data

Remember when you could only fit 10 songs on a cassette tape? Or store a couple of books on a floppy disc? It is getting harder to remember a time when you couldn't fit the whole TV series on to a gadget smaller than a matchbox.

That's just as well. It is becoming increasingly faster, cheaper and easier for scientists to collect vast amounts of data, whether it's about people's shopping habits, internet usage, or even their genetic make-up. The challenge now is to store, share and make sense of that

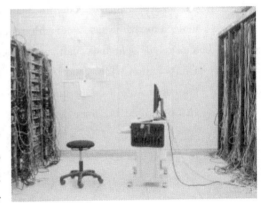

Figure 2.1 You can't just send 46 million gigabytes of data over the internet

information (Fig. 2.1). A new breed of cross-disciplinary researcher is meeting that challenge, and answering some of the toughest questions in science.

Around the world, geneticists and molecular biologists are busy sequencing proteins and genomes. Many of their results are sent to the European Bioinformatics Institute (EBI), based in Hinxton, UK, which stores the information in huge databases, readily accessible to all.

Over the past five years or so, much of the genetic data sent to the EBI was on viruses, bacteria and animals. "Now, the majority of sequencing is actually devoted to human beings," says Janet Thornton, director of the EBI.

Take the 1000 Genomes Project, for example. This international collaboration will make the full genomes of 2500 anonymous individuals freely available for research. In December 2012, the Prime Minister David Cameron announced plans for an even bigger set—the 100 000 Genomes Project, which should be completed by 2017. The project's goals include using the genetic data to help diagnose and treat illnesses such as cancer within the next four years.

The EBI has the capacity to store 46 petabytes of information (Table 2.1). That's 46 million gigabytes, or enough to fill about 10 million standard DVDs. "The size of the sequence data is becoming a challenge, technically, in terms of transferring it," says Thornton. "You can't just shift this data over the internet."

Table 2.1 Units of storage capacity

Full name	Abbreviation	Byte = 1
Bit	b	0.125
Byte	B	1
KiloByte	KB	2^{10}
MegaByte	MB	2^{20}
GigaByte	GB	2^{30}
TeraByte	TB	2^{40}
PetaByte	PB	2^{50}
ExaByte	EB	2^{60}
ZettaByte	ZB	2^{70}
YottaByte	YB	2^{80}
BrontByte	BB	2^{90}

What's more, the databases are growing rapidly. "Last year, our volume of data doubled," says Thornton.

Share and share alike

Elixir, an intergovernmental organization covering 17 European countries, is trying to find a way for scientists around the world to add to and share all that data. "At the moment, the EBI is the centrepiece, where all the big archives in Europe are kept," says Niklas Blomberg, director of Elixir.

"When biology data becomes big, it is not produced at a single site, like at the Large Hadron Collider," Blomberg says. "It's not just coming from one large hole beneath Geneva—it is coming from every university, and there are thousands of them in Europe. So we need to build an infrastructure that scales with that diversity and distribution."

Blomberg and his colleagues use two methods. The first involves renting out a **fibre-optic cable** that usually takes internet traffic between countries. "We can rent part of the network for a specific task," Blomberg says. That might be sending a particularly large number of genome sequences from the UK to Finland, for example.

The other involves creating temporary "digital embassies" at the EBI. If a research group wants to compare some secure information to the reference data at the EBI, it can do so by essentially creating a secure data cloud within the EBI. This allows researchers to access smaller amounts of information in a secure way, without having to download data.

This kind of collaboration is helping to answer all kinds of questions. Olivo Miotto and his colleagues at the Centre for Genomics and Global Health are collecting and mining another set of genetic data for clues about the spread of **drug-resistant malaria**. "We have brought together a network of collaborations to create a global resource of genomic data on genetic variation of the ***Plasmodium falciparum* parasite** which causes malaria," he says.

The center, funded by the UK Medical Research Council, is based in Oxford, and partners with MalariaGEN, a network of clinical researchers working all over the world. Miotto, who is in Bangkok, Thailand, is particularly concerned about the spread of drug-resistant malaria across South-East Asia. "We've seen a rise in resistance to **artemisinin**, the front-line antimalarial therapy worldwide," he says. "There is a major, justified concern that artemisinin-resistant malaria will spread from South-East Asia to Africa, which would cost many lives."

In an attempt to track the spread of resistance, Miotto's team collaborate with others in the region. Colleagues in health clinics take blood from people with malaria, isolate the parasites in the blood, and send the samples to Miotto's team. The team then sequences the parasite genomes and compares them to recording at the Wellcome Trust Sanger Institute in Hinxton, UK. "We are looking for points in the genome where there is a difference between parasites," Miotto says.

Once his team share this information with doctors in countries affected by malaria, they look at how patients are responding to treatments. They can compare the genomes of parasites found in people whose treatment was successful with those taken from people who aren't responding as well. This helps to determine which genes in the parasite might be conferring resistance. The team hope to be able to use this information to drive health policy. For example, if they spot a drug-resistant pathogen in a region previously unaffected by the problem, they could alert public health authorities, who might be able to intervene to prevent its spread.

The approach, known as genetic epidemiology, has only taken off in the last few years, Miotto says. "It's very much an emerging field, and is being applied to a variety of diseases," he says. "It is an exciting area that is here to stay."

Of course, big data isn't just about banks of computers. "The people who work at the EBI are the jewels of the institution," says Thornton. The work attracts a certain kind of person, says Miotto, a breed of researchers who are very multidisciplinary and willing to focus on the broader impacts of their work in biology, computing and statistics.

Miotto came to genetic epidemiology from a career in software engineering, while Blomberg initially studied biochemistry. "I had to sit down with a thick mathematics book, because there wasn't enough maths in my undergraduate degree," Blomberg recalls. Miotto's team write some of the software used to analyze the data. But biology underpins what they do. "A lot of this is very specific to malaria parasites," says Miotto. "It requires a lot of knowledge about malaria as well as statistics."

This blend of expertise is vital for the EBI and Elixir, too. "We've got people coming from physical sciences, computer sciences and life sciences," says Blomberg.

"The scientists making sense of big data can play an important role in global health," says Miotto. "Big data gets condensed into smaller size, but higher value, data, until it gets to a point where it is a decision," he says. This might mean changing the dose of a drug, for example. "If you're working in diseases that affect poor countries, there's no way that the local government health authority will have the skills or resources to analyze terabytes of data," he says. "You have to work on this translation to make it actionable—condensing terabytes into a single sentence."

Blomberg says it is very rewarding work. "This is great fun. It is where science is happening right now—you can really start to understand the genetic drivers behind both rare and complex diseases in a way that was unthinkable four or five years ago."

Glossary

fibre-optic cable
纤维光缆
An optical fiber cable is a cable containing one or more optical fibers that are used to carry light.

drug-resistant /dˈrʌgrɪzˈɪstənt/
耐药的；抗药的
Drug resistance is the reduction in effectiveness of a drug in curing a disease or condition.

malaria /mə'leriə/

疟疾

Malaria is a mosquito-borne infectious disease of humans and other animals caused by parasitic protozoans (原生动物) belonging to genus Plasmodium (疟原虫属).

Plasmodium falciparum

镰状疟原虫

Plasmodium falciparum is a protozoan parasite that cause malaria in humans. It is transmitted by the female *Anopheles mosquito* (按蚊).

parasite /ˈpærəsaɪt/

寄生虫

Parasitism is a non-mutual symbiotic (共生的) relationship between species, where one species, the parasite, benefits at the expense of the other, the host.

artemisinin /ɑːtɪmɪˈsaɪnɪn/

青蒿素

An antimalarial (抗疟疾的) drug derived from the sweet wormwood shrub, found as the active ingredient in traditional Chinese medical herbal treatment for malaria, chemically a sesquiterpene lactone (倍半萜内酯).

Notes to Difficult Sentences

"We've seen a rise in resistance to artemisinin, the front-line antimalarial therapy worldwide," he says. "There is a major, justified concern that artemisinin-resistant malaria will spread from South-East Asia to Africa, which would cost many lives."

"我们发现,作为全球首选的抗疟疾药物,青蒿素的耐药性却在不断增加,"他说,"我们有必要且合理地担忧,耐青蒿素的疟疾将从东南亚传播到非洲,从而夺走很多人的生命。"

拓展:青蒿素是一种几乎在任何地方都通用的值得信赖的治疗疟疾的药物。不过在2005年,柬埔寨西部首次确定了疟疾对青蒿素出现抗药性,抗药性不一定会导致青蒿素治疗的完全失败,但确实减缓了青蒿素清除患者血液中的恶性疟原虫。目前,研究人员已经在疟原虫的基因组中确定了与抗性相关的区域。

Lesson 2
Life Sciences in Big Data Era

Biologists are joining the big-data club. With the advent of high-throughput genomics, life scientists are starting to grapple with massive data sets, encountering challenges with handling, processing and moving information that were once the domain of astronomers and high-energy physicists.

1. Data explosion

With every passing year, they turn more often to big data to probe everything from the regulation of genes and the evolution of genomes to why coastal **algae** bloom, what **microbes** dwell where in human body **cavities** and how the genetic **make-up** of different cancers influences how cancer patients fare. EBI (the European Bioinformatics Institute) in Hinxton, UK, part of the European Molecular Biology Laboratory and one of the world's largest biology-data **repositories**, currently stores 20 petabytes of data and **back-ups** about genes, proteins and small molecules. Genomic data account for 2 petabytes of that, a number that more than doubles every year (Fig. 2.2).

This data pile is just one-tenth the size of the data store at CERN, Europe's particle-physics laboratory near Geneva, Switzerland. Every year, **particle-collision** events in CERN's Large Hadron Collider generate around 15 petabytes of data—the equivalent of about 4 million **high-definition** feature-length films. But the EBI and institutes like it face similar data-**wrangling** challenges to those at CERN, says Ewan Birney, associate director of the EBI. He and his colleagues now regularly meet with organizations such as CERN and the European Space Agency (ESA) in Paris to swap lessons about data storage, analysis and sharing.

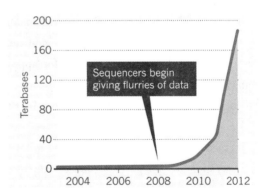

Figure 2.2 The amount of genetic sequencing data stored at the European Bioinformatics Institute takes less than a year to double in size

All labs need to manipulate data to yield research answers. As prices drop for high-throughput instruments such as automated genome sequencers, small biology labs can become big-data generators. And even labs without such instruments can become big-data users by accessing terabytes of data from public repositories at the EBI or the US National Center for Biotechnology Information in Bethesda, Maryland. Each day last year, the EBI received about 9 million online requests to query its data, a 60% increase over 2011.

Biology data mining has challenges all of its own. Biological data are much more **heterogeneous** than those in physics. They stem from a wide range of experiments that spit out many types of information, such as genetic sequences, interactions of proteins or findings in medical records. The complexity is daunting, says Lawrence Hunter, a computational biologist at the University of Colorado Denver. "Getting the most from the data requires interpreting them in light of all the relevant prior knowledge," he says.

That means scientists have to store large data sets, and analyse, compare and share them—not simple tasks. Even a single sequenced human genome is around 140 gigabytes in size. Comparing human genomes takes more than a personal computer and online file-sharing applications such as DropBox.

2. Opportunities and challenges

Moore's Law describes a trend coined by Intel co-founder Gordon Moore which states that "the number of transistors that can be placed on an integrated circuit board is increasing **exponentially**, with a doubling time of roughly 18 months". Put more simply: computers double in speed and half in size every 18 months. Similar phenomena have been noted for the capacity of hard disks (Kryder's Law) and **network bandwidth** (Nielsen's Law and Butter's Law). This trend has remained true for approximately 40 years, until the completion of the Human Genome project in 2003. Since then, a deluge of biological sequence data has been generated, a phenomenon largely spurred by the falling cost of sequencing.

Until recent years, Moore's law managed to keep ahead of the genomic curve, slightly outpacing the generation of biological sequence data by its growth in storage and processing capacity. However, since 2008, genomics data is outpacing Moore's Law. Biology's big data sets are now more expensive to store, process and analyse than they are to generate.

Indeed, the big data problem has been at the forefront of the technology sector over the last 5 ~ 8 years as a result of the widespread rollout of high speed wide area network access and a proliferation of next generation applications, combined with the advent of social media. The

Chapter 2 Big Data

advent of such large datasets, has significant storage and, more importantly, computational implications. Given that processing and analysis of such datasets may be bursty in nature e. g. , tasks such as read assembly is more computationally intensive than subsequent tasks, such high performance compute power may not be fully utilized over time. This has spurred the use of **cloud or utility computing** (elastic computing) where users can hire infrastructure on a "pay as you go" basis, thereby avoiding large capital infrastructure and maintenance costs. Due to advances in virtualisation, such customised hardware and computational power can now be provisioned instantaneously using user friendly web interfaces.

However, the solution does not lie in cloud computing alone. Big data presents problems in that it can deviate from traditional structured data (organised in rows and columns) and can be represented as semi-structured data such as XML, or unstructured data including flat files which are not compliant with traditional database methods.

Figure 2.3 data saientist is the sexiest job of the 21st century

Furthermore, cloud computing alone does not address the challenge of big data analytics where large scale processing is required, particularly when the scale of the data exceeds a single machine. In this case, it is necessary to develop applications that will execute in parallel on distributed data sets, a non-trivial task that has been the focus of **grid computing** research for many years. This explosion in big data and the need for the application of big data technologies has generated significant demand for "data scientists", computer scientists and mathematicians with expertise in big data, analytical techniques, statistics, data mining and computer programming. As evidence of this, the *Harvard Business Review* has heralded the Data Scientist as the "Sexiest Job of the 21st Century" (Fig. 2.3).

Glossary

algae /ˈældʒiː/
藻类
Algae is a large and diverse group of eukaryotic organisms which have chlorophyll as their primary photosynthetic pigment and lack a sterile covering of cells around their reproductive cells. Most are autotrophic and lack many of the distinct cell and tissue types found in land plants such as stomata, xylem and phloem.

microbe /ˈmaɪkroʊb/
细菌；微生物
Microbe is a microscopic living organism, which may be single celled or multicellular. They are very diverse and include all the bacteria and archaea and almost all the protozoa. They also include some fungi, algae, and certain animals, such as rotifers.

cavity /ˈkævəti/
（体）腔
A body cavity is a fluid filled space in many animals where organs typically develop.

make-up /ˈmeɪkˈʌp/
构造；排版；化妆品；补考
Genetic make-up (or genotype), is genetic formation of a cell, an organism, or an individual usually with reference to a specific characteristic under consideration.

repository /rɪˈpɑzətɔːri/
贮藏室，仓库；知识库；智囊团
Data repository is a facility that stores, maintains and shares certain kinds of data for future analysis and research.

back-up /ˈbækˈʌp/
备份；为…做备份
Back-up refers to the copying and archiving of computer data so it may be used to restore the original after a data loss event.

particle-collision /ˈpɑːrtɪkl kəˈlɪʒn/
粒子碰撞
Particle-collision refers to two or more particles (like protons) exerting forces on each other for a relatively short time and during this short period, available energy is released.

high-definition /ˈhaɪˌdefɪˈnɪʃn/
非常鲜明的；高清晰度
High-definition, sometimes abbreviated as Hi-def or HD, commonly refers to an increase in display or visual resolution over previously used standard.

wrangle /ˈræŋgl/
争论；争吵；辩驳
To argue or dispute, especially in a noisy or angry manner.

heterogeneous /ˌhetərəˈdʒiːniəs/
多相的；异种的；不均匀的
Heterogeneous means consisting of dissimilar elements or parts.

exponentially /ˌekspəˈnenʃəli/
以指数方式
exponent—exponential, exponentially
Exponential growth refers to where the growth rate of a mathematical function is proportional to the function's current value. Here are means that transistors are increasing rapidly.

network bandwidth /ˈnetwɜːk ˈbændˌwɪdθ/
网络带宽
Network bandwidth is the bit-rate of available or consumed information capacity expressed often in metric multiples of bits per second.

cloud or utility computing
云或效用计算
Cloud computing involves application systems which are executed within the cloud and operated through internet enabled devices. Purely cloud computing does not rely on the use of cloud storage as it will be removed upon users' download action.
Utility computing is a service provisioning model in

which a service provider makes computing resources and infrastructure management available to the customer as needed, and charges them for specific usage rather than a flat rate. Utility is the packaging of computing resources, such as computation, storage and services, as a metered service.

grid computing /grɪd kəmˈpjuːtɪŋ/
网格计算
Grid computing is the collection of computer resources from multiple locations to reach a common goal. The grid can be thought of as a distributed system with non-interactive workloads that involve a large number of file.

Notes to Difficult Sentences

(1) With every passing year, they turn more often to big data to probe everything from the regulation of genes and the evolution of genomes to why coastal algae bloom, what microbes dwell where in human body cavities and how the genetic make-up of different cancers influences how cancer patients fare.

随着时间的推移，他们（生物学家们）更频繁的求助于大数据，想从中挖掘任何有关基因调控、基因组进化的东西，以期解释为什么沿海藻类会大量爆发，人体不同体腔中生活着什么微生物，不同的癌症基因结构会对癌症病人产生怎样的影响等诸多未解之谜。

拓展："大数据"一词最初起源于互联网和 IT 行业，然而随着"人类基因组计划"的完成，它带动了生物行业的一次革命，高通量测序技术得到快速发展，使得生命科学研究获得了强大的数据产出能力，包括基因组学、转录组学、蛋白质组学、代谢组学等生物学数据。

(2) Indeed, the big data problem has been at the forefront of the technology sector over the last 5~8 years as a result of the widespread rollout of high speed wide area network access and a proliferation of next generation applications, combined with the advent of social media.

诚然，在过去 5~8 年时间里，由于高速广域网的普及和下一代应用程序的激增，同时伴随社会媒体的出现，大数据难题一直处在技术领域的最前沿。

拓展：社会媒体的数据不仅是海量的，而且是多元的，数据类型和结构存在很大差异，因而给大数据的收集和分析带来巨大挑战。

Lesson 3
Big Data Meets Public Health

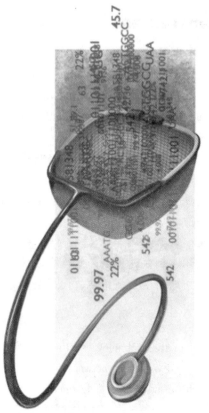

Figure 2.4 From validity to utility

In 1854, as **cholera** swept through London, John Snow, the father of modern **epidemiology**, painstakingly recorded the locations of affected homes. After long, laborious work, he implicated the Broad Street water pump as the source of the outbreak, even without knowing that a ***Vibrio*** organism caused cholera. "Today, Snow might have crunched **Global Positioning System** information and disease prevalence data, solving the problem within hours." That is the potential impact of "Big Data" on the public's health. But the promise of Big Data is also accompanied by claims that "the scientific method itself is becoming obsolete", as next-generation computers, such as IBM's Watson, sift through the digital world to provide predictive models based on massive information. Separating the true signal from the gigantic amount of noise is neither easy nor straightforward, but it is a challenge that must be tackled if information is ever to be translated into societal well-being.

The term "Big Data" refers to volumes of large, complex, linkable information. Beyond genomics and other "omic" fields, Big Data includes medical, environmental, financial, **geographic**, and social media information. Most of this digital information was unavailable a decade ago. This swell of data will continue to grow, stoked by sources that are currently unimaginable. Big Data stands to improve health by providing insights into the causes and outcomes of disease, better drug targets for precision medicine, and enhanced disease prediction and prevention. Moreover, citizen-scientists will increasingly use this information to promote their own health and wellness. Big Data can improve our understanding of health behaviors and accelerate the knowledge-to-diffusion cycle.

But "Big Error" can **plague** Big Data. In 2013, when **influenza** hit the United States hard and early, analysis of flu-related Internet searches drastically overestimated peak flu levels relative to those determined by traditional public **health surveillance**. Even more problematic is the potential for many false alarms triggered by large-scale examination of putative associations with disease outcomes. **Paradoxically**, the proportion of false alarms among all proposed "findings" may increase when one can measure more things. **Spurious** correlations and **ecological fallacies** may multiply. There are numerous such examples, such as "honey-producing **bee colonies** inversely correlate with juvenile arrests for **marijuana**."

The field of genomics has addressed this problem of signal and noise by requiring replication of study findings and by asking for much stronger signals in terms of statistical significance. This requires the use of collaborative large-scale epidemiologic studies. For nongenomic associations, false alarms due to **confounding variables** or other biases are possible even with very large-scale studies, extensive replication, and very strong signals. Big Data's strength is in finding associations, not in showing whether these associations have meaning. Finding a signal is only the first step.

Even John Snow needed to start with a plausible **hypothesis** to know where to look, i.e., choose what data to examine. If all he had was massive amounts of data, he might well have ended up with a correlation as spurious as the honey bee-marijuana connection. Crucially, Snow "did the experiment." He removed the handle from the water pump and dramatically reduced the spread of cholera, thus moving from correlation to causation and effective intervention. How can we improve the potential for Big Data to improve health and prevent disease? One priority is that a stronger epidemiological foundation is needed. Big Data analysis is currently largely based on convenient samples of people or information available on the Internet. When associations are probed between perfectly measured data (e.g., a genome sequence) and poorly measured data (e.g., administrative claims health data), research accuracy is dictated by the weakest link. Big Data are observational in nature and are fraught with many biases such as selection, confounding variables, and lack of **generalizability**. Big Data analysis may be embedded in epidemiologically well-characterized and representative populations. This epidemiologic approach has served the genomics community well and can be extended to other types of Big Data.

There also must be a means to integrate knowledge that is based on a highly **iterative process** of interpreting what we know and don't know from within and across **scientific disciplines**. This requires knowledge management, knowledge synthesis, and knowledge translation. Curation can be aided by machine learning algorithms. An example is the ClinGen project that will create centralized resources of clinically **annotated** genes to improve interpretation of genomic variation and optimize the use of genomics in practice. And new funding, such as the Biomedical Data to Knowledge awards of the U.S. National Institutes of Health, will develop new tools and training in this arena.

Another important issue to address is that Big Data is a hypothesis-generating machine, but even after robust associations are established, evidence of health-related utility (i.e., assessing balance of health benefits versus harms) is still needed. Documenting the utility of genomics and Big Data information will necessitate the use of **randomized clinical trials** and other experimental designs. Emerging treatments based on Big Data signals need to be tested in **intervention studies**. Predictive tools also should be tested. In other words, we should embrace (and not run away from) principles of evidence-based medicine. We need to move from clinical validity (confirming robust relationships between Big Data and disease) to clinical utility (answering the "who cares?" health impact questions) (Fig. 2.4).

As with genomics, an expanded translational research agenda for Big Data is needed that goes beyond an initial research discovery. In genomics, most published research consists of either basic scientific discoveries or preclinical research designed to develop health-related tests and interventions. What happens after that in the bench-to-bedside journey is a "road less traveled" with <1% of published research dealing with validation, evaluation, implementation, policy, communication, and outcome research in the real world. Reaping the benefits of Big Data requires a "Big Picture" view. Bringing Big Data to bear on public health is where the rubber meets the road. The combination of a strong epidemiologic foundation, robust knowledge integration, principles of evidence-based medicine, and an expanded translation research agenda can put Big Data on the right course.

Glossary

cholera /ˈkɑːlərə/
霍乱
Cholera is caused by a number of types of *Vibrio cholerae*, with some types producing more severe disease than others. It is spread mostly by water and food that has been contaminated with human feces containing the bacteria. Infectors may experience vomiting, diarrhea, have sunken eyes, cold skins and wrinkling of the hands and feet.

epidemiology /ˌepɪˌdiːmiˈɑːlədʒi/
流行病学；传染病学
epidemic—epidemics, epidemiology, epidemiological, epidemiologically
Epidemiology is the science that studies the patterns, causes, and effects of health and disease conditions in defined populations.
Vibrio /ˈvɪbrɪˌoʊ/
弧菌属

Global Positioning System
即 GPS，全球定位系统
geographic /ˌdʒiːəˈɡræfɪk/
地理的；地理学的
geography—geographic, geographer, geographical, geographically
Geography is a field of science dedicated to the study of the lands, the features, the inhabitants, and the phenomena of Earth.
plague /pleɪɡ/
瘟疫；灾祸
Plague is a deadly infectious disease (generally), especially the disease that is caused by the enterobacteria Yersinia pestis.
influenza /ˌɪnfluˈenzə/
流行性感冒；家畜流行性感冒
Influenza (also known as flu), is an infectious disease caused by the influenza virus. The most common symptoms include: a high fever, runny nose, sore throat, muscle pains, headache, coughing, and feeling tired.
health surveillance /helθ sɜːrˈveɪləns/
健康监护
Health surveillance is the surveillance (collection and analysis) of health data about a clinical syndrome that has a significant impact on public health, which is then used to drive decisions about health policy and health education.
paradoxically /ˌpærəˈdɒksɪkli/
自相矛盾地；似非而是地；反常地
spurious /ˈspjʊəriəs/
假的；伪造的；欺骗的
ecological fallacy /ˌiːkəˈlɒdʒɪkl ˈfæləsi/
生态谬误；生态学谬论
Ecological fallacy is a logical fallacy in the interpretation of statistical data where the inferences about the nature of individuals are deduced from inference for the group to which those individuals belong. Ecological fallacy sometimes refers to the fallacy of division which is not a statistical issue.
bee colonies /biː ˈkɑːləniz/
蜂群

marijuana /ˌmærəˈwɑːnə/
大麻
Marijuana (also known as cannabis) is a preparation of the Cannabis plant intended for use as a psychoactive drug and as medicine.
confounding variables /kənˈfaʊndɪŋ ˈveəriəblz/
混杂变量
Confounding variable is an extraneous variable in a statistical model that correlates (directly or inversely) with both the dependent variable and the independent variable.
hypothesis /haɪˈpɒθəsɪs/
（科学）假说
A hypothesis is a proposed explanation for a phenomenon. For a hypothesis to be a scientific hypothesis, the scientific method requires that one can test it. Scientists generally base scientific hypotheses on previous observations that can't satisfactorily be explained with the available scientific theories.
generalizability /dʒenərəlaɪzəˈbɪlɪtɪ/
普遍性；概括性
general—generally, generalize, generalizable, generalization, generalizability
iterative process /ˈɪtəˌreɪtɪv ˈprəʊses/
迭代过程
Iterative process is a process for arriving at a decision or a desired result by repeating rounds of analysis or a cycle of operations.
scientific discipline /ˌsaɪənˈtɪfɪk ˈdɪsɪplɪn/
科学学科
Scientific disciplines refer to the branches of science. They are commonly divided into three major groups: natural sciences, which study natural phenomena, formal sciences and social sciences.
annotated /ˈænəteɪtɪd/
（基因）注释
DNA annotation or genome annotation is the process of identifying the locations of genes and all of the coding regions in a genome and determining what those genes do.
randomized clinical trials
随机临床试验

Randomized controlled trial is a type of scientific (often medical) experiment, where the people being studied are randomly allocated one or other of the different treatments under study.

intervention studies /ˌɪntəˈvenʃn ˈstʌdiz/

干预性研究

Interventional studies are often performed in laboratories and clinical studies to establish beneficial effects of drugs or procedures. They are considered to provide the most reliable evidence in epidemiological research and be either preventative or therapeutic.

Notes to Difficult Sentences

Another important issue to address is that Big Data is a hypothesis-generating machine, but even after robust associations are established, evidence of health-related utility (i.e., assessing balance of health benefits versus harms) is still needed.

另一个需要注意的重要问题是，大数据只是一个假说制造机，即使（某些数据和现象）显示有密切联系，但我们仍需要健康相关的实例证据（如健康相关的利弊平衡的评估）进行进一步验证。

拓展：在一般做检验测试时，我们会界定一个值，叫做第一类统计错误率，它通常被设定为5%，也就是说每100次检验测试，我们允许有5次在统计学上实际无意义的数据被错误判断为统计学上有意义。也就是说，如果实际不存在相关性，我们允许100次假试检验中出现5次错误相关，从而出现虚假相关（或伪相关）。面对海量数据和超多维度的因素时，如果同时对一个数据进行许多检验测试，不可避免会出现虚假相关，如何解决这一问题，统计学上还在做着进一步的研究。

Reading Material 1

Big Data Matters

In 2012, 2.5 quintillion bytes of data were generated daily, and 90% of current data worldwide originated in the past two years. During 2012, 2.2 million TB of new data are generated each day. In 2010, the market for Big Data was $3.2 billion, and this value is expected to increase to $16.9 billion in 2015. As of July 9, 2012, the amount of digital data in the world was 2.7 ZB; Facebook alone stores, accesses, and analyzes 30+ PB of user-generated data. In 2008, Google was processing 20 000 TB of data daily. To enhance advertising, Akamai processes and analyzes 75 million events per day. Walmart processes over 1 million customer transactions, thus generating data in excess of 2.5 PB as an estimate.

More than 5 billion people worldwide call, text, tweet, and browse on mobile devices. The amount of e-mail accounts created worldwide is expected to increase from 3.3 billion in 2012 to over 4.3 billion by late 2016 at an average annual rate of 6% over the next four years. In 2012, a total of 89 billion e-mails were sent and received daily, and this value is expected to increase at an average annual rate of 13% over the next four years to exceed 143 billion by the end of 2016. In 2012, 730 million users (34% of all e-mail users) were e-mailing through mobile devices. Boston.com reported that in 2013, approximately 507 billion e-mails were sent daily. Currently, an e-mail is sent every 3.5×10^{-7} seconds. Thus, the volume of data increases per second as a result of rapid data generation.

Growth rates can be observed based on the daily increase in data. Until the early 1990s, annual growth rate was constant at roughly 40%. After this period, however, the increase was sharp and peaked at 88% in 1998. Technological progress has since slowed down. In late 2011, 1.8 ZB of data were created as of that year, according to IDC. In 2012, this value increased to 2.8 ZB. Globally, approximately 1.2 ZB of electronic data are generated per year by various sources. By 2020, enterprise data is expected to total 40 ZB, as per IDC. Based on this estimation, business-to-consumer (B2C) and internet-business-to-business (B2B) transactions will amount to 450 billion per day. Thus, efficient management tools and techniques are required (Fig. 2.5).

The current international population exceeds 7.2 billion, and over 2 billion of these people are connected to the Internet. Furthermore, 5 billion individuals are using various mobile devices, according to McKinsey. As a result of this technological revolution, these millions of people are generating tremendous amounts of data through the increased use of such devices. In particular, remote sensors continuously produce much heterogeneous data that are either structured or unstructured. This data is known as Big Data. Big Data is characterized by three aspects:

(1) the data are numerous;

(2) the data cannot be categorized into regular relational databases;

(3) the data are generated, captured, and processed very quickly.

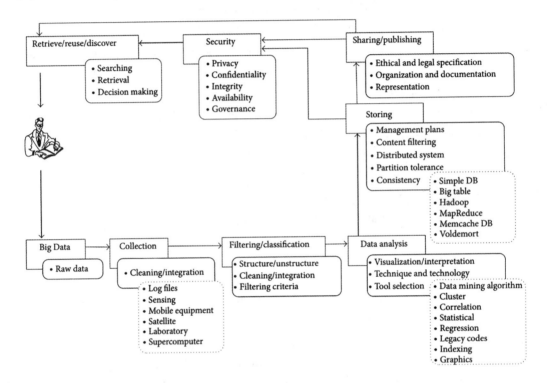

Figure 2.5　Proposed data life cycle using the technologies and terminologies of Big Data

Big data refers to very large datasets with complex structures that are difficult to process using traditional methods and tools. The term process includes, capture, storage, formatting, extraction, curation, integration, analysis, and visualization. A popular definition of big data is the "3V" model proposed by Gartner, which attributes three fundamental features to big data: high volume of data mass, high velocity of data flow, and high variety of data types. The notion of big data can be traced back to the 1970s when scientists realized that they lacked the tools to analyze datasets of large size. In those days, big data was merely several to hundreds of megabytes; now datasets of terabytes are common. Therefore, the "big" in big data reflects the limits of data storage and computational power existing at a given point in time.

Big Data has generated significant interest in various fields, including the manufacture of healthcare machines, banking transactions, social media, and satellite imaging. Traditionally, data is stored in a highly structured format to maximize its informational contents. However, current data volumes are driven by both unstructured and semistructured data. Therefore, end-to-end processing can be impeded by the translation between structured data in relational systems of database management and unstructured data for analytics.

In computational sciences, Big Data is a critical issue that requires serious attention. Thus far, the essential landscapes of Big Data have not been unified. Furthermore, Big Data cannot be processed using existing technologies and methods. Therefore, the generation of incalculable data by the fields of science, business, and society is a global problem. With respect to data analytics, for instance, procedures and standard tools have not been designed to search and analyze large datasets. As a result, organizations encounter early challenges in creating, managing, and manipulating large datasets. Systems of data replication have also displayed some security weaknesses with respect to the generation of multiple copies, data governance, and policy. These policies define the data that are stored, analyzed, and accessed. They also determine the relevance of these data. To process unstructured data sources in Big Data projects, concerns regarding the scalability, low latency, and performance of data infrastructures and their data centers must be addressed.

The extraction of valuable data from large influx of information is a critical issue in Big Data. Qualifying and validating all of the items in Big Data are impractical; hence, new approaches must be developed. From a security perspective, the major concerns of Big Data are privacy, integrity, availability, and confidentiality with respect to outsourced data. Large amounts of data are stored in cloud platforms. However, customers cannot physically check the outsourced data. Thus, data integrity is jeopardized. Given the lack of data support caused by remote access and the lack of information regarding internal storage, integrity assessment is difficult. Big Data involves large systems, profits, and challenges. Therefore, additional research is necessary to improve the efficiency of integrity evaluation online, as well as the display, analysis, and storage of Big Data.

Reading Material 2

DNA Sequencing Caught in Deluge of Data

BGI, based in China, is the world's largest genomics research institute, with 167 DNA sequencers producing the equivalent of 2000 human genomes a day (Fig. 2.6). BGI churns out so much data that it often cannot transmit its results to clients or collaborators over the Internet or other communications lines because that would take weeks. Instead, it sends computer disks containing the data, via FedEx. "It sounds like an analog solution in a digital age," conceded Sifei He, the head of cloud computing for BGI, formerly known as the Beijing Genomics Institute. But for now, he said, there is no better way.

The field of genomics is caught in a data deluge. DNA sequencing is becoming faster and cheaper at a pace far outstripping Moore's law, which describes the rate at which computing gets faster and cheaper. The result is that the ability to determine DNA sequences is starting to outrun the ability of researchers to store, transmit and especially to analyze the data.

Figure 2.6 BGI's TH-1A supercomputers used to analyze sequencing data

"Data handling is now the bottleneck," said David Haussler, director of the center for biomolecular science and engineering at the University of California, Santa Cruz. "It costs more to analyze a genome than to sequence a genome."

That could delay the day when DNA sequencing is routinely used in medicine. In only a year or two, the cost of determining a person's complete DNA blueprint is expected to fall below $1000. But that long-awaited threshold excludes the cost of making sense of that data, which is becoming a bigger part of the total cost as sequencing costs themselves decline. "The real cost in the sequencing is more than just running the sequencing machine," said Mark Gerstein, professor of biomedical informatics at Yale. "And now that is becoming more apparent."

But the data challenges are also creating opportunities. There is demand for people trained in bioinformatics, the convergence of biology and computing. Numerous bioinformatics companies, like SoftGenetics, DNAStar, DNAnexus and NextBio, have sprung up to offer software and services to help analyze the data. EMC, a maker of data storage equipment, has found life sciences a fertile market for products that handle large amounts of information. BGI is starting a journal, *GigaScience*, to publish data-heavy life science papers.

Sequencing involves determining the order of the bases, the chemical units represented by the letters A, C, G and T, in a stretch of DNA. The cost has plummeted, particularly in the last four years, as new techniques have been introduced.

The cost of sequencing a human genome—all three billion bases of DNA in a set of human chromosomes—plunged to $10 500 last July from $8.9 million in July 2007, according to the National Human Genome Research Institute. That is a decline by a factor of more than 800 over four years. By contrast, computing costs would have dropped by perhaps a factor of four in that time span.

The lower cost, along with increasing speed, has led to a huge increase in how much sequencing data is being produced. World capacity is now 13 quadrillion DNA bases a year, an amount that would fill a stack of DVDs two miles high, according to Michael Schatz, assistant professor of quantitative biology at the Cold Spring Harbor Laboratory on Long Island.

There will probably be 30 000 human genomes sequenced by the end of this year, up from a handful a few years ago, according to the journal *Nature*. And that number will rise to millions in a few years.

In a few cases, human genomes are being sequenced to help diagnose mysterious rare diseases and treat patients. But most are being sequenced as part of studies. The federally financed Cancer Genome Atlas, for instance, is sequencing the genomes of thousands of tumors and of healthy tissue from the same people, looking for genetic causes of cancer.

One near victim of the data explosion has been a federal online archive of raw sequencing data. The amount stored has more than tripled just since the beginning of the year, reaching 300 trillion DNA bases and taking up nearly 700 trillion bytes of computer memory.

Straining under the load and facing budget constraints, federal officials talked earlier this year about shutting the archive, to the dismay of researchers. It will remain open, but certain big sequencing projects will now have to pay to store their data there.

If the problem is tough for human genomes, it is far worse for the field known as metagenomics. This involves sequencing the DNA found in a particular environment, like a sample of soil or the human gut. The idea is to take a census of what microbial species are present.

E. Virginia Armbrust, who studies ocean-dwelling microscopic organisms at the University of Washington, said her lab generated 60 billion bases—as much as 20 human genomes—from just two surface water samples. It took weeks to do the sequencing, but nearly two years to then analyze the data, she said. "There is more data that is infiltrating lots of different fields that weren't particularly ready for that," Professor Armbrust said. "It's all a little overwhelming."

The Human Microbiome Project, which is sequencing the microbial populations in the human digestive tract, has generated about a million times as much sequence data as a single human genome, said C. Titus Brown, a bioinformatics specialist at Michigan State University. "It's not at all clear what you do with that data," he said. "Doing a comprehensive analysis of it is essentially impossible at the moment."

Other scientific fields, like particle physics and astronomy, handle huge amounts of data. In those fields, however, much of the data is generated by a few huge accelerators or observatories, said Eugene Kolker, chief data officer at Seattle Children's Hospital. "In the life sciences, anyone can produce so much data, and it's happening in thousands of different labs throughout the world," he said.

Moreover, DNA is just part of the story. To truly understand biology, researchers are gathering data on the RNA, proteins and chemicals in cells. That data can be even more voluminous than data on genes. And those different types of data have to be integrated.

"We have these giant piles of data and no way to connect them," said H. Steven Wiley, a biologist at the Pacific Northwest National Laboratory. He added, "I'm sitting in front of a pile of data that we've been trying to analyze for the last year and a half."

Still, many say the situation will be manageable. Jay Flatley, chief executive of Illumina, the leading supplier of sequencing machines, said he did not think information handling was a bottleneck or that it was causing people to hold off on buying new sequencers.

Sequencers produce huge amounts of raw data that then has to be analyzed and processed by software to produce the result. With the field still young, many researchers store all the raw data, so it can be re-analyzed if better software is developed in the future. But there is now so much raw data that it is becoming not feasible to re-analyze it. So researchers will increasingly store just the final results. In the case of human genomes, they might store even less—only the difference between a particular genome and some reference genome.

Professor Brown of Michigan State said: "We are going to have to come up with really clever ways to throw away data so we can see new stuff."

Chapter 3   Personal Genomics & Personalized Medicine

Personalized medicine is a broad and rapidly advancing field of health care that is informed by each person's unique clinical, genetic, genomic, and environmental information. Health care that embraces personalized medicine is an integrated, coordinated, and evidence-based approach for individualizing patient care across the continuum from health to disease. Personalized medicine utilizes our molecular understanding of disease to enhance preventive health care strategies while people are still well and begin drug therapies at the earliest stages of disease. The overarching goal of personalized medicine is to optimize medical care and outcomes for each individual, resulting in an unprecedented customization of patient care.

Lesson 1
The Advent of Personal Genome Sequencing

Complete human genome sequencing is becoming available at increasing scale and decreasing cost, thanks to massively parallel genomic micro- and **nanoarrays**. The number of genomes sequenced has grown dramatically over the last few years from < 100 in 2009 to > 2000 in 2010 and is projected by the journal *Nature* to reach approximately 25 000 this year, including low-coverage genomes. It would not be surprising if within the next 5 years, we see the annual number of complete human genomes sequenced rise to over a million. Obtaining complete genetic and epigenetic information at this scale, coupled with routine transcriptome sequencing and various functional studies, will lead to an increasingly comprehensive understanding of disease development at the molecular level.

These DNA sequencing advances are making large-scale personal genome sequencing (PGS) a rapidly approaching reality (Fig. 3.1). Experts predict that the consumer price to sequence a complete human genome will drop to $1000 in 2014. In our opinion, this will be achieved with existing DNA nanoarray techno-logies. We further believe that the existing DNA nanoarray technologies, with expected engineering advances, are capable of driving the cost per genome to significantly below $1000 in the following years. By 2020, with improved technology and reduced cost, we may expect tens of millions of personal genomes to be sequenced

Figure 3.1　Rersonal Genome Sequencing

worldwide. It is important that society at large start preparing for this rapidly approaching genomic **tsunami**.

1. Understanding the human genome: deriving the biological context of genetic variants

Although large-scale genome sequencing is an exciting proposition, the need to convert the resulting data into actionable reports remains a daunting challenge. The genetic programs governing human development, adaptive functioning, and maintenance consist of complex regulatory and signal processing networks and pathways. Any segment of the genome sequence derives context from the other sequences in that genome (including parental sequences), environmental conditions, and stochastic events such as **somatic** mutations. These complex interactions explain why isolated genetic variants (e. g., **single-nucleotide polymorphisms**) that are statistically associated with various diseases most often show only incomplete **penetrance**. To understand the intricate regulatory networks and the biological context of any given variant, it will be necessary to obtain complete and accurate genomic, transcriptomic, and **epigenetic** sequence data from thousands of individuals: patients, family members, and healthy controls. Similarly, understanding regulatory networks will also require additional systems approaches, many focused studies, collection of **phenotypic** data, and an enormous amount of computer modeling.

It is critical to achieve all four of these data measures: completeness, accuracy, volume, and diversity. For a molecular understanding and improved prevention and treatment of thousands of diverse diseases and conditions, it is critical that reliable and affordable services in genomic data generation and processing are available to the broad scientific and medical communities. The storage of these data in a digital format, preferably as part of an individual's electronic medical record, is essential to enable manageability and continuous analysis. We expect that advances in electronics will allow permanent lifelong storage of personal genetic variants (1 GB/person) for less than $10.

2. Medical benefits and remaining challenges

Large-scale PGS coupled with a proper interpretation of the results will permit a deep understanding of disease mechanisms, allowing for more rational interventions. This has already occurred to some extent using targeted gene studies. PGS is also likely to permit increased identification of at-risk patients, such as those with mutation in a **tumor suppressor gene**, who should be monitored more frequently for disease development.

PGS information may also improve the drug development process by identifying genetically predisposed nonresponders and individuals who are at greater risk of experiencing a **side effect** from the treatment before they enter a clinical trial. By excluding those subjects, trial sponsors can greatly increase the likelihood that the study will be successful and achieve its endpoints. This genetic information will ultimately make drugs safer and more effective because they will be targeted at patients who are more likely to benefit from them and will be **contraindicated** for people more likely to develop adverse events.

For patients with cancer, PGS of hundreds of patients from each tumor type will lead to a detailed understanding of the diverse molecular processes in cancer development and **metastasis** and will enable the development of improved tumor diagnosis and the classification and selection of more effective treatments based on complete genome and transcriptome sequencing of each **biopsy**. This improved understanding of the disease pathways involved may also allow existing drugs to be repurposed for other indications. We have to be mindful of the complexities of these developments and the amount of time required to complete proper clinical studies before these advances are adopted as routine medical practice.

Similarly, PGS is expected to help diagnose, better understand, and select optimal treatment for children and other patients with undefined diseases. We believe that the initiation of a national project enabling immediate DNA sequencing and interpretation of the whole genomes of these affected children and their parents could be of great utility as one of the primary diagnostic procedures for these patients.

Finally, PGS can serve as a universal genetic test, carried out once, and used for life. PGS would combine tests for rare and metabolic diseases—such as predisposition to cancer and various **late-onset** diseases, drug response and adverse reactions, carriers of **recessive** mutations, and human **leukocyte antigen** typing for **immunological** compatibility, to mention a few of the known biomarkers.

The limited understanding of the genome today does not mean that PGS should not be used today. There are at least 3000 genes for which interpretative information would be immediately useful. Furthermore, personal genome variants may be repeatedly reanalyzed in the light of new genomic and functional knowledge. For most people, no serious disease-causing genetic variants will be detected, even in advanced analysis. This is to be expected for any **presymptomatic** risk reduction test. It is important to treat this as a positive outcome, because it will still allow disease prevention recommendations to be made and better treatments prescribed for potentially millions of people.

However, with these benefits come certain risks. The most serious perhaps is the potential overinterpretation of results based on a limited understanding of contextual information. For example, a risk that is estimated at 1.2 times normal should probably not be reported. It could spur unnecessary medical actions and cause unwarranted **psychological** distress. Validated genome interpretation software using conservative reporting standards is a potential solution. To further minimize this risk, physician and patient education programs need to be introduced, so that the genotypic data are understood within a broader biological and statistical context—for example, personal medical history, family history, and other behavioral or molecular phenotypic data. There is also the risk of genetic **discrimination**, which has just begun to be addressed by the Genetic Information Nondiscrimination Act. The implementation of this law and other supporting nondiscriminatory policies needs to be continued and reinforced.

PGS is being enabled by unprecedented advances in complete genome sequencing technology. Medical genomics software advances are also occurring rapidly, driven by the need to interpret the influx of data from thousands of genome sequences. Together these advancements will enable a wider use of PGS in medical practice starting in a few years. It is our opinion that any revealed risk will be manageable through education, appropriate policies, and conservative data reporting standards. On the other hand, it is unlikely that the current increase in US health care costs will be sustainable even in the foreseeable future. These circumstances may work together to motivate decision makers and payers to adopt new methods of preventive and predictive personalized medicine based on complete genetic knowledge. We are witnessing the exciting and promising beginnings of genomic medicine.

Glossary

nanoarray /ˈnænoʊˌəˈreɪ/
纳米阵列
Nanoarray is an array of nanosized objects, especially one of nanosized spots that have unusual optical characteristics.

tsunami /tsuːˈnɑːmi/
海啸
Tsunami is a series of waves in a body of water caused by the displacement of a large volume of water, generally in an ocean or a large lake.

somatic /soʊˈmætɪk/
躯体的；肉体的；体壁的
Somatic refers to the cells of the body in contrast to the germ line cells.

single-nucleotide polymorphisms
单核苷酸多态性
A Single Nucleotide Polymorphism (SNP) is a DNA sequence variation occurring commonly within a population (e.g., 1%) in which a single nucleotide—A, T, C or G—in the genome (or other shared sequence) differs between members of a biological species or paired chromosomes.

penetrance /ˈpenətrəns/
外显率
The penetrance of a disease-causing mutation is the proportion of individuals with the mutation who exhibit clinical symptoms.

epigenetic /ˌepədʒəˈnetɪk/
后生的，表观的
Epigenetics is the study of cellular and physiological trait variations that are not caused by changes in the DNA sequence; epigenetics describes the study of dynamic alterations in the transcriptional potential of a cell.

phenotypic /ˈfiːnətɪpɪk/
表型的
phenotype—phenotypic, phenology
A phenotype is the composite of an organism's observable characteristics or traits, such as its morphology, development, biochemical or physiological properties, phenology, behavior, and products of behavior (such as a bird's nest).

tumor suppressor gene
肿瘤抑制基因
A tumor suppressor gene, or antioncogene (抗癌基因), is a gene that protects a cell from one step on the path to cancer.

side effect /saɪd ɪˈfekt/
副作用
A side effect is an effect, whether therapeutic or adverse, that is secondary to the one intended; although the term is predominantly employed to describe adverse effects, it can also apply to beneficial, but unintended, consequences of the use of a drug.

contraindicate /ˌkɒntrəˈɪndəˌkeɪt/
禁忌（某种疗法或药物）
A contraindication is a condition or factor that serves as a reason to withhold a certain medical treatment due to the harm that it would cause the patient. Contraindication is the opposite of indication, which is a reason to use a certain treatment.

metastasis /məˈtæstəsɪs/
（远端）转移
Metastasis, or metastatic disease, is the spread of a cancer or disease from one organ or part to another not directly connected with it.

biopsy /ˈbaɪɑːpsi/
活组织检查；活组织切片检查
A biopsy is the medical removal of tissue from a living subject to determine the presence or extent of a disease. The tissue is generally examined under a microscope by a pathologist, and can also be analyzed chemically.

late-onset /ˈleɪtˈɒnset/
晚发性的；迟发性的
Late-onset diseases are a kind of diseases that shown up later in life.

recessive /rɪˈsesɪv/
隐性的
Dominance in genetics is a relationship between alleles of one gene, in which the effect on phenotype of one allele masks the contribution of a second allele at the same locus. The first allele is dominant and the second allele is recessive.

leukocyte /ˈluːkəˌsaɪt/
白细胞
White blood cells (WBCs, leukocytes or leucocytes) are the cells of the immune system that are involved in protecting the body against both infectious disease and foreign invaders. All leukocytes are produced and derived from a multipotent cell in the bone marrow known as a hematopoietic stem cell.

antigen /ˈæntɪdʒən/
抗原
Antigen (antibody generator) is any structural substance which serves as a target for the receptors of an adaptive immune response, TCR or BCR or its secreted form antibody, respectively.

immunological /ˌɪmjunəˈlɒdʒɪkl/
免疫学的
immune—immunology, immunological, immunity, immunize
Immunology is a branch of biomedical science that covers the study of all aspects of the immune system in all organisms. It deals with the physiological functioning of the immune system in states of both health and diseases; malfunctions of the immune system in immunological disorders (autoimmune diseases, hypersensitivities, immune deficiency, transplant rejection).

presymptomatic /ˌprɪsɪmptəˈmætɪk/
症状发生前的
Presymptomatic is of or relating to the early phases of a disease when accurate diagnosis is not possible because symptoms of the disease have not yet appeared.

psychological /ˌsaɪkəˈlɒːdʒɪkl/
心理的；精神上的
Psychological distress (or mental distress) is a term used to describe a range of symptoms and experiences of a person's internal life that are commonly held to be troubling, confusing or out of the ordinary.

discrimination /dɪˌskrɪmɪˈneɪʃn/
歧视；区别；辨别；识别力
Genetic discrimination occurs when people are treated differently (often be estranged, isolated) because they have or are perceived to have a gene mutation that causes or increases the risk of an inherited disorder.

Notes to Difficult Sentences

(1) Any segment of the genome sequence derives context from the other sequences in that genome (including parental sequences), environmental conditions, and stochastic events such as somatic mutations.

基因组上的任意片段都能从该基因组上的其他序列（包括父母的序列）、环境条件、随机事件例如体细胞突变获得新的内容。

拓展：在这里，基因组上的任意片段获得新的内容是指基因变异，基因变异可以在体内和体外进行。导致基因变异的因素很多，如 DNA 体内复制时产生畸变，一些化学物质会导致基因复制时发生错误从而引起突变，辐射引起的基因变异更是为人们所熟知。

(2) PGS information may also improve the drug development process by identifying genetically predisposed non-responders and individuals who are at greater risk of experiencing a side effect from the treatment before they enter a clinical trial.

个人基础组测序数据还能改善药物研发过程，它能筛选出由遗传因素决定的那些对药物不起作用的个体和有可能产生更大副作用的个体，并把他们排除在临床试验之外。

拓展：genetically predisposed 表示由遗传决定的。基因是一个很神奇的东西，它不仅决定人的外在体态相貌特征，还从一定程度上决定人的内在的智商、情商和性格特征。有些人天生对某些化合物更敏感，有些人天生对某些病毒、细菌更易感，而另外一些人天生就对某些危险物质有抗性，这些也都有基因/遗传的"功劳"。

Lesson 2
The Future of Personal Genomics

On 31 May 2007, James Watson was handed a miniature hard drive containing his personal genome sequence, which was subsequently uploaded onto publicly accessible databases. Craig Venter's personal genome was published a few months later. These projects represent research milestones. They also present an opportunity to examine the **ethical**, social, and **clinical** implications of personal genomics (Fig. 3.2).

Excitement over these projects has been tremendous. Many are willing to pay a hefty price to be next. Scientists predict that within 5 years DNA sequencing technologies will be affordable enough that personal genomics will be integrated into routine clinical care. Companies are responding by offering their services for ancestry tracing, **forensics**, nutritional advice, **reproductive** assistance, and even social networking. It will not be long before companies are able to offer a "Face-book-like service centered around our genomes". The medical community needs to consider the ways in which routine generation of this information will affect our health system and how this information might be used outside the medical context.

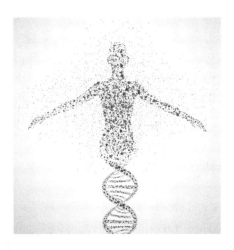

Figure 3.2　Personal Genomics

Despite limited treatment options for many genetic conditions, genetic testing has revolutionized the clinical management of patients for many disorders. Building on this history, companies and genetic testing laboratories have begun to develop technologies for genetic testing on a broader scale. For example, Baylor College of Medicine offers **microarray** analyses to evaluate a **fetus** for over 65 disorders or for genomic errors associated with **autism** or mental retardation.

We currently face an inflection point in clinical medicine as we move from specific **diagnostic** tests for particular disorders to much broader assays for **variants** whose effects we do not yet fully understand. In addition, the effects of any single gene on common diseases are generally small, and their interactions with environmental factors remain largely unknown. For example, despite enthusiasm about recent genome-wide association studies that report an association between **coronary** heart disease and a common variant on chromosome 9, the actual risk of heart disease was only increased from 1% to 1.6% in **homozygotes**.

These studies are invaluable for understanding disease **pathogenesis**, but the present utility of this information for making treatment decisions is limited. Just because an association between genetic variation and disease is statistically significant does not mean that it is clinically meaningful. Moreover, simply knowing genetic risks and disease **predispositions** may not lead to better health decisions. For some, it might lead to **fatalism** and reduced compliance with healthy choices. As a result, many clinicians are "not at all enthusiastic about rushing out to test people in the clinic" for these genes. Although the scientific value of genomic research has been enormous, these emerging technologies have only had marginal impact on health care to date, at least at the population level.

Some fear that personal genomes may become the genetic version of whole-body magnetic resonance imaging scans, which might lead to a population of "worried well" seeking follow-up investigations that could burden already-strained health-care systems. **Physicians** knowledgeable in genetics are the best guard against this concern. However, physicians are ill-prepared for current genetic testing information. The deluge of risk information from widespread use of whole-genome sequencing would greatly magnify this dilemma. Research and training for health-care providers is necessary for personal genomic information to affect patient care.

Only clinically meaningful genomic test results should be integrated into medical decision-making. Clinical practice guidelines should be developed, considering how best to use and present genomic information, and whether and how to withhold information that patients do not want to know. Failure to anticipate what may become standard of care could result in these issues being decided through malpractice litigation.

As personal genomics advances, questions about social justice and the cost of whole-genome sequencing will loom large, especially in countries (including the United States) where there is limited access to basic health-care services for many. Should private health insurance companies and public health systems pay for DNA sequencing, genetic analysis, counseling, and follow-up clinical care? Will physicians be reimbursed for the additional time spent educating patients about the significance of genetic risk information? Payers will likely decline coverage for genomic testing and counseling until it can be associated with improved patient outcomes and quality of care.

The potential clinical application of genomic information is great, as exemplified by the recent

U. S. Food and Drug Administration approval of a label change for **warfarin** to include information on how genetic variations may affect drug response. However, successful integration of personal genomics into routine clinical care will require clear standards, multidisciplinary collaboration, and careful consideration of the ethical, social, and clinical implications (Fig. 3.3).

Figure 3.3　Personal Genome Project

The Personal Genome Project (PGP) is a long term, large cohort study which aims to sequence and publicize the complete genomes and medical records of 100 000 volunteers, in order to enable research into personal genomics and personalized medicine. It was initiated by Harvard University's George M. Church and announced in 2005. As of August 1, 2014, more than 3500 volunteers have joined the project.

Glossary

ethical /ˈeθɪkl/
伦理的；道德的
Ethical is used to describe standards of behavior between individuals, while moral or immoral can describe any behavior.

clinical /ˈklɪnɪkl/
临床的
Dealing with how to practically manage patients, contrasting with prehealth sciences.

forensic /fəˈrensɪks/
鉴证；辩论术；辩论练习
Relating to the use of science and technology in the investigation and establishment of facts or evidence in a court of law.

reproductive /ˌriːprəˈdʌktɪv/
生殖的
reproductive—reproduction
Reproduction (or procreation) is the biological process by which new individual organisms—"offspring"—are produced from their "parents".

microarray /ˌmaɪkroʊəˈreɪ/
微矩阵
A microarray is a multiplex lab-on-a-chip. It is a 2D array on a solid substrate (usually a glass slide or silicon thin-film cell) that assays large amounts of biological material using high-throughput screening miniaturized, multiplexed and parallel processing and detection methods.

fetus /ˈfiːtəs/
胎；胎儿
A fetus is a prenatal mammal or other viviparous vertebrate between its embryonic state and its birth.

autism /ˈɔːtɪzəm/
自闭症；孤独症
Autism is a neurodevelopmental disorder characterized by impaired social interaction, verbal and non-verbal communication, and restricted and repetitive behavior.

diagnostic /ˌdaɪəgˈnɑːstɪk/
诊断的；特征的
diagnostic—diagnosis

Diagnosis is the identification of the nature and cause of a certain phenomenon.

variant /ˈveriənt/
变体；变异型
A different sequence of a gene (locus).

coronary /ˈkɔːrəneri/
冠状动脉或静脉的
Encircling something (like a crown), especially with regard to the arteries or veins of the heart.

homozygote /ˌhɑːməˈzaɪɡoʊt/
纯合子；纯合体；同质接合体；均质接合体
A cell is said to be homozygous for a particular gene when identical alleles of the gene are present on both homologous chromosomes. The cell or organism in question is called a homozygote.

pathogenesis /ˌpæθəˈdʒenɪsɪs/
发病机制；致病原因
The pathogenesis of a disease is the biological mechanism (or mechanisms) that lead to the diseased state.

predisposition /ˌpriːdɪspəˈzɪʃn/
倾向；癖性；（易患病的）体质
The state of being predisposed or susceptible to something, especially to a disease or other health problem.

fatalism /ˈfeɪtəlɪzəm/
宿命论
Fatalism is a philosophical doctrine stressing the subjugation of all events or actions to fate.

physician /fɪˈzɪʃn/
内科医生
A physician is a professional who practices medicine, which is concerned with promoting, maintaining or restoring human health through the study, diagnosis, and treatment of disease, injury, and other physical and mental impairments.

warfarin /ˈwɔːrfərɪn/
杀鼠灵；华法令阻凝剂
Warfarin is an anticoagulant normally used in the prevention of thrombosis and thromboembolism, the formation of blood clots in the blood vessels and their migration elsewhere in the body, respectively.

Notes to Difficult Sentences

Some fear that personal genomes may become the genetic version of whole-body magnetic resonance imaging scans, which might lead to a population of "worried well" seeking follow-up investigations that could burden already-strained health-care systems.

有些人担心个人基因组测序可能成为基因版的全身磁共振扫描成像，导致人们产生"健康焦虑症"，从而给本就很有压力的卫生保健系统带来更重的负担。

拓展：健康焦虑症，或称为疑病症，属于心理疾病范畴。其实疑病心理是人们关心自己身体健康的一种正常表现，但若是过度疑病，就会对自己的正常生活造成影响，成为真正的"病人"，患上疑病症。个人基因组测序的确会助长这种疾病的发生，因为每个人的基因组中或多或少都会存在一些"高风险"的致病基因，当这些"高风险"基因出现在检测报告中，人们就会惊慌失措，认为自己是不是"有病"。其实，"高风险"基因要起作用并引起真正的疾病，是一个很复杂的、受多因素影响的过程，只要专业医生或遗传咨询师能给报告所有者进行全面的检测报告解读和正确的健康指导，就能避免疑病症的产生。

Lesson 3
Obstacles to the Translation of Personalized Medicine into the Clinic

Advances in personalized medicine will create a more unified treatment approach specific to the individual and their genome. Personalized medicine may provide better diagnoses with ealier intervention, and more efficient drug development and therapies (Fig. 3.4). However, innovative solutions to the many challenges of personalized medicine are required if the dream is to be fulfilled.

1. Scientific challenges

It is only in the recent past that drug development has been revolutionized by the understanding of **oncogene addictions**. Although this understanding is **rudimentary**, utilization of companion biomarkers is expected to provide advantageous results. Not every altered protein or **pathway** is a pathogenic mutation representing a therapeutic target. Unraveling driver mutations from bystander mutations is a fundamental challenge and begins with comprehension of complex mechanisms of action, as well as undertaking complex bioinformatic analysis of genomic data.

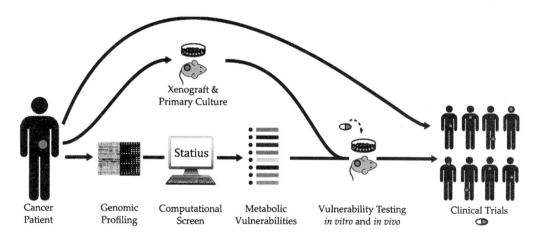

Figure 3.4 Potential applications to personalized and/or precision cancer therapy

Therapeutics must effectively engage the target. This was exemplified by the failed Phase III trial of **iniparib** in triple-negative breast cancer. In addition, some targets with a sound basis for disease biology, such as mutated RAS proteins and transcription factors, such as c-MYC or

HIF, are technically extremely challenging targets for drug developers. This is compounded by the fact that not all **preclinical** hypotheses translate into clinically meaningful developments (e.g., HSP90 inhibitors). Overcoming **intratumor heterogeneity**, which complicates the matching of driver mutations to therapies and contributes to drug resistance, is obligatory. Lastly, smart clinical trials that successfully determine whether these drugs create improvements in clinical outcomes for patients are essential.

2. Challenges of biomarker development

Identification of robust, predictive and **prognostic** biomarkers is essential and, to date, has proved problematic. Beyond the challenge of scientific discovery, biomarkers must be verified, have assay qualification and statistical validation, and be used successfully in clinical trials and then in the clinic. Prognostic biomarkers require modest retrospective data, yet, despite this, many candidates fail at independent validation studies. In comparison predictive markers require large multicenter randomized trials for validation and prove challenging from this perspective. As a result limited breast cancer biomarkers exist.

3. Challenge of uptake into clinical practice

Despite high rates of genomic and molecular data generation, the translation into clinical practice has remained slow. It takes approximately 17 years for 14% of scientific discoveries to enter day-to-day practice. This is explained by fragmentation and lack of a systematic approach to the translation of genomics into clinical medicine. Many personalized medicine discoveries have not demonstrated clinical utility and cost benefits above and beyond current practices; as a result, government agencies are unable to endorse or reimburse the instrument.

4. Challenges in clinical trial design & end points

Failure at the very costly Phase III stage is a consequence of conventional trial design and drug evolution strategies, and their application to targeted therapeutics. Improvements include validated alternative end points, either clinical or biomarker, and the **neoadjuvant** setting to test early drug signals. "Window" trials, such as NeoSPHERE, have accurately predicted the outcome of large Phase III trials in breast cancer, such as CLEOPATRA, which substantiates this claim. It is vital that regulatory and government bodies encourage flexibility and innovation in trial design when approving new therapies, particularly in small patient population subgroups.

5. Collaborative challenges

Pioneering research networks between **pharmaceutical** companies, biotechnology companies and academia are a necessity to facilitate the development and application of personalized breast cancer therapy in clinical practice. The pharmaceutical industry, currently the main contributor to new drug therapies, is facing mounting economic pressures due to the substantial investment required for drug maturity, limited drug pipelines, reduced regulatory approval of new therapies and loss of patents. The fallout is the pressure to produce new "blockbuster" therapies and potentially abandoning drugs with niche therapeutic indications owing to a limited potential market share. Collaborations with academia and biotechnology companies offer the potential for improved innovation and new revenues generated through licensing, spinoffs or sales and **divestitures**. Barriers to these networks include a lack of clearly defied models of collaborations, and conflicts with intellectual property rights and primary goals/objectives.

6. Data sharing challenges

It is apparent that data generated from clinical trials is inefficiently employed. Part of the reason for this lies in lack of secondary use of data, **interoperability** between data sets and poorly developed bioinventories, as well as a lack of collaboration between researchers. Currently, cutting edge biomedical advances are limited by intensive data acquisition, storage and computational capacity. Projects such as the European Commission project, INTEGRATE, offer potential solutions. Further utilization of existing resources, such as the electronic health record, offers an exciting opportunity for genomic medicine, both as a tool and as a resource. It represents an efficient means for obtaining phenotypic data and an effective method for patient recruitment and biosample acquisition.

7. Legislative & administrative challenges

The rapid growth of personalized medicine has resulted in ongoing debate and a shifting structure regarding the appropriate level of regulation of these technologies. Mechanisms need to be established that can facilitate re-use and sharing of medical data and **biospecimens** obtained from signed informed consents. Standardization of testing and conditions are required. One of the greatest challenges facing personalized breast cancer medicine is determining a level of regulation that both protects patients and encourages innovation.

8. Financial considerations & challenges

The obvious question of the budgetary impact of technologies and therapy developed in the era of personalized medicine needs to be addressed. Determinations of cost-effectiveness require ascertaining high-quality models and frameworks to determine the value of genomic tests and targeted therapies. As examples, both MammaPrint and Oncotype DX have been found to reduce the overall cost of patient treatment by US $2800 and $2000, respectively. In addition, the translation into noncontrolled settings needs to be accounted for. In 2007, Lo et al. sampled physicians and patients who had employed Oncotype DX and, while both groups found the test useful, the absolute drop in **chemotherapy** use was only 2%.

9. Ethical considerations & challenges

The evolution of personalized cancer medicine in general requires adequate provision of an ethical and legal framework, which calls for new legislation. This framework should encompass data and sample collection, storage and sharing of data, as well as policies governing patient consent. In addition, genetic tests may challenge anatomized data concepts depending on how comprehensive the test is. These elements represent obligatory patient protection considerations.

Glossary

oncogene addiction /ˈɒŋkəˌdʒiːn əˈdɪkʃn/
癌基因成瘾性
Oncogene addiction refers to the apparent dependency of some cancers on one or a few genes for maintenance of the malignant phenotype.
rudimentary /ˌruːdɪˈmentri/
基本的；初步的；退化的；未发展的
pathway /ˈpæθweɪ/
通路；路径
Pathway here refers to the signal transduction pathway. Signal transduction occurs when an extracellular signaling molecule activates a specific receptor located on the cell surface or inside the cell. In turn, this receptor triggers a biochemical chain of events inside the cell, creating a response. Depending on the cell, the response alters the cell's metabolism, shape, gene expression, or ability to divide.
iniparib /ɪnɪˈpærɪb/
一种抗癌药物
preclinical /priˈklɪnɪkəl/
临床前的；潜伏期的
In drug development, preclinical development, is a stage of research that begins before clinical trials (testing in humans) can begin, and during which important feasibility, iterative testing and drug safety data is collected.
intratumor /ˌɪntrɑːtˈjuːmər/
瘤内的
heterogeneity /ˌhetərəˈdʒəˈniːəti/
异质性
Homogeneity（同质性）and heterogeneity are concepts often used in the sciences relating to the

uniformity in a substance or organism. A material that is homogeneous is uniform in composition or character (i.e. color, shape, size, weight, height, distribution, etc); one that is heterogeneous is distinctly nonuniform in one of these qualities.

prognostic /prɒɡˈnɒstɪk/
预兆；预言；预后症状
Prognosis（预后，预知）is a medical term for predic- ting the likely outcome of one's current standing.

neoadjuvant /niːəʊədʒˈjʊvənt/
新辅助疗法
Neoadjuvant therapy is the administration of therapeutic agents before a main treatment. Neoadjuvant therapy aims to reduce the size or extent of the cancer before using radical treatment intervention, thus making procedures easier and more likely to succeed, and reducing the consequences of a more extensive treatment technique that would be required if the tumor wasn't reduced in size or extent.

pharmaceutical /ˌfɑːrməˈsuːtɪkl/
药物；制药（学）
A pharmaceutical drug (also referred to as a medicine, medication, or medicament) is a drug used to diagnose, cure, treat, or prevent disease.

divestiture /dəˈvestətʃə/
剥夺

interoperability /ˈɪntərɒpərəˈbɪlətɪ/
互操作性；互用性
In healthcare, interoperability is the ability of different information technology systems and software applications to communicate, exchange data, and use the information that has been exchanged.

biospecimen /ˈbaɪəʊˈspesɪmən/
生物样本；生物标本
Biospecimen is a biological laboratory specimen held by a biorepository for research. Such a specimen would be taken by sampling so as to be representative of any other specimen taken from the source of the specimen. When biological specimens are stored, ideally they remain equivalent to freshly-collected specimens for the purposes of research.

chemotherapy /ˌkiːmoʊˈθerəpi/
化学疗法
Chemotherapy is a category of cancer treatment that uses chemical substances, especially one or more anti-cancer drugs that are given as part of a standardized chemotherapy regimen. Chemotherapy may be given with a curative intent, or it may aim to prolong life or to reduce symptoms (palliative chemotherapy).

Notes to Difficult Sentences

Many personalized medicine discoveries have not demonstrated clinical utility and cost benefits above and beyond current practices; as a result, government agencies are unable to endorse or reimburse the instrument.

因为一些个性化医疗成果并没有立即展现出临床应用潜力，也没能体现出超过当前技术的经济收益，因此政府机构不予拨款或报销。

拓展：美国约一半的科研经费用于生命科学研究，可见基础研究是一切科研工作的根本。基础研究和转化可谓厚积而薄发，切不可拔苗助长。即便如此，仍有很多实验室由于研究课题不够有吸引力（应用前景）而被迫叫停。

Reading Material 1

What is Personalized Medicine and What Should It Replace

Medicine improves in gradual steps and quantum leaps. Medical practice is established within a conceptual framework that is based on the current understanding of a disease and gradually improves as new knowledge fills in the details. After 100 years of incremental progress, new technologies and discoveries in the past 20~25 years have revealed major inconsistencies and inadequacies within the existing 20th century framework. Personalized medicine is a new conceptual framework that represents the quantum leap from the 20th century paradigm of Western medicine to medicine for the 21st century. The personalized medicine paradigm retains the advances of the 20th century but also effectively addresses complex disorders.

1. 20th century medicine

In the 20th century, the conceptual framework for medicine was based on the germ theory of disease. The fundamental assumption was that acquired diseases were caused by a single pathologic factor that resulted in a complex syndrome. The scientific method that was established for medical education and medical research early in the 20th century was observation, generation of hypotheses and experimental testing to determine whether an association between a single factor and a disease syndrome existed. Disease taxonomy (disease description, nomenclature and classification) was built on tissue pathology, and the diagnosis of a disease was made on the basis of the identification of pathology within a tissue sample or by using surrogate signs and symptoms. If a "germ" or other single aetiological factor was not identified, the disease was defined by the type of pathology (inflammation or metaplasia, etc.) rather than the aetiology. A treatment was then prescribed on the basis of the diagnosis and evidence that previous patients within a similar disease classification often improved under that therapeutic regimen.

2. New technologies

Instead, the framework for medicine in the 21st century should begin with mechanistic and predictive modelling of normal biological systems before determining which genetic, environmental and structural factors, or combination of these factors, alter "normal" beyond the capacity of the system to adapt and therefore result in disease. A model is a simplified representation of the system that is designed to help researchers understand the real system. The model should define all the critical elements of the real system. Simulation involves modelling the processes of the system over time and enables the investigator to understand the interaction of the parts and predict outcomes on the basis of results obtained by manipulating the model. Modelling and simulation of complex disorders is critical because complex interactions and evolving processes cannot be understood by studying a single variable or even multiple but independent variables. Simulating the disease risk or trajectory enables the effect of interventions to be evaluated *in silico*, on the basis of the combination of risk factors specific to each individual patient (Table 3.1).

Table 3.1 Personalized medicine differs from the 20th century paradigm in many ways

Domain	20th century	Personalized Medicine
Overarching goal	Treatment of disease	Prevention of disease
Enabling technology	Microscope, culture techniques, biopsies	NGS, biomarkers, computers
Disease model	Germ theory	Complex risk, variant response to stress
Paradigm-shifting force	Flexner Report of 1910	Economics
Education focus	Disease diagnosis and classification	Normal responses, assessment of variants
Scientific focus	Determine associations	Determine mechanisms
Scientific approach	Koch's Postulates, global statistics	Modelling and simulation, performance characteristics
Disease classification	Tissue pathology, syndromes	Genetic and environmental risks, surrogate endpoints
Disease time frame	Static, cross-sectional	Dynamic, longitudinal
Physician focus	Overall organ dysfunction	Activity and trajectory of dysfunctional systems
Assessment	Disease classification	Outcome prediction
Treatment	Trial and error	Targeted, optimized
Success measures	Population based	Individual based
Utility of the paradigm	Infectious diseases, Mendelian genetics, single agent disorders, cancer detection	Inflammatory disease, complex genetics, functional disorders, cancer control

3. A new paradigm is required

Four advances in technology illustrate the limitations of the outdated 20th century framework.

These advances are critical to ensure that patients with complex disorders receive appropriate care.

3.1 Imaging and diagnostic biopsies

A diagnosis based on tissue pathology was the foundation of medicine in the 20th century. However, advances in obtaining high quality biopsy samples from an anatomical location using exploratory surgery, laparoscopy, endoscopy and advanced imaging have not led to increased effectiveness of treatments for complex inflammatory disorders or cancers. In the case of cancer, where the character of the disease and patient outcomes are determined by aberrant genetics within the tumour, a personalized medicine approach is needed to identify the genetic signatures that define the mechanisms underlying the pathology in a particular patient. This approach means that the behavior of a tumour can be predicted, and appropriate targets for therapy identified. However, for complex inflammatory disorders such as chronic pancreatitis, tissue evaluation tells us about disease activity, but not about aetiology, mechanisms, or why some people develop pancreatitis whereas others do not.

3.2 Evidence-based medicine

The explosion of clinical and basic research publications in the last half of the 20th century resulted in data overload for physicians. Evidence-based medicine is an analysis framework that was developed by clinical epidemiologists in the early 1990s to evaluate, synthesize and present clinical research reports in a standardized fashion that could be understood and acted upon by clinicians and policy makers. In addition, evidence-based medicine that utilizes retrospective analysis of old clinical studies that approached complex medical disorders using a binary (germ theory) method and disease classifications cannot generate fundamentally new insights or mechanistic breakthroughs, and actually diminishes the usefulness of existing information. Thus, the "next generation" of evidence-based methods is needed to evaluate the mechanistic evidence underlying complex disorders and the performance of new computational tools.

3.3 Genome-wide association studies

A genome-wide association study (GWAS) uses thousands to millions of common single nucleotide polymorphisms (SNPs) in the human genome as chromosome location markers to pinpoint the genetic location of a gene that contributes to a particular disease. Genetic data from large cohorts of patients with and without a defined disease feature are compared through an unbiased statistical approach to discovering the genetic basis of an inherited trait. The underlying assumptions are that humans are related at some level, that pieces of chromosomes that carry disease risk are inherited in subsets of people, and that the culprit gene can be discovered through a nearby genetic marker that can be tracked through various populations of patients with the disease. Early results from GWAS confirm that no single gene causes complex syndromes, but instead reveals that dozens and dozens of factors are associated with complex disorders.

3.4 Next-generation sequencing

Next-generation sequencing (NGS) is a rapidly evolving technology that uses massive parallel sequencing with computer reconstruction of DNA sequence fragments to generate a partial or full genomic sequence. NGS is a major advance over GWAS, because it reveals disease-causing genetic variants rather than nearby markers and is faster and costs less than traditional Sanger sequencing of a single large gene. Clinical application of NGS reveals a tremendous amount of genetic variation among individuals, with many new mutations and multiple susceptibly risk factors seen in each patient. These realities highlight the near impossibility of resolving the complexity of a patient's genome using epidemiology, statistics and patient subclassification strategies within the framework of 20th century medicine. However, integration of NGS into new paradigms will be the foundation of medicine in the 21st century.

Using expensive technology to diagnose patients on the basis of the old framework is inefficient and ineffective, because the complex data sets cannot be adequately interpreted. What is needed is a new framework so that new types of data relevant to individual patients can be integrated into a treatment plan that targets the true aetiology precisely.

4. Personalized medicine

In contrast to current practice, health care should no longer focus on disease, but on health; not on disease status, but on trajectory; not on treatment based on pathology, but on avoiding pathology; not on treatment trial and error, but on selection of best treatment with continuous optimization.

The process of developing disease models is challenging but can be accomplished using reverse engineering, an approach used to understand other complex systems. The system is broken into its component parts, the function of each component is modeled, the modeled components are reintegrated, and the effects of the integrated components on overall processes are simulated under multiple conditions. In medicine, we know a lot about the components of complex disorders, including the specialized cells, organs, signaling and regulation under normal and stress conditions, which we can model and simulate. The advantage of such modelling and simulation is that it can be done on a patient-by-patient basis, incorporating the unique variables that each patient possesses.

Fortunately, we do not need to model each biological step in every pathway to develop useful disease models. Through detailed evaluation of a series of patients with a complex disease involving a known system, and by isolating and evaluating individual parts, the components that are commonly dysfunctional can be identified. Then, the dysfunctional mechanism can be simulated and brought back to the larger model. At this point, the effect of any combination of variables in a single patient can be calculated, and the effect of a therapeutic intervention can be simulated.

Reading Material 2

"Me" Medicine Could Undermine Public Health Measures

Advocates of personalized medicine claim that healthcare isn't individualized enough.

Backed up by the glamour of new biotechnologies such as direct-to-consumer genetic testing, personalized medicine—what I call "Me Medicine"—appears to its advocates as the inevitable and desirable way to go (Fig. 3.5). Barack Obama, when still a US senator, declared that "in no area of research is the promise greater than in personalized medicine".

Figure 3.5 "Me Medicine" versus "We Medicine"
(By Andrzej krauze)

This trend towards Me Medicine is led by the US, but it is growing across the developed world.

In contrast, "We Medicine"—public-health programmes such as flu shots or childhood vaccination—is increasingly distrusted and vulnerable to austerity cuts. Yet historically this approach has produced the biggest increase in lifespan. Even today, countries with more social provision of healthcare and less individualistic attitudes have better health outcomes across all social classes.

Contrary to the claims of its proponents, the personalized approach hasn't yet delivered a paradigm shift in medicine. A 2012 Harris poll of 2760 US patients and physicians found that doctors had recommended personal genetic tests for only 4 per cent of patients. The Center for Health Reform & Modernization, run by U.S. healthcare company United Health, put the figure at just 2 per cent.

But money is still pouring into Me Medicine. In July, the UK government announced that it would offer private companies a subsidy from a £300 million fund to encourage investment in its personalized medicine initiative, Genomics England. Last year the U.S. administration increased the National Institutes of Health budget for personalized medicine, while cutting the budget for the Centers for Disease Control and Prevention's Office of Public Health Genomics by 90 per cent.

Of course it would be nice if we could afford both, but in reality there's a growing risk that "me" will edge out "we". If it does, it won't be because the science is better or the outcomes more beneficial. In some instances of Me Medicine, clinical outcomes are worse than the We equivalent. For example, according to the UK's Royal College of Obstetricians and Gynaecologists, private umbilical cord blood banks, which ostensibly provide a personal "spare parts kit" for the baby, produce poorer outcomes than public cord blood banking.

It is true that in some areas of Me Medicine, such as genetically individualized drug regimes for cancer care (technically known as pharmacogenetics), there has been genuine progress. For example, vemurafenib, a drug for aggressive melanoma, was reported in a 2012 *New England Journal of Medicine* article to extend the lifespan of 1 in 4 patients by seven months if they carry a specific genetic mutation in their cancer.

But only about half of those with the "right" type of tumour responded, and the mutation in question only occurs in about half of such melanomas. What is more, pharmaceutical firms will probably charge more for such drugs than for mass-market ones. They will be expensive, may benefit only a subset of the population and could leave cash-strapped state healthcare systems facing difficult decisions about where to allocate resources.

A month after the melanoma study, much less encouraging results for pharmacogenetics were reported in another NEJM article. A genome-wide analysis of biopsies on four people with kidney cancer showed that separate samples from the same tumour can have different mutations, so a drug that targets one may leave other parts of the tumour untreated.

Given that the scientific evidence alone doesn't explain all the interest in personalized medicine, what does? Many retail genetics companies have "me" in their name—notably 23andMe, DeCODEme and Knome—so does it boil down to narcissism? I doubt it. There's nothing narcissistic about pharmacogenetics.

Another possible explanation is the favourable connotations of "personal" and "choice". "We" measures such as childhood vaccination are routinely attacked as an invasion of parental choice, while accounts by people who have paid to have genetic profiles drawn up often include themes of individual self-discovery.

A third explanation is commercial: that in personalized medicine, pharmaceutical companies see a way to rescue themselves from the demise of profitable patents on mass-market drugs, so they promote the shift from We to Me.

As Mark Levin, former CEO of Millennium Pharmaceuticals, put it in 2012: "Business incentives must be put in place to encourage private investment and further develop the pipeline of new personalized medicine products."

The landscape has clearly changed. Twenty years ago, who could have predicted that people would pay to have a spit sample genetically tested or to bank their child's umbilical cord blood?

As well as unpicking and unpacking the science, we need to consider the social and economic context behind Me Medicine. How can we balance the role of the individual and the communal in healthcare? And how did we move from the original vision of genetic biomedicine as a communitarian endeavour—the Human Genome Project was ostensibly for the benefit of all humankind—to the personalized medicine paradigm?

These are big questions that need to be asked. If we do embrace personalized medicine, it should only be after a thorough review of the evidence and careful analysis of the social landscape in which we're making that choice.

Chapter 4   Animal & Plant Genome Research and Its Agricultural Applications

Advances in genomics, the study of all the genetic material (i. e., the genome) of an organism, have been remarkable in recent years. Publication of the first draft of the human genome in 2001 was a milestone, quickly followed by that of the first crop (rice) in 2002 and the first farm animal (chicken) in 2004. Huge technological advancements have meant that sequencing has become dramatically quicker and cheaper over time, so the genomes of many of the important crops, livestock, forest trees, aquatic animals and agricultural pests are now already sequenced or soon will be. Next generation sequencing also enables us to detect functional genes and markers of important traits to facilitate molecular breeding and improve agriculture production and conservation. Application of genomics in food and agriculture include: (I) genetic improvement of populations; (II) characterization and management of genetic resources for food and agriculture; (III) food and agricultural product authentication; (IV) pathogen detection and (V) vaccine development.

Chapter 4 Animal & Plant Genome Research and Its Agricultural Applications

Lesson 1
Plant and Animal Sequencing

1. *De novo* plant and animal sequencing

Whether a research project is focused on a novel species or just one that has never been investigated before using genetic tools, *de novo* sequencing is a first step toward understanding the genetic **underpinnings** of a plant or animal's functions and its interaction with the environment. With long-paired and mate-paired sequence data, some researchers use the assembled genome to assign map positions and stack diverse breed information for subsequent resequencing to discover SNPs and other genetic variations.

2. Whole-genome resequencing

When a species' reference genome is available, whole-genome resequencing is an efficient approach for discovering genes, SNPs, and structural variants, while simultaneously determining genotypes. Information from these studies will fill in the gaps that exist in the genetic maps of many plant and animal species, improving plant breeding and selection, and enabling definitive comparative genomic analyses within and across species.

3. Transcriptome analysis in plants and animals

RNA sequencing is revolutionizing the exploration of gene expression in plants and animals, providing novel insights into changing expression levels that occur in development, and during disease and stress conditions. It can be used to elucidate gene and protein function and interactions, identify tissue-specific list of RNA transcripts produced by an animal or plant genome (mRNAs, non-coding RNAs, and small RNAs), and for SNP discovery.

4. Plant and animal epigenetics

Adaptive responses to changes in the environment (food availability, drought conditions, etc.) can trigger phenotypic changes in plants and animals that affect their viability and reproductive fitness. By using sequencing to identify changes in DNA methylation, chromatin structure, and small RNA expression, researchers can better understand how epigenetic factors contribute to controlling these and other traits in a species of interest.

5. Targeted resequencing

Targeted resequencing digs deeper into the exome or specific genomic regions of interest identified from large-scale association or linkage studies. This efficient and economical method sequences predetermined areas of genetic variation over a large number of samples, identifying common and rare variants (SNPs, CNVs, etc.). These variants may represent beneficial mutations that can help inform breeding decisions and may reveal causative mutations responsible for plant or animal disease, or parasite susceptibility.

6. Genotyping by sequencing

Genotyping by sequencing, or next-generation genotyping (NGG), provides a low-cost genetic screening method to discover novel plant and animal SNPs and perform genotyping studies, often simultaneously in many specimens. With a low-cost tool for routine screening, researchers can accelerate the return on investment in breeding practice. Applications of this method include **genetic mapping**, screening backcross lines, purity testing, constructing **haplotype** maps, and performing association and genomic evaluation for plant **agrigenomic** studies.

7. Soil and agricultural metagenomics

Sequencing has transformed **metagenomics**, enabling the study of large microbial communities directly in their natural environment without prior culturing. These studies can yield important information about the complex and diverse populations of microbes associated with animal and plant development, from **rumen flora** that enhance animal digestion to root-associated bacteria involved in nitrogen fixation. Next-generation sequencing (NGS) has been instrumental in advancing microbiology research. With NGS, you can measure changes anywhere in the genome without prior knowledge, which is critical for unculturable organisms. Single-base resolution allows tracking of microbial adaptation over short periods of time, both in the laboratory and in the environment

8. Case study

8.1 Cucumber *de novo* sequencing

The genome sequence of *C. sativus* var. *sativus* L. was assembled using a novel combinational method of traditional Sanger and next-generation Illumina GA sequencing technologies, resulting in a 72X total genome coverage. The study established that five of cucumber's seven chromosomes arose by fusions of ten ancestral chromosomes after speciation from melon lineage (Fig. 4.1). Insights were also afforded into sex determination, unique cucumber biosynthetic pathways, as well as important evolutionary traits, such as **tendril** formation and the evolution of the plant **vascular system**. The cucumber genome provides a resource for developing of elite **cultivars** with improved **agronomic** traits, and for the study of the evolution and function of the plant vascular system. (*Nature Genetics* publication)

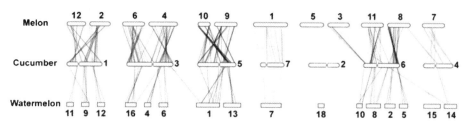

Figure 4.1 Comparative analysis of the melon and watermelon genetic maps with the cucumber sequence map

8.2 Giant Panda *de novo* sequencing

The giant panda genome was successfully sequenced and assembled using next-generation sequencing technology. The assembled contigs (2.25 Gb) cover approximately 94% of the whole genome, and over 2.7 million heterozygous SNPs in the **diploid** genome were indentified. A history of the panda population size over a period of twenty thousand to several million years ago was provided (Fig. 4.2). The data and analyses demonstrate the feasibility for using next-generation sequencing technologies for accurate, cost-effective, and rapid *de novo* assembly of large **eukaryotic** genomes. (*Nature* publication)

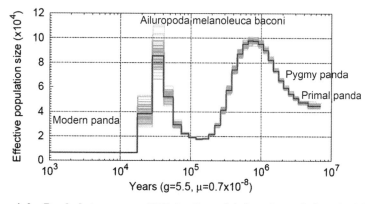

Figure 4.2 Panda heterozygous SNP density and inferred population size history

8.3 Rice resequencing

25 representative cultivated rice and 25 wild rice accessions were resequenced. The first genome variation maps for cultivated and wild rice which contain about 8.4 million SNPs is developed. The genome variation data suggested the rice genome might originate from two ancient wild rice populations. Based on the variation maps, a conservative list of 511 genes showing strong selection signals in cultivated rice were detected as candidate **domestication** genes (Fig. 4.3). Many of these genes have functions related to plant growth, **architecture**, maturity, productivity or resistance. The population genomics approach combining the new sequencing technology with selection detection methods could be very useful in identifying domestication genes and tracing evolutionary history of species. (*Nature* publication)

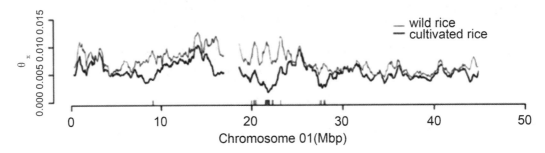

Figure 4.3 Possible artificial selection signals in the genomes of cultivated rice

(Candidate domestication genes are marked on the x-axis in vertical lines)

Glossary

underpinning /ˌʌndərˈpɪnɪŋ/
基础；基础材料
Underpinning is the process of strengthening the foundation of an existing building or other structure.

genetic mapping /dʒəˈnetɪk ˈmæpɪŋ/
遗传作图
Genetic mapping is any method used for determining the location of gene and relative distances between genes on a chromosome.

haplotype /ˈhæploʊtaɪp/
单体型
A haplotype is a portmanteau for haploid genotype. A haplotype is a collection of specific alleles in a cluster of tightly-linked genes on a chromosome that are likely to be inherited together.

agrigenomic /ˌæɡrɪdʒəˈnɒmɪk/
农业基因组学的
agrigenomics = agricultural genomics

metagenomics /ˌmetədʒəˈnɒmɪks/
宏基因组学
Metagenomics is the study of genetic material recovered directly from environmental samples.

rumen /ˈruːmen/
瘤胃
Rumen forms the larger part of the reticulorumen, which is the first chamber in the alimentary canal (消化道) of ruminant (反刍) animals.

flora /ˈflɔːrə/
植物群；真菌/细菌群
flora = plant
Sometimes bacteria and fungi are also referred to as flora.

tendril /ˈtendrəl/
卷须；蔓；卷须状物
A tendril is a specialized stem, leaf or petiole with a threadlike shape that is used by climbing plants for support, attachment and cellular invasion by parasitic plants, generally by twining around suitable hosts.

vascular system /ˈvæskjələr ˈsɪstəm/
维管系
In plant vascular system, the primary components of vascular tissue are the xylem (木质部) and phloem (韧皮部). These two tissues transport fluid and nutrients internally.

cultivar /ˈkʌltɪvɑːr/
栽培品种；栽培品系
A cultivar is a plant or grouping of plants selected for desirable characteristics that can be maintained by propagation.

agronomic /ˌægrəˈnɒmɪk/
农事的；农艺学的
Agronomy is the science and technology of producing and using plants for food, fuel, fiber, and land reclamation.

diploid /ˈdɪplɔɪd/
二倍体
Diploid cells have two homologous copies of each chromosome, usually one from the mother and one from the father.

eukaryotic /ˌuːkeəriˈɒtɪk/
真核的；真核生物的
A eukaryotic organism (eukaryote) is any organism whose cells contain a nucleus and other organelles enclosed within membranes.

domestication /dəˌmestɪˈkeɪʃn/
驯养；教化
Domestication is the cultivating or taming of a population of organisms in order to accentuate traits that are desirable to the cultivator or tamer.

architecture /ˈɑːrkɪtektʃər/
建筑学；建筑风格；建筑式样
Plant architecture or plant morphology is the study of the physical form and external structure of plants.

Notes to Difficult Sentences

Whether a research project is focused on a novel species or just one that has never been investigated before using genetic tools, *de novo* sequencing is a first step toward understanding the genetic underpinnings of a plant or animal's functions and its interaction with the environment.

不论一个研究课题是否着眼于某一新的物种或仅仅一个未曾用基因工具研究过的物种，从头测序往往是了解一个动物、植物功能和该物种与环境间相互作用的基因基础的第一步。

拓展：对某一物种进行基因组测序通常分两种情况。第一种是已经有参考序列（reference-based）的重测序（resequencing），指在已知物种基因组的情况下，对物种内的不同个体或某个个体的不同组织进行基因组重测序，可以在全基因组水平上发现不同个体或组织细胞之间的差异。另一种就是这里提到的没有任何序列资料的从头测序（*de novo* sequencing），它不依赖于任何已知基因组序列信息对某个物种的基因组进行测序，然后应用生物信息学手段对测序序列进行拼接和组装，最终获得该物种基因组序列图谱。

Lesson 2
Animal Code: Our Favorite Genomes

Every part of our bodies and every action of our cells is exquisitely controlled by the billion base pairs that make up our DNA. These **nucleotides** are the building blocks of genes, the part of the genome that holds the information our cells turn into proteins.

Since the first gene was suggested by Gregor Mendel in the 1860s, scientists have been searching for ways to decode them, to figure out how this code creates the end product: An **organism**. That organism can be an animal, plant, virus or bacteria that lives, reproduces and spreads its genome. Uncovering the secrets locked in each species' genomes will teach researchers how to harness the power of genes, from the longevity of the naked mole rate and the fat processing abilities of the **orangutan**. Dozens of animal, plant and microbe genomes have been sequenced. Here are LiveScience's favorite 10 genome projects.

1. Culturing cow

Itching for a tastier slice of beef? Look no further than the cow's genome (Fig. 4.5). After being sequenced in 2009, analysis of the cow's genes could lead to higher quality milk and better beef and tells an interesting tale of how human domestication has impacted the evolution of the once-wild animal. The analysis of the cow's 22 000 genes has also shown that while we humans are more closely related to **rodents** than to cows in terms of the family tree, our genome more closely resembles those of cows because the tiny lifespan of rodents requires them to have many more babies in a much quicker timeframe, accelerating evolution. The cows also have many additional immune system genes, ones that could defend against **pathogens** that live in their extra stomachs. Analysis of other breeds also determined that the cows showed specific patterns of genetic changes depending on whether they were

Figure 4.5 *Bos Taurus*
(Credit: Wikimedia Commons user Jim Champion)

breed for meat or milk.

2. First amphibian, the African clawed frog

The first amphibian genome to be sequenced belongs to the frog *Xenopus tropicalis*, a slimy rotund amphibian also known as the African clawed frog (Fig. 4.6). The genome study enables researchers to compare genes in mammals to those of the amphibians to see which genes stay the same and which have changed since mammals and amphibians parted 360 million years ago, which pinpoints the important basic genes that all complex life needs, including genes involved in the heart and lungs.

Figure 4.6 *Xenopus tropicalis*
(Credit: Michael Linnenbach at the German language Wikipedia)

3. The tasty turkey

The turkey genome was published in the journal *PLoS One* in November of 2010, just in time for the Thanksgiving meal (Fig. 4.7)! The turkey clocked in at 1.1 billion base pairs, about a third the size of the human genome, and bears a close resemblance to its relative, the chicken, whose genome was completed in 2004. This work could lead to meatier, healthier birds, according to the researchers, by providing a better understanding of the turkey's muscles and taste and can help farmers improve disease resistance and treatment.

Figure 4.7 *Meleagris gallopavo*
(Credit: American Livestock Breeds Conservancy)

4. Our cousin the orangutan

A study in the journal *Nature* in 2011 released the genes of the orangutan Susie (and five of her wild brethren) of the Texas Zoo (Fig. 4.8). The genes revealed that orangutans have been evolving much more slowly than **chimps** and humans; their genes change around much less frequently. This could mean that chimps and humans have accelerated their evolution since separating from the rest of the **primates**. The orangutans were evolving in one respect: their fat breakdown molecules were changing quicker than expected. This is probably why they make better use of the energy they take in.

Figure 4.8 *Pongo abelii*
(Credit: Adam van Casteren)

5. Spiny, spineless sea urchin

Humanity's evolutionary cousin, the spiny but spineless sea **urchin**, received the honor of having its genome sequenced in 2006 and published in the journal *Science* (Fig. 4.9). Seventy percent of the urchins' 23 300 genes (made from 814 million pairs of genetic bases) are similar to those in humans, more than many other lab organisms like fruit flies. The urchins' genes also hold details where the urchins get their unique immune system, and the secrets of their 100-year-

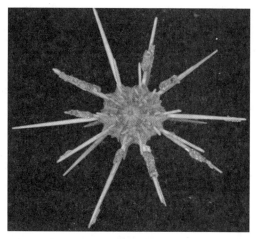

Figure 4.9 *Strongylocentrotus purpuratus*
(Credit: NOAA)

long lives. The genes of the innate immune system, our body's first line of defense, multiplied in the urchin, giving them a larger toolbox to combat **infections**. Though they lack eyes and ears, the researchers discovered that the urchins sport genes associated with vision and hearing as well as taste, smell and even balance.

6. Rhesus monkey

The first primate to get rocketed into space and to be cloned, the rhesus monkey, had its genome sequenced in 2007 (Fig. 4.10). The rhesus monkey genome has about 93 percent similarity with that of humans, which is important since it is often used in medical testing for human drugs and **therapies**. The researchers identified roughly 200 genes that appear to be key players in what defines the differences between our species. These include genes involved in hair formation, sperm-egg fusion, immune response and changes to cell membrane proteins. The rhesus monkey shows the same mysterious rearrangements that are seen in the human lineage's X chromosome following the branching off of the chimpanzee which gives us new evidence of the unusual role of this sex chromosome in primate evolution.

Figure 4.10 *Macaca mulatta*
(Credit: Shutterstock)

7. Marsupials versus mammals

Marsupials, our mammalian brethren, are found mostly in Australia and New Guinea. They have many weird features that separate them from other mammals, including a very short **pregnancy**, after which they shelter their very immature offspring in a pouch (Fig. 4.11). Sequences of the kangaroo and other marsupials have shed light on how these features have developed after the **placental** mammal-marsupial split 150 million years ago. The genome sequencing of an opossum and a small kangaroo species called the tammar wallaby show that the group may have evolved in South America, not Australia. Analysis of the

Figure 4.11 *Macropus eugenii*
(Credit: Wikimedia Commons user Thomas)

tammar wallaby genome indicates that large areas of the marsupial genome are similar to the genome of normal, placental mammals.

8. Nematodes

One of the first multi-cellular organisms to have its genome decoded, way back in 1998, the **nematode** is a staple in many research labs (Fig. 4.12). The nematode and its simple-minded cousins have about 20 000 genes. While similar in number to those of other animals, the nematode's genome contains only 100 million base pairs of DNA; one tenth the size of an average mammalian genome. This is because more evolved organisms tend to have more non-protein coding regions that regulate how, when and how much of a gene is expressed in different types of cells, and not necessarily have more genes. This fine-tuned regulation seems to play an important part in what makes mammals and other organisms unique.

Figure 4.12 *Caenorhabditis elegans*
(Credit: Christopher Chandler, Iowa State University, Michigan State University)

9. Human

The first human genome was sequenced in 2001, and currently over 60 complete human genomes have been sequenced. These include the genome of researcher J Craig Venter, James Watson (who helped discover the double helix shape of DNA), a Han Chinese, a Yoruban Nigerian, a female **leukemia** patient and a Korean individual.

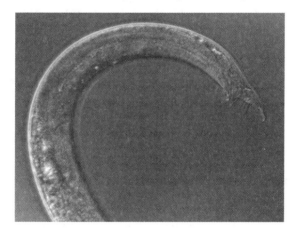

Figure 4.13 Human Evolution
(Credit: Shutterstock)

Comparison of these genomes to the genome

of the chimpanzee and other organisms and looked at which seem to disappear in humans give us insights into human origin and evolution (Fig. 4.13). These genes are likely to play an important role in what makes us humans, though only one held the code for an actual protein, the rest were involved in regulation or had other functions. They found differences in the handling of several proteins, including ones in the brain, and ones that respond to male hormones. These changes resulted in bigger brains and changes in **penis** shape in response to a decrease in **polyandry** in humans.

10. The enigmatic naked mole rat

The newly deciphered genome of the hairless, underground-dwelling, long-lived and cancer-resistant naked mole rat could help researchers unravel the creature's secrets, and may help improve human health along the way. The researchers found that the naked mole rat had turned off several genes related to vision since they live in the dark (Fig. 4.14). They also saw a mutation in the gene dubbed "hairless", previously seen to cause

Figure 4.14 *Heterocephalus glaber*
(Credit: Rochelle Buffenstein, City College of New York)

baldness in mice and humans, which could explain how they lost their fur. While a quick cursory look at the genome sequencing is already shedding light on changes that may lead to the naked mole rat's exquisite uniqueness, the information is also useful for human health. Stroke and heart attack deprive parts of the body from oxygen. Discovering how the mole rats survive in their low-oxygen burrows can help scientists design treatments to improve outcomes. By comparing this genome with those of other mole rats, including solitary ones, scientists could also tease out how the animal's genes influence their behaviors.

Glossary

nucleotide /ˈnjuːklɪəˌtaɪd/
核苷酸
Nucleotides are organic molecules that serve as the monomers, or subunits, of nucleic acids like DNA and RNA.

organism /ˈɔːrɡənɪzəm/
有机体；生物体
In biology, an organism is any contiguous living system, such as a vertebrate, insect, plant or bacterium.

Chapter 4   Animal & Plant Genome Research and Its Agricultural Applications

orangutan /oʊˈræŋuːˌtæn/
猩猩
The orangutans (also spelled orang-utan, orangu-tang, or orang-utang) are the two exclusively Asian species of extant great apes.

rodent /ˈroʊdnt/
啮齿动物
Rodents are mammals of the order rodentia, which are characterized by a single pair of unremittingly growing incisors in each of the upper and lower jaws.

pathogen /ˈpæθədʒən/
病原体
In biology, a pathogen in the oldest and broadest sense is anything that can produce disease, a term which came into use in the 1880s.

chimp /tʃɪmp/
（非洲）黑猩猩
Chimpanzees, colloquially called chimps, are two extant hominid species of apes in the genus Pan.

primate /ˈpraɪmeɪt/
灵长类动物
A primate is a mammal of the order Primates. In taxonomy, primates include two distinct lineages, strepsirrhines and haplorhines.

urchin /ˈɜːrtʃɪn/
海胆
Sea urchins are spiny sea creatures that are round and prickly like hedgehogs.

infection /ɪnˈfekʃn/
传染；传染病
Infection is the invasion of an organism's body tissues by disease-causing agents, their multiplication, and the reaction of host tissues to these organisms and the toxins they produce.

therapy /ˈθerəpi/
疗法；治疗
Therapy (often abbreviated tx or Tx) is the attempted remediation of a health problem, usually following a diagnosis.

marsupial /mɑːrˈsuːpiəl/
有袋动物
Marsupials are an infraclass of mammals living primarily in Australasia and the Americas. A distinctive characteristic, common to most species, is that the young are carried in a pouch.

pregnancy /ˈpregnənsi/
怀孕；妊娠
Pregnancy, also known as gravidity or gestation, is the time during which one or more offspring develops inside a woman.

placental /pləˈsentl/
有胎盘哺乳动物
The placentals are primarily distinguished from other mammals in that the fetus is carried in the uterus of its mother where it is nourished via a placenta, until the live birth of a fully developed offspring occurs.

nematode /ˈnemətoʊd/
线虫类
The nematodes or roundworms constitute the phylum Nematoda. They are a diverse animal phylum inhabiting a very broad range of environments. Nematodes have tubular digestive systems with openings at both ends.

leukemia /luːˈkiːmɪə/
白血病
Leukemia is a group of cancers that usually begins in the bone marrow and results in high numbers of abnormal white blood cells.

penis /ˈpiːnɪs/
阴茎；阳物
A penis (plural penises or penes) is the primary sexual organ that male and hermaphrodite animals use to inseminate sexually receptive mates (usually females and hermaphrodites respectively) during copulation.

polyandry /ˌpɑːliˈændri/
一妻多夫制；一雌多雄配合
Polyandry is a form of polygamy whereby a woman takes two or more husbands at the same time.

Notes to Difficult Sentences

These genes are likely to play an important role in what makes us humans, though only one held the code for an actual protein, the rest were involved in regulation or had other functions.

虽然这些基因中只有一个能编码出功能性蛋白，其他的仅参与调控或行使其他功能，但这些基因很可能在解决人之所以是人这一问题中起到重要作用。

拓展：非编码DNA序列是指基因组中不编码蛋白质的DNA序列。这些序列可以结合调节因子、转录为功能性RNA、单独或协同地调节生理活动和病理过程。在庞大的人类基因组中，蛋白质编码序列所占比例不到2%，其余约98%的DNA序列都是不编码蛋白质的，曾一度被认为是基因组里的垃圾，因而也被冠以"垃圾DNA"的称号。然而，随着时间的推移，非编码DNA的功能不断被发现并逐渐得到证实。

Lesson 3
Sequencing of Animal/Plant Genomes and Its Application

Next-generation sequencing (NGS) has revolutionized plant and animal research, allowing us to decode the whole genomes of many species. NGS also enables us to detect functional genes and markers of important traits to facilitate molecular **breeding** and improve agriculture production and conservation (Fig. 4.15). BGI has been a pioneer in this field and is highly experienced in applying NGS to the study of plant and animal genomes, with state-of-the-art technologies and computing power, rapid turn-around time, as well as strong **bioinformatics** know-how. To date, BGI Tech has sequenced 656 plant and animal reference genomes, including 421 animal genomes and 235 plant genomes.

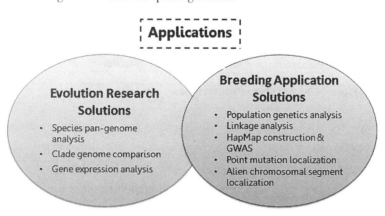

Figure 4.15 Applications of genome sequencing for plants and animals

1. Evolution and diversity

De novo sequencing allows us to study genomes within the same species (Species Pan-genome) or decode genomes in the same family or genus (**Clade** Genomes) (Fig. 4.16). Population evolution based on whole-genome re-sequencing can be used for **phylogenetic**, linkage disequilibrium, genetic structure analyses, as well as population genetic structure and species formation, to explore mechanisms of biological evolution. Discovering the secrets of biological evolution will clarify the origin of species and the diversity of life on earth.

Figure 4.16 Evolution research based on *de novo* sequencing

In addition to genomics, whole transcriptome analyses are very important to understanding how altered expression of genetic variants contributes to complex plant phenotypes. BGI offers an extensive service portfolio for gene expression analyses, from transcriptome sequencing (including miRNA and noncoding RNA analyses) to **epigenomics** research.

2. Molecular breeding

Molecular breeding applies molecular biology tools to accelerate the breeding process (Fig. 4.17). One of the most important molecular breeding methods is marker-assisted selection (MAS), the use of tightly linked DNA markers that target loci as a substitute to assist in phenotypic screening. Recent improvements in NGS have simplified the discovery of DNA markers, making it much more cost-effective. As the largest genomics center in the world, BGI has developed new services that advance NGS applications in the molecular breeding area. With their services, scientists can complete their breeding projects, which would take six to eight years using traditional strategies, in just one year. This approach provides dramatic time and financial savings.

Chapter 4 Animal & Plant Genome Research and Its Agricultural Applications

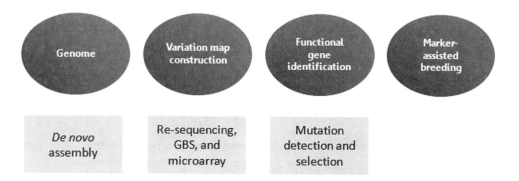

Figure 4.17 Research strategies of molecular breeding

Currently, **genotyping** by sequencing (GBS) is becoming increasingly important as a unique, cost-effective tool for associate studies and genomics-assisted breeding, particularly in plant species with complex genomes that lack a reference sequence. The key components of this system include reduced sample handling, fewer PCR and purification steps, no size fractionation, and inexpensive barcoding.

3. Advantages of GBS

(1) Faster, simpler protocol than traditional methods.
(2) Simplified computational analyses.
(3) High accuracy of SNP calling.
(4) Low cost makes it an attractive option for large numbers of markers or individuals.
(5) Decreased amounts of input DNA.

4. Example—cucumis melon breeding

Melon (*Cucurbitaceae cucumis*) is cultivated worldwide and is an important agricultural crop. China has the largest cultivation region and the highest yield in the world. Although numerous varieties of melon have been developed through traditional **crossbreeding** techniques, shortcomings and deficiencies remain. While maintaining the yield of **hybrid** and wide **adaptability** traits, other traits were directionally improved, including background peel and flesh color. BGI helped scientists generate several new varieties that combined the desired traits of the parents. Using NGS-based molecular breeding, an improved variety with yellow rind, thick crazing, yellow **pulp**, and higher yield had been obtained (Fig. 4.18).

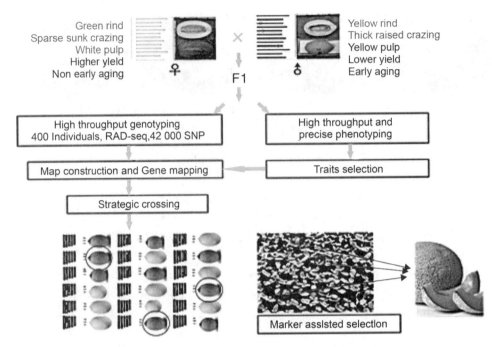

Figure 4.18　Research strategy of cucumis melon breeding

Glossary

breeding /ˈbriːdɪŋ/
繁殖；育种
Breeding is the reproduction that is producing of offspring, usually animals or plants.

bioinformatics /ˌbiːəʊɪnˈfɔːmətɪks/
生物信息学
Bioinformatics is an interdisciplinary field that develops methods and software tools for understanding biological data.

clade /kleɪd/
进化枝；分化枝
A clade or monophylum is a life-form group consisting of a common ancestor and all its descendants—representing a single "branch" on the "tree of life".

phylogenetic /ˌfaɪləʊdʒəˈnetɪk/
系统发生的；动植物演化史的；动植物种类史的
In biology, phylogenetics is the study of evolutionary relationships among groups of organisms (e.g. species, populations), which are discovered through molecular sequencing data and morphological data matrices.

epigenomics /ˌepaɪdʒəˈnɒmɪks/
表观基因组学
Epigenomics is the study of the complete set of epigenetic modifications on the genetic material of a cell, known as the epigenome.

genotyping /ˈdʒenəʊˌtaɪpɪŋ/
基因分型
Genotyping is the process of determining differences in the genetic make-up (genotype) of an individual by examining the individual's DNA sequence using biological assays and comparing it to another individual's sequence or a reference sequence. It reveals the alleles an individual has inherited from their parents.

crossbreeding /ˈkrɒsbriːdɪŋ/
杂交育种
crossbreeding-crossbreed
A crossbreed or crossbred usually refers to an organism with purebred parents of two different breeds, varieties, or populations.
hybrid /ˈhaɪbrɪd/
杂种；杂交种
Hybrid, an offspring resulting from cross—breeding.

adaptability /əˌdæptəˈbɪləti/
适应性
In ecology, adaptability has been described as the ability to cope with unexpected disturbances in the environment.
pulp /pʌlp/
果肉
The soft center of a fruit.

Notes to Difficult Sentences

Population evolution based on whole-genome re-sequencing can be used for phylogenetic, linkage disequilibrium, genetic structure analyses, as well as population genetic structure and species formation, to explore mechanisms of biological evolution.

基于全基因组重测序的种群演化策略可以用于进行系统发育、连锁不平衡、基因结构等分析，研究种群遗传结构和物种形成机理，从而阐明生物进化的机制。

拓展：全基因组重测序是对已知基因组序列的物种进行不同个体的基因组测序，并在此基础上对个体或群体进行差异性分析，可以全面挖掘基因序列的差异和结构变异。同时，在全基因组水平上扫描并检测与生物体重要性状相关的基因位点，具有重大的科研价值和产业价值。全基因组重测序的个体，通过序列比对，可以找到大量的单核苷酸多态性位点（SNP）、插入缺失位点（Insertion/Deletion，InDel）、结构变异位点（Structure Variation，SV），达到基因挖掘或分子机制研究等目的，进而快速、高效、精准地推动遗传学研究。

Reading Material 1

Recent Advances of Genome Mapping and Marker-Assisted Selection in Aquaculture

Aquaculture is the fastest growing sector in agriculture. Substantial genetic gains have been achieved in a few cultured species using conventional selective breeding approaches. However, the majority of fish and shellfish species remain in their wild state. Due to the recognition of the enormous potential of marker-assisted selection (MAS) to speed up genetic gain through early selection, aquaculture scientists have constructed linkage maps in over 40 species and mapped quantitative trait loci (QTL) for important traits in over 20 species since the 1990s. Although MAS and genomic selection (GS) have not been widely used in aquaculture, their application in breeding programmes is expected to be a fertile area of research.

1. Linkage mapping

A linkage map is an ordered listing of genetic markers located along the length of the chromosomes in the genome. Construction of a linkage map requires four major components: polymorphic markers, genotyping platforms, reference families and software for analysis of linkage between pairwise markers and among markers.

1.1 DNA markers and genotyping

DNA markers are variable DNA sequences in a genome that can be differentiated using biochemical methods. There are three types of DNA markers widely used in linkage mapping. (I) Microsatellites are short tandemly repeated (1~6 bp) DNA sequences found throughout a genome. Most laboratories are using DNA sequencers (e.g., ABI3130 and ABI3730xl) for genotyping microsatellites. (II) SNP describes polymorphisms caused by point mutations at a given nucleotide position within a locus. The genomes of at least 11 aquaculture species are being sequenced. From these sequencing efforts, a large number of SNPs is expected to be identified. (III) CNV corresponds to relatively large regions of the genome that have been deleted or duplicated on certain chromosomes. As CNVs in human were associated with a number of human diseases, they are also potentially associated with important traits in aquaculture species. CNVs can be genotyped using Taqman technology, microarray and next-generation sequencing.

1.2 Reference families for linkage mapping

Constructing a linkage map requires one or more reference populations/families where DNA markers segregate. Population sizes used in constructing a linkage map ranges from dozens to a few hundred individuals. However, for high-resolution mapping, a large number of individuals (> 500 individuals) are required to detect rare recombinants. F1 families generated by crossing genetically diverse individuals can be used for linkage mapping. Using several reference populations, more markers can be mapped as markers could be informative in at least one of the populations. However, using more populations for mapping means that it is necessary to merge the maps from different populations. F2 populations derived from F1 hybrids, and backcross populations derived by crossing the F1 hybrid to one of the parents, are the commonly used types of mapping populations.

1.3 Linkage analysis of markers

After genotyping all individuals in the reference populations with markers, the next step is to conduct pairwise and multipoint linkage analysis for constructing a linkage map using computer programs. To determine whether two markers are linked or not, LOD (a logarithm of odds) score is used. To detect a greater level of linkage, LOD values may be lowered, whereas to place additional markers within constructed maps, higher LOD values may be applied.

2. Mapping of quantitative trait loci

Most economically important traits such as growth, flesh quality and disease resistance are controlled by a number of genes, environmental factors and their interactions. The underlying single genes usually have small effects. QTL are chromosomal regions (single gene or gene clusters) determining a quantitative character. The purpose of mapping QTL is to understand the numbers and effects of genes that determine a trait and to assist in selective breeding to accelerate genetic improvement of important traits.

2.1 Important traits in QTL analyses in aquaculture species

Growth traits including growth rate, body weight and length are the most important traits in aquaculture species. They can be easily measured. Due to their high heritability in most aquaculture species, they can be improved using traditional selection methods. QTL analysis for growth traits has been conducted in almost all species, in which QTL analyses have been performed, such as Asian seabass, rainbow trout and tilapia.

In most aquaculture species, feed accounts for about 65 ~ 75% of the total production cost. Therefore, food conservation rate (FCR) is another important trait. Feed intake of each individual is generally difficult to measure in aquaculture species due to unequal feed intake over days and the requirement of a single tank to raise each fish in each of the reference families. No QTL analysis on FCR has been conducted in aquaculture species so far.

Meat quality traits include fat percentage and distribution, fatty acid profiling, color, texture and dressing percentage. In most cases, accurate measurements of these traits can only be conducted in slaughtered individuals. QTL for fat percentage and distribution as well as flesh color were mapped on the genome of salmon.

Disease resistance is one of the most frequently researched traits in QTL studies as diseases represent one of the major challenges and bottlenecks in aquaculture. To quantify the resistance of each individual to pathogens, challenge experiments were often conducted. Usually, survival, death and the time of survival are recorded. QTL for disease resistance have been mapped in several aquaculture species, such as salmon, trout species, Japanese flounder and oysters.

2.2 Families for mapping QTL

In many cultured fish species, large numbers of offspring can be generated during spawning, thus any kinds of families can be easily obtained. Although F2 families are commonly used for QTL mapping, in marine fishes such as Pacific oyster, Asian seabass and Japanese flounder, F1 families have been used in QTL mapping. This is mainly because in these species, the parents used for constructing the reference families segregate at both DNA markers and phenotypic values. To increase the power for QTL mapping, parents can be selected based on genotypes at marker loci. Another issue related to the power of the QTL mapping is the family size. The optimum number of family size in the QTL mapping population depends on the intrinsic power of the experiment. Usually, large family sizes (> 300 individuals) are needed for detecting QTL of small effects.

3. Marker-assisted selection

The advantages of MAS are obvious as compared with the conventional selective breeding. MAS is especially useful for traits that are difficult to measure, exhibit low heritability and/or are expressed late in development. Implementation of MAS requires DNA markers that are tightly linked to QTL for traits of interest based on QTL mapping or association studies. Ideally, the DNA markers should be the causative mutation underlying the phenotypic variation. QTL studies in aquaculture species covered a wide range of traits including growth, meat quality, egg production, disease resistance, stress resistance, reproduction and other traits. The results of these studies provide a good starting point to search for QTL within breeding populations. Of the QTL from experimental crosses, only a small number of them have been followed up by confirmation and fine-mapping. The responsible mutations in genes have not been described for detected QTL. However, there are already a few applications of MAS in commercial breeding programmes in aquaculture species.

The application of MAS in breeding programmes means that brooders are now able to be selected according to both genotypes and performance records, rather than on performance alone. However, to date, little is known about the economic benefits gained from MAS in aquaculture species. Information of this nature is essential because the additional genetic gains depend on the magnitude of the allelic effects, and thus, the marginal increase should offset the costs of applying the technology (e. g., genotyping and manpower costs).

4. Future directions

Because the QTL approaches only detect QTL with moderate-to-large effects for MAS, the QTL with small effects may be missed. Therefore, researchers are now working towards identifying huge numbers of DNA variations associated with traits in the whole-genome sequences in humans, model organisms and agronomic species, that is, genome-wide association studies (GWAS). GWAS, also called as whole-genome association study, is an examination of a large number of variations (e. g., >500 000 SNPs) in the whole genome of a large number (e. g., >2000) of individuals of a particular species to see how many variations differ from individual to individual. Different variations are then associated with different traits, such as diseases and growth. The main advantage of GWAS is their high ability to detect very small effects of marker-trait associations, as they are based on linkage disequilibrium. The MAS using genetic markers associated with traits of interest, which are identified in GWAS, is called genomic selection (GS). Simulation results and limited experimental results suggest that breeding values can be predicted with high accuracy using SNPs along the whole genomes. GS is better suited to breeding programmes of aquaculture species, which aims to maintain a large genetic variation to maintain the sustainability of breeding programmes, that is, brooder stocks with a large number of families. In contrast, the QTL approach is ideal for within-family selection because most QTL detected are family specific, and only a few are universal. To our best knowledge, GWAS are being started in a few aquaculture species. On the other hand, QTL mapping remains largely a research tool to improve our understanding of the number, distribution and mode of action of QTL controlling economically important traits in aquaculture species. QTL can also play a role in GWAS as a vehicle for validating and confirming significant SNP correlations identified in association populations. In the near future, GWAS promise to yield numerous SNP markers that could be used in GS for early selection of superior alleles associated with a wide range of traits. As the efficiency of techniques for DNA sequencing, SNP discovery, genotyping and other molecular procedures improves further and experimental costs decrease, the opportunities to incorporate GS into breeding programmes for aquaculture species will surely increase.

Reading Material 2

Marker Assisted Breeding for Rice Improvement

The development of DNA (or molecular) markers has irreversibly changed the disciplines of plant genetics and plant breeding. While there are several applications of DNA markers in breeding, the most promising for cultivar development is called marker assisted selection (MAS). MAS refers to the use of DNA markers that are tightly-linked to target loci as a substitute for or to assist phenotypic screening. By determining the allele of a DNA marker, plants that possess particular genes or quantitative trait loci (QTLs) may be identified based on their genotype rather than their phenotype.

1. What are the advantages of marker-assisted selection?

Marker-assisted selection may greatly increase the efficiency and effectiveness for breeding compared to conventional breeding. The fundamental advantages of MAS compared to conventional phenotypic selection are:
(1) Simpler compared to phenotypic screening.
(2) Selection may be carried out at seedling stage.
(3) Single plants may be selected with high reliability.

For example, time and labor savings may arise from the substitution of difficult or time-consuming field trials (that need to be conducted at particular times of year or at specific locations, or are technically complicated) with DNA marker tests. Furthermore, selection based on DNA markers may be more reliable due to the influence of environmental factors on field trials. In some cases, using DNA markers may be more cost effective than the screening for the target trait. Another benefit from using MAS is that the total number of lines that need to be tested may be reduced. Since many lines can be discarded after MAS at an early generation, this permits a more effective breeding design. Moreover, background markers may also be used to accelerate the recovery of recurrent parents during marker-assisted backcrossing.

2. What is the importance of QTL mapping for MAS?

The identification of genes and QTLs and DNA markers that are linked to them is accomplished via QTL mapping experiments. QTL mapping thus represents the foundation of the development of markers for MAS. Previously, it was generally assumed that markers could be directly used in MAS. However, there are many factors that influence the accuracy of QTL mapping such as population size and type, level of replication of phenotypic data, environmental effects and genotyping errors. Therefore, in recent years it has become widely-accepted that QTL confirmation, validation and/or additional marker testing steps may be required after QTL mapping and prior to MAS. These steps may include:

(1) Marker conversion—may be required such that the marker genotyping method is technically simpler for MAS or so that the reliability is improved.

(2) QTL confirmation testing the accuracy of results from the primary QTL mapping study.

(3) QTL validation—to verify that a QTL is effective in different genetic backgrounds.

(4) Marker validation testing the level of polymorphism of most tightly-linked markers within a narrow window (say 5~10 cm) spanning a target locus and also testing the reliability of markers to predict phenotype.

3. MAS schemes in plant breeding

3.1 Marker assisted backcrossing

There are three levels of selection in which markers may be applied in backcross breeding (Fig. 4.19). In the first level, markers may be used to screen for the target trait, which may be useful for traits that have laborious phenotypic screening procedures or recessive alleles. The second level of selection involves selecting backcross progeny with the target gene and tightly-linked flanking markers in order to minimize linkage drag. We refer to this as recombinant selection. The third level of MAB involves selecting backcross progeny (that have already been selected for the target trait) with background markers. In other words, markers can be used to select against the donor genome, which may accelerate the recovery of the recurrent parent genome.

3.2 Marker assisted pyramiding

Pyramiding is the process of simultaneously combining multiple genes/QTLs together into a single genotype. This is possible through conventional breeding but extremely difficult or impossible at early generations. Using conventional phenotypic selection, individual plants must be phenotypically screened for all traits tested. Therefore, it may be very difficult to assess plants from certain population types or for traits with destructive bioassays. DNA markers may facilitate selection because DNA marker assays are non-destructive and markers for multiple specific genes/QTLs can be tested using a single DNA sample without phenotyping. The most widespread application for pyramiding has been for combining multiple disease resistance genes in order to develop durable disease resistance (Fig. 4.20).

Chapter 4 Animal & Plant Genome Research and Its Agricultural Applications

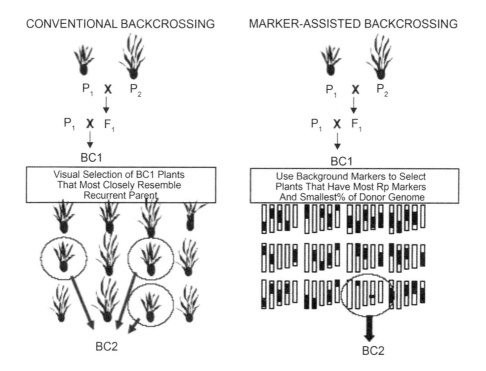

Figure 4. 19 Comparing conventional and marker-assisted backcrossing

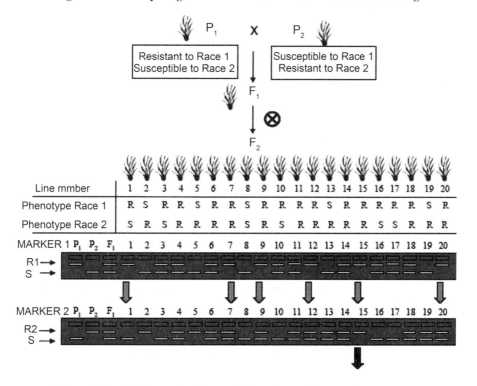

Figure 4. 20 Marker assisted pyramiding of two disease resistance genes

3.3 Early generation marker assisted selection

One of the most intuitive stages to use markers to select plants is at an early generation. The main advantage is that many plants with unwanted gene combinations, especially those that lack essential disease resistance traits and plant height, can be simply discarded. This has important consequences in the later stages of the breeding program because the evaluation for other traits can be more efficiently and cheaply designed for fewer breeding lines.

3.4 Combined approaches

In some cases, a combination of phenotypic screening and MAS approach may be useful.
(1) To maximize genetic gain (when some QTLs have been unidentified from QTL mapping).
(2) Level of recombination between marker and QTL (marker is not 100% accurate).
(3) To reduce population sizes for traits where marker genotyping is cheaper or easier than phenotypic screening.

4. Current obstacles for the adoption of MAS

There are many barriers to the adoption of MAS in plant breeding. Currently, one of the most important barriers for MAS in rice today is the prohibitive cost. Although there are only a small number of reports analyzing the economics of MAS versus conventional breeding in the literature, the cost-effectiveness of using MAS compared to conventional plant breeding varies considerably between studies. Two additional factors need to be considered for cost-analysis:
(1) equipments and consumables required to establish and maintain a marker lab is considerable;
(2) there is a large initial cost in the development of markers which is seldom reported.

For marker assisted backcrossing, the initial cost of using markers would be more expensive compared to conventional breeding in the short term however time savings could lead to an accelerated variety release which could translate into greater profits in the medium to long term. Another important factor obstructing the successful application of markers for line development is the low reliability of markers to determine phenotype. This is often attributable to the thoroughness of the primary QTL mapping study. Even QTLs that are detected with high LOD scores and explain a large proportion of the phenotype may be affected by sampling bias, and therefore may not be useful for MAS. Furthermore, the effect of a QTL may depend on the genetic background. This emphasizes the importance of testing the QTL effects and the reliability of markers before MAS is undertaken. Finally the level of integration between molecular geneticists and plant breeders may not be adequate to ensure that markers are effectively applied for line development.

5. Future of MAS in rice breeding

We believe that despite the relatively small adoption of markers in rice breeding to date, there will be a greater level of adoption within the next decade and beyond. Factors that should lead to a greater adoption of MAS in rice include: (I) establishment of facilities for marker genotyping and staff training within many rice breeding institutes in different countries, (II) currently available (and constantly increasing) data on genes/QTLs controlling traits and the identification of tightly-linked markers, (III) development of effective strategies for using markers in breeding, (IV) establishment and curation of public databases for QTL/marker data, (V) available resource for generating new markers from DNA sequence data arising from rice genome sequencing and research in functional genomics.

It is also critical that future endeavors in MAS are based upon lessons that have been learnt from past successes and failures in using MAS. Further optimization of marker genotyping methods in terms of cost-effectiveness and a greater level of integration between molecular and conventional breeding represent the main challenges for the greater adoption and impact of MAS on rice breeding in the near future.

Chapter 5 Metagenomics

Metagenomics has emerged as a powerful tool that can be used to analyze microbial communities regardless of the ability of member organisms to be cultured in the laboratory. Metagenomics is based on the genomic analysis of microbial DNA that is extracted directly from communities in environmental samples. This technology—genomics on a huge scale—enables a survey of the different microorganisms present in a specific environment, such as water or soil, to be carried out. By integrating the information gleaned with information about biological functions within the community, the structure of microbial communities can potentially be probed. Metagenomics could also unlock the massive uncultured microbial diversity present in the environment to provide new molecules for therapeutic and biotechnological applications.

Chapter 5   Metagenomics

Lesson 1
Metagenomics: The Science of Biological Diversity

For approximately 4.5 billion years, the Earth has been evolving from a **barren** volcanic landscape into the vibrant globe full of life that it is today. The first forms of life, small microorganisms, have been found in fossils from 3.5 billion years ago. Around 1.5 billion years ago, motile microorganisms emerged allowing life to migrate to different environments with different environmental conditions like increased exposure to **ultraviolet radiation** or higher temperatures. Microorganisms began to evolve with the changing environmental conditions of the planet.

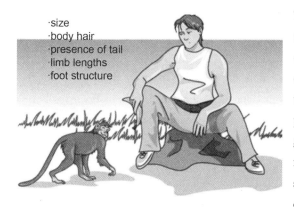

Figure 5.1   Visible differences:
human vs. monkey

These new environmental conditions, acting as selective pressures, drove the evolutionary process. They forced new species of organisms to evolve that were better suited to survival under particular environmental pressures. The evolution of new species generates biological diversity, which is represented by the number of different species in an environment. Over time, the evolutionary process has led to the development of more complex life forms such as trees, fish, and humans. A simple example of biological diversity is a comparison between a human and a monkey (Fig. 5.1).

Both species (human and monkey) are eukaryotes, multicellular, **vertebrates**, mammals, and primates. However, significant differences between humans and monkeys are immediately visible such as body hair and arm length. Other differences such as amino acid synthesis cannot be perceived by casual observation. The basis of this biological difference lies in the organization and expression of the genetic material of each species.

1. Genetic diversity

DNA is responsible for encoding the physical characteristics of an organism. Differences in

DNA sequences between organisms create genetic diversity. These changes are also responsible for the subtle differences (such as hair or eye color) between organisms of the same species. This genetic diversity is able to manifest itself as biological diversity through the structure, organization, regulation, and expression of DNA. These effects determine how organisms develop physically, **assimilate** nutrients, interact with the environment, and even, in some cases, how they behave.

It is these properties of genetic diversity that support the effective stability of natural environments. Multiple biological and non-biological components interact through intricate nutrient cycling webs to create a **macroscopic** global environment. This global environment can be imagined as a pyramid in which the entire structure depends on each of the small blocks that are used to create and support the larger structure. For this reason, it is often useful to examine the environmental impacts of small ecological components such as microorganisms. As noted above, microorganisms are believed to be the origins of life on the planet. This theory is supported by the fact that they display the highest degree of biological diversity.

2. Metagenomics

To understand the biochemical processes of life, it is often easier to study them in a simple system (like a microorganism) instead of a complex one (like humans). Microorganisms have many of the same properties as more complex organisms such as amino acid biosynthesis. They also contain unique properties such as the ability to degrade waste products. As a result, the genetic and biological diversity of microorganisms is an important area of scientific research. Unfortunately, scientists are able to grow less than 1% of all microorganisms observable in nature under standard laboratory conditions. This leaves scientists unable to study more than 99% of the biological diversity in the environment. Metagenomics is a new field combining molecular biology and genetics in an attempt to identify, and characterize the genetic material from environmental samples and apply that knowledge. The genetic diversity is assessed by isolation of DNA followed by direct cloning of functional genes from the environmental sample.

Metagenomics is described as "the comprehensive study of nucleotide sequence, structure, regulation, and function". Scientists can study the smallest component of an environmental system by extracting DNA from organisms in the system and inserting it into a model organism. The model organism then expresses this DNA where it can be studied using standard laboratory techniques.

Metagenomics is employed as a means of systematically investigating, classifying, and manipulating the entire genetic material isolated from environmental samples. This is a multistep process that relies on the efficiency of four main steps. The procedure consists of (I) the isolation of genetic material, (II) manipulation of the genetic material, (III) library construction, and the (IV) the analysis of genetic material in the metagenomic library (Fig. 5.2).

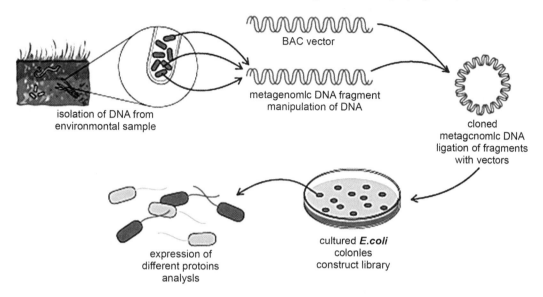

Figure 5.2 The standard steps of a metagenomics experiment

The first step of the procedure is the isolation of the DNA. First, a sample is collected that represents the environment under investigation because the biological diversity will be different in different environments. The samples contain many different types of microorganism, the cells of which can be broken open using chemical methods such as **alkaline** conditions or physical methods such as **sonication**. Once the DNA from the cells is free, it must be separated from the rest of the sample. This is accomplished by taking advantage of the physical and chemical properties of DNA. Some methods of DNA isolation include density **centrifugation**, affinity binding, and solubility/**precipitation**.

Once the DNA is collected, it is manipulated so that it can be used in the model organism. Genomic DNA (the genetic material of an organism) is relatively large so it is cut up into smaller fragments using enzymes called **restriction endonucleases**. These are special enzymes that cut DNA at a particular sequence of base pairs. The enzymes move along the long fragments until they recognize these sequences where they cut both strands of the DNA. This results in the smaller, linear fragments of DNA depicted in Figure 5.2. The fragments are then combined with vectors. Vectors are small units of DNA that can be inserted into cells where they can replicate and produce the proteins encoded on the DNA using the machinery that the cells use to express normal genes. The vectors also contain a selectable marker. Selectable markers provide a growth advantage that the model organism would not normally have (such as resistance to a particular antibiotic) and are used to identify which organisms contain vectors and which ones do not.

The third step is to introduce the vectors with the metagenomic DNA fragments into the model organism. This allows the DNA from organisms that would not grow under laboratory conditions to be grown, expressed, and studied. The DNA inserted in the vector is transformed into cells of a model organism, typically *Escherichia coli*. Transformation is the physical insertion of foreign DNA into a cell, followed by stable expression of proteins. It can be done by chemical, electrical, or biological methods. The method of transformation is determined based on the type of sample used and the required efficiency of the reaction. The metagenomic DNA in the vectors are all in the same sample initially but the vectors are designed so that only one kind of DNA fragment from the sample will be maintained in each individual cell. The transformed cells are then grown on selective media so that only the cells carrying vectors will survive. Each group of cells that grows is called a colony. Each colony consists of many cloned cells that originated from one single cell. These samples of cells containing all of the metagenomic DNA samples on vectors are called metagenomic libraries. Each colony can be used to create a stock of cells for future study of a single fragment of the DNA from the environmental sample.

The fourth and final step in the procedure is the analysis of the DNA from the metagenomic libraries. The expression of DNA determines the physical and chemical properties of organisms so there are many potential methods of analysis. A phenotype is the physical attribute associated with expression of a gene. An example of metagenomic analysis would be to look for an unusual colour or shape in the model organism. An aspect of the phenotype that is not readily observed is chemical reaction. The chemical properties of the expressed metagenomic DNA can be examined by performing chemical assay on products created by the model organism. This would investigate whether the model organism gained an enzymatic function that it was previously lacking such as use of an unusual nutrient source for growth under conditions that limit normal nutrient availability.

Metagenomic libraries are typically used to search for new forms of a known gene. First, the metagenomic DNA is inserted into a model organism that lacks a specific gene function. Restoration of a physical or chemical phenotype can then be used to detect genes of interest. A genotype is the specific sequence of the DNA and provides another means of analyzing the metagenomic DNA fragment. The sequence of the bases in the DNA can be compared to databases of known DNA to get information regarding the structure and organization of the metagenomic DNA. Comparisons of these sequences can provide insight into how the gene products (proteins) function.

Genotypic analysis is usually performed after phenotypic analysis. A typical metagenomic analysis involves several subsequent rounds of the procedure in order to definitively isolate target genes from environmental samples and to effectively characterize the information encoded by the DNA sequence. The information gained from the metagenomic procedure provides information regarding the structure, organization, evolution, and origin of the DNA and can be used in scientific applications for the benefit of society and the environment

3. Applications of Metagenomics

Many microorganisms have the ability to degrade waste products, make new drugs for medicine, make environmentally friendly plastics, or even make some of the ingredients of food we eat. By isolating the DNA from these organisms, it provides us with the opportunity to optimize these processes and adapt them for use in our society. As a result of ineffective standard laboratory culture techniques, the potential wealth of biological resources in nature (like microbes) is relatively untapped, unknown, and uncharacterized. Metagenomics represents a powerful tool to access the abounding biodiversity of native environmental samples. The valuable property of metagenomics is that it provides the capacity to effectively characterize the genetic diversity present in samples regardless of the availability of laboratory culturing techniques. Information from metagenomic libraries has the ability to enrich the knowledge and applications of many aspects of industry, therapeutics, and environmental sustainability. This information can then be applied to society in an effort to create a healthy human population that lives in balance with the environment. Metagenomics is a new and exciting field of molecular biology that is likely to grow into a standard technique for understanding biological diversity.

Glossary

barren /ˈbærən/
不育的，贫瘠的
A barren organism is a person, animal or plant without the ability to reproduce by natural means. A barren land is a land without nutrition or growing no plants.

ultraviolet radiation /ˌʌltrəˈvaɪələtˌ reɪdiˈeɪʃn/
紫外线
Ultraviolet (UV) light is an electromagnetic radiation with a wavelength from 400 nm to 100 nm, shorter than that of visible light but longer than X-rays.

vertebrate /ˈvɜːrtɪbrət/
脊椎动物
Vertebrates are animals that are any species of animals within the subphylum Vertebrata (chordates with backbones).

assimilate /əˈsɪməleɪt/
吸收；使同化
Biological assimilation, or bio assimilation, is the combination of two processes to supply cells with nutrients.

macroscopic /ˌmækrəˈskɒpɪk/
宏观的；肉眼可见的
The macroscopic scale is the length scale on which objects or phenomena are large enough to be visible practically with the naked eye, without magnifying devices.

alkaline /ˈælkəlaɪn/
碱性的；碱的
Alkalinity is the name given to the quantitative capacity of an aqueous solution to neutralize an acid.

sonication /ˌsɒnəˈkeɪʃən/
声波降解法
Sonication is the act of applying sound energy to agitate particles in a sample, for various purposes. Ultrasonic frequencies (>20 kHz) are usually used, leading to the process also being known as ultrasonication.

centrifugation /sentrɪfjʊˈgeɪʃən/
离心分离
Centrifugation is a process which involves the use of the centrifugal force for the sedimentation of heterogeneous mixtures with a centrifuge. This process is used to isolate targeted components from immiscible liquids.

precipitation /prɪˌsɪpɪˈteɪʃn/
沉淀
Precipitation is the condensation of a solid from a solution.

restriction endonuclease
/rɪˈstrɪkʃn ˌendoʊˈnjuːkliːˌeɪs/
限制性（核酸）内切酶
A restriction endonuclease is an enzyme that cuts DNA at or near specific recognition nucleotide sequences known as restriction sites.

Notes to Difficult Sentences

This global environment can be imagined as a pyramid in which the entire structure depends on each of the small blocks that are used to create and support the larger structure. For this reason, it is often useful to examine the environmental impacts of small ecological components such as microorganisms.

我们可以把全球环境想象成一座金字塔，金字塔内部整体结构依赖于每一个能创造和支持更大结构的小模块。因而，研究微生物等小生态元件对环境的影响显得意义重大。

拓展： 生态金字塔把生态系统中各个营养级有机体的个体数量、生物量或能量，按营养级位顺序排列并绘制成图，其形似金字塔，故称生态金字塔或生态锥体。它指各个营养级之间某种数量关系，这种数量关系可采用生物量单位、能量单位或个体数量单位来表示，采用这些单位构成的生态金字塔分别称为生物量金字塔、能量金字塔和数量金字塔。微生物作为生态系统中的分解者，能将动植物遗体、排泄物分解，对物质循环起着重要作用。

Lesson 2
How Gut Bacteria Help Make Us Fat and Thin

For the 35 percent of American adults who do daily battle with **obesity**, the main causes of their condition are all too familiar: an unhealthy diet, a sedentary lifestyle and perhaps some unlucky genes. In recent years, however, researchers have become increasingly convinced that important hidden players literally lurk in human bowels: billions on billions of **gut** microbes (Fig. 5.3).

Figure 5.3 Bacteria in gut
(By Rafa Alvare Z)

Throughout our evolutionary history, the microscopic denizens of our **intestines** have helped us break down tough plant fibers in exchange for the privilege of living in such a nutritious broth. Yet their roles appear to extend beyond digestion. New evidence indicates that gut bacteria alter the way we store fat, how we balance levels of **glucose** in the blood, and how we respond to **hormones** that make us feel hungry or full. The wrong mix of microbes, it seems, can help set the stage for obesity and **diabetes** from the moment of birth.

Fortunately, researchers are beginning to understand the differences between the wrong mix and a healthy one, as well as the specific factors that shape those differences. They hope to learn how to cultivate this inner ecosystem in ways that could prevent—and possibly treat—obesity, which doctors define as having a particular ratio of height and weight, known as the body mass index, that is greater than 30. Imagine, for example, foods, baby formulas or supplements devised to promote virtuous microbes while suppressing the harmful types. "We need to think about designing foods from the inside out," suggests Jeffrey Gordon of Washington University in St. Louis. Keeping our gut microbes happy could be the elusive secret to weight control.

1. An inner rain forest

Researchers have long known that the human body is home to all manner of microorganisms, but only in the past decade or so have they come to realize that these microbes outnumber our own cells 10 to 1. Rapid gene-sequencing techniques have revealed that the biggest and most diverse metropolises of "microbiota" reside in the large intestine and mouth, although impressive communities also flourish in the **genital tract** and on our skin.

Each of us begins to assemble a unique congregation of microbes the moment we pass through the **birth canal**, acquiring our mother's bacteria first and continuing to gather new members from the environment throughout life. By studying the genes of these various microbes—collectively referred to as the **microbiome**—investigators have identified many of the most common residents, although these can vary greatly from person to person and among different human populations. In recent years researchers have begun the transition from mere census taking to determining the kind of jobs these minute inhabitants fill in the human body and the effect they have on our health.

An early hint that gut microbes might play a role in obesity came from studies comparing intestinal bacteria in obese and lean individuals. In studies of twins who were both lean or both obese, researchers found that the gut community in lean people was like a rain forest brimming with many species but that the community in obese people was less diverse—more like a nutrient-overloaded pond where relatively few species dominate. Lean individuals, for example, tended to have a wider variety of Bacteroidetes, a large tribe of microbes that specialize in breaking down bulky plant starches and fibers into shorter molecules that the body can use as a source of energy.

Documenting such differences does not mean the discrepancies are responsible for obesity, however. To demonstrate cause and effect, Gordon and his colleagues conducted an elegant series of experiments with so-called humanized mice, published last September in *Science*. First, they raised genetically identical baby rodents in a germ-free environment so that their bodies would be free of any bacteria. Then they populated their guts with intestinal microbes collected from obese women and their lean twin sisters (three pairs of **fraternal** female twins and one set of identical twins were used in the studies). The mice ate the same diet in equal amounts, yet the animals that received bacteria from an obese twin grew heavier and had more body fat than mice with microbes from a thin twin. As expected, the fat mice also had a less diverse community of microbes in gut.

Gordon's team then repeated the experiment with one small twist: after giving the baby mice microbes from their respective twins, they moved the animals into a shared cage. This time both groups remained lean. Studies showed that the mice carrying microbes from the obese human had picked up some of their lean roommates' gut bacteria—especially varieties of

Bacteroidetes—probably by consuming their feces, a typical, if unappealing, mouse behavior. To further prove the point, the researchers transferred 54 varieties of bacteria from some lean mice to those with the obese-type community of germs and found that the animals that had been destined to become obese developed a healthy weight instead. Transferring just 39 strains did not do the trick. "Taken together, these experiments provide pretty compelling proof that there is a cause-and-effect relationship and that it was possible to prevent the development of obesity," Gordon says.

Gordon theorizes that the gut community in obese mice has certain "job vacancies" for microbes that perform key roles in maintaining a healthy body weight and normal metabolism. His studies, as well as those by other researchers, offer enticing clues about what those roles might be. Compared with the thin mice, for example, Gordon's fat mice had higher levels in their blood and muscles of substances known as **branched-chain amino acids** and **acylcarnitines**. Both these chemicals are typically elevated in people with obesity and type 2 diabetes.

Another job vacancy associated with obesity might be one normally filled by a stomach bacterium called *Helicobacter pylori*. Research by Martin Blaser of New York University suggests that it helps to regulate appetite by modulating levels of **ghrelin**—a hunger-stimulating hormone. *H. pylori* was once abundant in the American digestive tract but is now rare, thanks to more **hygienic** living conditions and the use of **antibiotics**, says Blaser, author of a new book entitled Missing Microbes.

Diet is an important factor in shaping the gut ecosystem. A diet of highly processed foods, for example, has been linked to a less diverse gut community in people. Gordon's team demonstrated the complex interaction among food, microbes and body weight by feeding their humanized mice a specially prepared unhealthy chow that was high in fat and low in fruits, vegetables and fiber (as opposed to the usual high-fiber, low-fat mouse kibble). Given this "Western diet," the mice with obese-type microbes proceeded to grow fat even when housed with lean cagemates. The unhealthy diet somehow prevented the virtuous bacteria from moving in and flourishing.

The interaction between diet and gut bacteria can predispose us to obesity from the day we are born, as can the mode by which we enter the world. Studies have shown that both formula-fed babies and infants delivered by **cesarean section** have a higher risk for obesity and diabetes than those who are breast-fed or delivered vaginally. Working together, Rob Knight of the University of Colorado Boulder and Maria Gloria Dominguez-Bello of N. Y. U. have found that as newborns traverse the birth canal, they swallow bacteria that will later help them digest milk. C-section babies skip this bacterial baptism. Babies raised on formula face a different disadvantage: they do not get substances in breast milk that nurture beneficial bacteria and limit colonization by harmful ones. According to a recent Canadian study, babies drinking formula have bacteria in their gut that are not seen in breast-fed babies until solid foods are introduced. Their presence before the gut and immune system are mature, says Dominguez-Bello, may be one reason these babies are more susceptible to **allergies**, **asthma**, **eczema** and **celiac** disease, as well as obesity.

A new appreciation for the impact of gut microbes on body weight has intensified concerns about the profligate use of antibiotics in children. Blaser has shown that when young mice are given low doses of antibiotics, similar to what farmers give livestock, they develop about 15 percent more body fat than mice that are not given such drugs. Antibiotics may annihilate some of the bacteria that help us maintain a healthy body weight. "Antibiotics are like a fire in the forest," Dominguez-Bello says. "The baby is forming a forest. If you have a fire in a forest that is new, you get extinction." When Laurie Cox, a graduate student in Blaser's laboratory, combined a high-fat diet with the antibiotics, the mice became obese. "There's a synergy," Blaser explains. He notes that antibiotic use varies greatly from state to state in the U.S., as does the prevalence of obesity, and intriguingly, the two maps line up—with both rates highest in parts of the South.

2. Beyond probiotics

Many scientists who work on the microbiome think their research will inspire a new generation of tools to treat and prevent obesity. Still, researchers are quick to point out that this is a young field with far more questions than answers. "Data from human studies are a lot messier than the mouse data," observes Claire Fraser of the University of Maryland, who is studying obesity and gut microbes in the Old Order Amish population. Even in a homogeneous population such as the Amish, she says, there is vast individual variation that makes it difficult to isolate the role of microbiota in a complex disease like obesity.

Even so, a number of scientists are actively developing potential treatments. Dominguez-Bello, for example, is conducting a clinical trial in Puerto Rico in which babies born by cesarean section are immediately swabbed with a gauze cloth laced with the mother's vaginal fluids and resident microbes. She will track the weight and overall health of the infants in her study, comparing them with C-section babies who did not receive the gauze treatment.

A group in Amsterdam, meanwhile, is investigating whether transferring feces from lean to overweight people will lead to weight loss. U.S. researchers tend to view such "fecal transplants" as imprecise and risky. A more promising approach, says Robert Karp, who oversees National Institutes of Health grants related to obesity and the microbiome, is to identify the precise strains of bacteria associated with leanness, determine their roles and develop treatments accordingly. Gordon has proposed enriching foods with beneficial bacteria and any nutrients needed to establish them in the gut—a science-based version of today's **probiotic** yogurts. No one in the field believes that probiotics alone will win the war on obesity, but it seems that, along with exercising and eating right, we need to enlist our inner microbial army.

Glossary

obesity /əʊˈbiːsəti/
肥胖的
obese—obesity
Obesity is a medical condition in which excess body fat has accumulated to the extent that it may have a negative effect on health, leading to reduced life expectancy and/or increased health problems.

gut /gʌt/
肠道

intestine /ɪnˈtestɪn/
肠道
Gut or intestine, is a tube by which bilaterian animals (两侧对称动物) (including humans) transfer food to the digestion organs.

glucose /ˈgluːkoʊs/
葡萄糖

hormone /ˈhɔːrmoʊn/
荷尔蒙;激素
A hormone is any member of a class of signaling molecules produced by glands in multicellular organisms that are transported by the circulatory system to target distant organs to regulate physiology and behavior.

diabetes /ˌdaɪəˈbiːtiːz/
糖尿病
Diabetes mellitus (DM), commonly referred to as diabetes, is a group of metabolic diseases in which there are high blood sugar levels over a prolonged period.

genital tract /ˈdʒenɪtl trækt/
生殖道;产道

birth canal /bɜːrθ kəˈnæl/
生殖道,产道

microbiome /ˈmaɪkroʊˈbaɪoʊm/
微生物群落
Microbiome is the ecological community of commensal (共生的), symbiotic and pathogenic microorganisms that literally share our body space.

fraternal /frəˈtɜːrnl/
兄弟姐妹的

branched-chain amino acids
支链氨基酸
A branched-chain amino acid (BCAA) is an amino acid having aliphatic side-chains with a branch (a central carbon atom bound to three or more carbon atoms).

acylcarnitine /əsɪlkɑːnɪˈtaɪn/
酰基肉碱

ghrelin /rəˈlɪn/
饥饿素;生长素
Ghrelin, the "hunger hormone", is a peptide produced by ghrelin cells in the gastrointestinal tract (胃肠道) which functions as a neuropeptide (神经肽) in the central nervous system.

hygienic /haɪˈdʒenɪk/
卫生的;保健的
Hygiene is a set of practices performed for the preservation of health.

antibiotics /ˌæntɪbaɪˈɒtɪks/
抗生素
antibiotic—antibiosis, antibiotics
Antibiotics are a type of antimicrobial used in the

treatment and prevention of bacterial infection.

cesarean section

剖腹产术

A cesarean section is a surgical procedure in which one or more incisions are made through a mother's abdomen and uterus to deliver one or more babies.

allergy /ˈælərdʒi/

过敏症

An allergy is a hypersensitivity disorder of the immune system.

asthma /ˈæzmə/

哮喘

Asthma is a common chronic inflammatory disease of the airways characterized by variable and recurring symptoms, reversible airflow obstruction and bronchospasm（支气管痉挛）.

eczema /ɪɡˈziːmə/

湿疹

Eczema is inflammation of the skin. It is characterized by itchy（发痒）, erythematous（红斑）, vesicular（水泡）and crusting patches（结痂）.

celiac /ˈsiːlɪˌæk/

腹腔的

Coeliac disease is an autoimmune disorder（自身免疫疾病）of the small intestine（小肠）that occurs in genetically predisposed people of all ages from middle infancy onward.

probiotic /ˌproʊbaɪˈɑːtɪk/

益生素的；益生菌的

Probiotics are microorganisms that are believed to provide health benefits when consumed. The term probiotic is currently used to name ingested microorganisms associated with beneficial effects to humans and animals.

Notes to Difficult Sentences

New evidence indicates that gut bacteria alter the way we store fat, how we balance levels of glucose in the blood, and how we respond to hormones that make us feel hungry or full.

新的证据表明肠道细菌改变了我们储存脂肪、平衡血液葡萄糖水平的方式，并改变着我们对调节饥饿和饱足感的激素的反应。

拓展：目前，肠道菌群中可培养细菌有400余种，其中优势菌群（dominant flora）包括类杆菌属、优杆菌属、双歧杆菌属、瘤胃球菌属和梭菌属等专性厌氧菌，通常属于原籍菌群。次要菌群（secondary dominant flora）主要为需氧菌或兼性厌氧菌，如大肠杆菌和链球菌等，此类菌群流动性大，有潜在致病性，大部分属于外籍菌群或过路菌群。

Lesson 3
Next-generation Sequencing Propels Environmental Genomics to the Front Line of Research

So far in the 21st century, next-generation sequencing (NGS) has been the major technological breakthrough in biology, promoting the emergence of a new multi-disciplinary approach: environmental genomics. Environmental genomics captures the structure and dynamics of a range of molecular components, including DNA and RNA in (meta-) genomes and (meta-) transcriptomes. In combination with other high-throughput approaches, called (meta-) omics, it addresses an integrated understanding of complex biological systems at various organization levels (individual, population and community) and in different dimensions of time and space (Fig. 5.4). NGS allows us to delve deeper to uncover biological systems, permitting measurement of species richness, abundance, and hence how species can interact when sharing and competing for resources. The cryptic, as well as the rare but active fraction of biodiversity are now accessible to study in all environments.

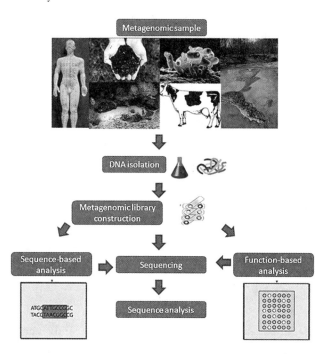

Figure 5.4　Schematic representation of the different steps for metagenomic analysis

Understanding the evolutionary history of organisms, as well as identifying genes or genomic structures that are involved in adaptive evolution (that is, in response to natural selection) can be answered by NGS approaches. The identification of important functional variants requires the integration of multiple approaches including molecular population genetics, phylogenetics and formal genetics. NGS technologies allow us to address evolutionary and population issues hitherto unthinkable, and even those considered part of the field of theoretical biology.

This special issue, coming from biennal symposia launched by French National Network on Environmental Genomics, exemplifies the use of NGS in prokaryotes and eukaryotes, from single organisms to complex communities living in marine, terrestrial and atmospheric environments. It comprises three review articles and eight original papers reporting scientific and technical advances in genomics to decipher biological diversity and species delineation, functional genomics, as well as genome evolution through the study of environmental selection and strategies for extracting relevant biological knowledge in non-model species.

Schlotterer et al. (2014) revisit the "evolve and resequence" approach to highlight genes and SNPs under selection through sequencing of pools of individuals. Experimental evolution has long been used as a traditional approach to uncover selective processes at the origin of population polymorphisms. The challenge is to increase the power and accuracy in the detection of genomic polymorphisms, reducing false positives and at a limited cost. The authors discuss optimal experimental and analytical strategies using Pool-Seq method through various biological examples, comparing this method with other genome-wide association methods.

Genome-wide evolutionary analyses are the focus of the two following papers investigating biological diversity at the species level. Peyretaillade et al. (2014) review the role of the obligate intracellular parasites, that is, *Microsporidia fungae*, in the food web at various trophic levels. Using different omics tools, the authors evaluate their diversity and abundance, and discuss their impact on ecosystem functioning. The study of Pante et al. (2014) investigates the Rad-seq method to delineate species within a rapidly diverged group for which very little genomic information is available. It focuses on deep-sea octocorals, *Chrysogorgia*, known to be widely distributed and to exhibit conflicting patterns between morphological and molecular data. By comparing their results with those on **cetacean**, **beetles**, **swordtail** and **platyfish**, the authors pointed out limitations of Rad-seq for phylogenetic reconstructions, which may be taxon dependent and may interfere with **molecular clocks.**

The next three papers investigate the structure, **dynamics** and functioning of bacterial populations and communities in different environments. An et al. (2014) highlight the changes caused by bacterial communities transported along with the dust in atmospheric sandstorms, over planetary distances. The authors hypothesize that the origin of the sandstorms may be explained by variations among sites with regards to wind sources and trajectories. They outline the potential contribution of atmospheric sandstorm bacterial communities in the sand deposited by the sandstorm that may drastically alter human health, in conjunction with other transported mineral or chemical **pollutants**. Terrat et al. (2014) compare an existing DNA fingerprint method (ARISA) and NGS metabarcoding to evaluate the taxa-area relationships among microbial communities in soil. The authors conclude that NGS metabarcoding provides a very accurate evaluation of soil microbial community assemblies in broad-scale **biogeographic** studies. Kwaziborski et al. (2015) combine genomics and transcriptomics to investigate bacterial (*Pectobacterium ~ Rhodococcus*) interactions within the plant environment. The authors analyze how chemical communication among bacteria may coordinate or alter gene expression of members of plant microbiotes. This work sheds new light on mechanisms that may be further developed as biocontrol agents in the course of plant protection against pathogens.

The following two papers present methodologies that will be useful in studies dealing with the characterization of adaptive genes in evolutionary ecology. Ferrandiz-Rovira et al. (2015) present methodologies for reliably genotyping large numbers of individuals, for example in the case of parental relationships or population genomics that may be used in any genetic system and in any organism. Genotyping was obtained using NGS at four MHC loci in wild Alpine marmots. The limitations, according to genome characteristics (for example, high copy number variation), loci of interest and commercial suitable platforms, are discussed. Gouin et al. (2014) rescue unmapped reads generally discarded from NGS analyses. The authors highlight the potential loss of information that these may bring. This approach is particularly important in non-model species or organisms whose reference genome is of poor quality and where the level of divergence between the reads and the reference genome is relatively high. Using re-sequencing approaches and an original pipeline, this study discovered variation in **symbiotic** composition during ecological **speciation** in Aphids among individual host genomes that are linked to the origin of the **biotypes** from which they arise.

The following three papers highlight the benefits of different NGS methods, and their combination, to understand the evolutionary response of organisms facing environmental changes. Porcelli et al. (2015) provide a review of emerging patterns of putative adaptive genomic responses, using the case of heat stress in metazoans. Thanks to a combination of both genomic and transcriptomic information, they uncover specific classes of genes under selection, from the regulation of gene transcription to mRNA translation. Future directions are discussed, and include combining RNA-seq with either proteomics or metabolomics to elucidate genetic networks plus regulatory and metabolic responses during adaptation to different thermal environments. The impact of genetic architecture on species evolution and adaptation is investigated in the following studies. Using standard linkage mapping methods after RAD-seq, Huber et al. (2015) examine species diversification linked to mimicry polymorphism in a clade of South American Heliconius species. Thanks to a combined set of QTL methods, from multivariate quantitative genetics to fine-mapping candidate genes, the authors confirmed the complex genomic architecture of wing patterning in this genus and explored the evolution of genetic architecture within a larger comparative framework. Lopes et al. (2015) investigate ecological mechanisms involved in the avoidance of competition between closely related **sympatric** species through a DNA metabarcoding diet analysis. Hi-seq sequencing was performed using markers characterizing the majority of the plant richness, as well as the **mollusks** and **arthropods** from the original habitat of two **parapatric** species of subterranean rodents living in the southern Brazilian coastal plain, and then compare with total DNA extraction from **feces** and **stool** samples. The results confirm the **herbivorous** status of the species and suggested a dietary partitioning in the sympatric region.

Global change, coming from natural phenomena and human activities, can drastically impact biological systems at unprecedented speeds. The diversity of NGS approaches, together with bioinformatics developments, open new areas that go more deeply in the characterization of biological systems, ranging from complex regulatory networks within communities up to metabolomics network within a single cell. Knowing what is there, what functions are performed and how regulatory pathways are activated, are challenging questions for which environmental genomics can provide important insights.

Glossary

cetacean /sɪˈteɪʃn/
鲸类动物
The infraorder Cetacea (鲸目) includes the marine mammals commonly known as whales, dolphins, and porpoises.

beetle /ˈbiːtl/
甲虫
Beetles are a group of insects which are classified in the order Coleopetera (鞘翅目).

swordtail /ˈsɔːrdˌteɪl/
剑尾鱼

platyfish /ˈplætiːˌfɪʃ/
新月鱼；阔尾鱼

molecular clocks
分子钟
The molecular clock (based on the molecular clock hypothesis (MCH)) is a technique in molecular evolution that uses fossil constraints and rates of molecular change to deduce the time in geologic history when two species or other taxa diverged.

dynamics /daɪˈnæmɪks/
动力学
Every object experiences some form of motion which is the result of different forces acting on the object. Dynamics is the study of the forces which are responsible for this motion.

pollutant /pəˈluːtənt/

污染物

A pollutant is a substance or energy introduced into the environment that has undesired effects, or adversely affects the usefulness of a resource.

biogeographic /biːəʊdʒɪəgˈræfɪk/

生物地理的

Biogeography is the study of the distribution of species and ecosystems in geographic space and through geological time. Organisms and biological communities often vary in a regular fashion along geographic gradients of latitude, elevation, isolation and habitat area.

symbiotic /ˌsɪmbaɪˈɒtɪk/

共生的

Symbiosis is close and often long-term interaction between two or more different biological species.

speciation /ˌspiːsiːˈeɪʃən/

物种形成

species—speciation

Speciation is the evolutionary process by which new biological species arise.

biotype /ˈbaɪəʊtaɪp/

生物型；同型小种

Biotype refers to a group of organisms having the same specific genotype.

sympatric /sɪmˈpætrɪk/

同域的

In biology, two species or populations are considered sympatric when they exist in the same geographic area and thus regularly encounter one another.

mollusk /ˈmɒləsk/

软体动物

The mollusks or molluscs compose the large phylum of invertebrate animals known as the Mollusca（软体动物门）.

arthropod /ˈɑːrθrəpɑːd/

节肢动物门

An arthropod is an invertebrate animal having an exoskeleton (external skeleton), a segmented body, and jointed appendages.

parapatric /ˌpærəˈpeɪtrɪk/

邻接群体的

parapatry is the relationship between organisms whose ranges do not significantly overlap but are immediately adjacent to each other; they only occur together in a narrow contact zone.

feces /ˈfiːsiːz/

粪便

stool /stuːl/

粪便

herbivorous /hɜːˈbɪvərəs/

食草的

herb(草)-(de)vo(u)r(吞食)-ous

A herbivore is an animal anatomically and physiologically adapted to eating plant material, for example foliage, for the main component of its diet.

Notes to Difficult Sentences

The diversity of NGS approaches, together with bioinformatics developments, open new areas that go more deeply in the characterization of biological systems, ranging from complex regulatory networks within communities up to metabolomics network within a single cell.

下一代测序方法的多样化及生物信息学的发展为更深入地描述生物系统（无论是群体内的复杂调控网络还是单个细胞内的代谢网络）开辟了新的领域。

拓展：在生物系统中包含很多不同层面和不同组织形式的网络，基因调控网络、新陈代谢网络、信号传导网络、蛋白质相互作用网络是最常见的生物分子网络。2004 年，Barabasi 和 Oltvai 在 *Nature Review Genetics* 上提出了"网络生物学（Network Biology）"这一概念，这必然成为系统生物学一个新的重要研究方向。

Chapter 5 Metagenomics

Reading Material 1

Exploring Diversity with Single-cell Genomics

Metagenomic studies have greatly enhanced our understanding of bacterial and archaeal diversity. However, environmental metagenomic data often do not allow the genomes of individual species to be assembled, and therefore most complete genome sequences have been obtained from cultured microorganisms. Now, two new large-scale studies have used single-cell genomics to recover bacterial and archaeal genomes directly from uncultured environmental samples.

Rinke et al. used fluorescence activated cell sorting to isolate 9600 single cells from nine environmental samples, including ocean water, fresh water, hydrothermal sites and sediments, from which 3330 single amplified genomes (SAGs) were obtained by multiple displacement amplification (Fig. 5.5).

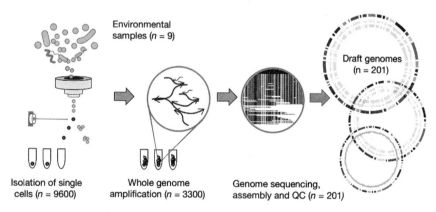

Figure 5.5 Single-cell sequencing workflow

Environmental samples were processed using a fluorescence-activated cell sorter allowing the isolation of 9600 single cells. Each cell was lysed and the genome amplified yielding 3300 successful amplifications. Resulting SAGs were screened by SSU rRNA gene PCR and sequencing to resolve taxonomic identities. SAGs belonging to major novel lineages were selected for genome sequencing and assembly resulting in 201 draft genomes. QC, quality control. (Christian Rinke, et al. 2013)

To identify genomes representing uncultured organisms, the SAGs were screened by 16S rRNA gene PCR, and 201 SAGs were selected for sequencing and draft genome assembly, with an average estimated genome completeness of 40%. Phylogenetic analysis of these single-cell genomes revealed many new groupings, including two new proposed superphyla: Patescibacteria, containing the phyla Microgenomates, Parcubacteria and Gracilibacteria; and DPANN, containing phyla Diapherotrites, Parvarchaeota, Aenigmarchaeota, Nanohaloarchaeota and Nanoarchaeota.

Furthermore, novel metabolic capabilities were identified: two bacterial lineages were shown to use archaeal PurP enzymes instead of bacterial PurH1 enzymes for purine synthesis, and one archaeal genome was found to encode a eukaryotic oxidoreductase, indicating a possible horizontal gene transfer event between a eukaryote and an archaeon. Intriguingly, several archaeal genomes were shown to encode bacterial-like σ-factors, and the authors also speculated that an archaeal murein transglycosylase could have an antibacterial function.

Swan et al. used similar techniques to sequence 56 genomes of single bacterioplankton cells isolated from several surface ocean sites. In contrast to the first study, here most of the SAGs obtained belonged to phyla for which cultured representatives are available, so it was possible to compare the genomes of cultured and uncultured, free-living marine bacteria. In comparison to cultured marine microorganisms, the uncultured bacterioplankton lineages, which dominate marine ecosystems, have smaller genomes and a lower GC content, as well as fewer duplicated genes, non-coding nucleotides, and genes involved in transcription and signal transduction, indicating that genome streamlining is prevalent in the resource-poor natural habitats.

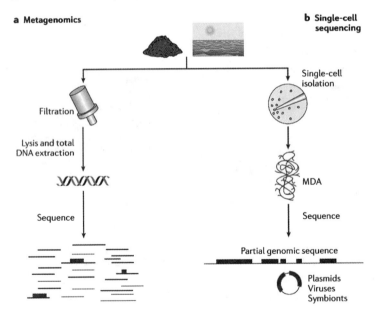

Figure 5.6 Metagenomics and single-cell sequencing

a. In metagenomics, a mixture of bacterial cells from the environment is lysed, and total DNA is subjected to shotgun sequencing. **b.** In single-cell sequencing, single cells are isolated from environmental samples and lysed, and the single genome copy is amplified by multiple displacement amplification (MDA) and sequenced. Only some of the genomic sequence is recovered by MDA. However, these fragmentary sequences are genetically linked, having originated from the same cell. In a process termed fragment recruitment, the genetically linked sequences from single cells can be used to query metagenomic databases to identify reads that are from the same species. (Roger S. Lasken, 2012)

Both studies show that single-cell genomics is a powerful approach to identify new phylogenetic relationships, interdomain gene transfers and genome adaptation to environmental conditions, all of which would be challenging to identify in standard metagenomic studies (Fig. 5.6).

In the few years since single-cell sequencing was introduced, it has steadily gained acceptance in the scientific community. The available methods for sequencing and assembling genomes from amplified DNA have been improved. Several genomes have been obtained from major bacterial taxa that had lacked sequenced representatives. The sequencing of the biosynthetic pathways for novel secondary metabolites with therapeutic potential has also demonstrated the value of the method. The rapidly growing number of applications that use limiting quantities of DNA in genomic detection and analysis underscores the continued need for innovation in the field of DNA amplification. Advancements in the enzymology used for DNA amplification can be expected over the next 5 years. If the history of biotechnology is a good guide, progress in single-cell sequencing will be driven by the discovery of new DNA replication enzymes or the modification of known enzymes, by the further automation and miniaturization of sequencing processes, and by the development of new methods that are required for emerging research needs. Perhaps even the ultimate goal in the biotechnology of DNA amplification—complete chromosomal replication *in vitro*—will be achieved.

Reading Material 2

Scientists Map 5000 New Ocean Viruses

In the few decades since viruses were first found in the oceans, scientists have only been able to identify a handful of species. A new survey has uncovered nearly all the rest (Fig. 5.7).

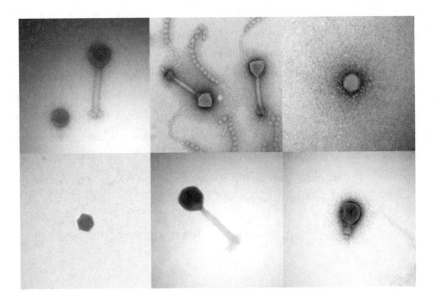

Figure 5.7 A few of the more than 5000 viruses discovered during the Tara Oceans Expedition

In March 2011, the Tara, a 36-meter schooner, sailed from Chile to Easter Island—a three-week leg of a five-year global scientific expedition. At the stern of the Tara, a shipping container was bolted to the deck, with a door and a tiny window cut through the metal walls. One of the scientists, Melissa Duhaime, spent most of the voyage inside the dark, tiny cell, where she fought off an endless bout of seasickness.

Inside her cell, Duhaime sat next to a hose as wide as an outstretched hand. A pump drew water through the hose from several meters below the boat and then pushed it through a series of filters. Each filter was finer than the last, blocking smaller and smaller life forms. The setup stopped animals first, then zooplankton and algae. The last filter in the hose, with pores just 220 nanometers wide, was fine enough to block bacteria. Scrubbed of all these living things, the water finally flowed into three 30-liter vats. To the untrained eye, these vats might seem to be full of sterile water. But they were seething with ocean life—or life-like things, at the very least. The three vats held up to 1 trillion viruses.

Scientists estimate that there are 1 000 000 000 000 000 000 000 000 000 000 virus particles in all the world's seas. Duhaime and her colleaguesgathered enough samples to confidently estimate the total number of distinct populations of viruses in the sunlit upper reaches of the ocean. Out of the 5476 populations they identified, only 39 were previously known to science.

1. An explosion of viruses

Scientists first discovered viruses in sickly tobacco plants in the late 1800s. Yet for nearly a century, marine biologists assumed that the oceans were virtually virus-free. In the 1980s, a biologist named Lita Proctor decided to take a more careful, systematic look. Her surveys of water from places like the Caribbean and the Sargasso Sea revealed a surprising abundance of viruses.

Then in the 1990s, a new way to survey life emerged. Scientists would add chemicals to a sample of seawater that would rip apart all the proteins and membranes it contained. Out of that detritus, the scientists could extract all the DNA from the sample in a jumble of fragments. The researchers then sequenced the fragments and pieced them together into larger DNA segments. Finally, they could compare these genetic sequences to those of known species—finding either an exact match, or a sequence from a closely related species. This method, known as metagenomics, quickly gave scientists a wave of new discoveries about bacteria and other microbes.

But ocean viruses don't surrender their secrets so easily to metagenomics. When scientists gather genes from a virus that's new to science, they often find that almost none of its genes bear any resemblance to any previously discovered viral gene. In addition, viruses often pick up new genes, either from other species of viruses, or from their hosts. When scientists isolate one piece of genetic material from an unknown virus, it can be difficult to determine where it came from.

In recent years, scientists have managed to bring some order to this chaos. Matthew Sullivan, an environmental virologist at the University of Arizona, and his colleagues have developed a method to identify new species of viruses. They start with viruses that share some of the same genes. Then they measure how similar their DNA is. When they plot those measurements on a graph, the viruses do not spread out into a hazy, inscrutable cloud. Instead, they huddle in tight clumps, which represent distinct species of viruses.

Sullivan joined the leadership of the Tara Oceans project to put these new methods to work on a global scale. His team of researchers filtered seawater in every ocean on Earth, along with the Red Sea, the Mediterranean and the Adriatic, visiting 43 sites in all. They processed the water with iron chloride to make the viruses stick together in particles, filtered the water again, and shipped the virus-clogged filters to labs around the world.

Sullivan and his colleagues examined the viruses under microscopes and sequenced their genes. All told, they extracted 2.16 billion pieces of DNA, each piece containing 101 base pairs on average. The scientists found that many of the pieces overlapped with each other. In jigsaw-puzzle fashion, they assembled long stretches of DNA and began to recognize the full sequence of virus genes. As they compiled this genetic catalog, they began to sort it. Closely related genes, or genes that encode for similar proteins were placed into cluster, and a total of 1 323 921 clustersgenes were identified.

Now they were left with a crucial question: What fraction of all the virus genes in the world's oceans had they collected? Had they just skimmed the surface, or did these 1.3 million clusters represent most of the viral genes in existence?

There's a clever statistical trick scientists can use to answer a question like this. Sullivan and his colleagues began by randomly picking a gene from their catalog. Then they picked another one and noted whether the two genes belonged to the same cluster, or to two different ones. Then they picked out a third gene and compared it to the first two. At each step, they marked their progress by plotting a point on a graph, where every novel gene made the graph tick up.

At first the curve was steep, because each new gene typically didn't belong to any cluster identified so far. But after a while, the curve flattened as the new genes fell into existing clusters. By the end of the process, it was rare for the scientists to pick a gene that was new. Repeating this exercise over and over again with randomly selected genes produced the same flattened curve. This flattened curve told something profound: that they have probably found almost all the virus genes in the upper oceans of the entire planet. There are not billions of additional genes lurking out there, waiting to be sucked into a hose.

The scientists then used this catalog to figure out how many different kinds of viruses there are in the world's oceans. By comparing the genes in the clusters to one another, the scientists were able to identify 5476 distinct populations. When Sullivan and his colleagues tried to match their 5476 populations to species that scientists have already documented, they succeeded just 39 times. In other words, 99 percent of the viruses they discovered were new to science.

But Sullivan is quick to point out that the total number of species of ocean viruses will turn out to be more than 5476. In recent years, for example, scientists have found a number of so-called "giant viruses" that are as big as bacteria. The filters that Duhaime and others used on the Tara Oceans Survey prevented any giant viruses from getting into the vats they studied. In addition, the scientists sequenced only viruses that use DNA to encode their genes. By one estimate, as many as half of the viruses in the ocean are RNA viruses. What's more, the Tara Oceans survey only took samples from the surface of the ocean. The deeper regions have viruses, too, as does the sediment at the bottom of the sea.

2. What viruses do

With such a comprehensive picture of ocean viruses, we can start drawing some broad conclusions about them. Each virus population is more common in some areas than in others, for example. That's likely due to the fact that their hosts thrive at certain temperatures or with certain levels of oxygen.

But Sullivan and his colleagues found viruses from most populations everywhere they looked. In other words, every part of the ocean is like a seed bank for viruses. As soon as the right host comes along, a relatively rare virus will infect it and replicate itself into a huge population.

Now that scientists have such a clear picture of the diversity of ocean viruses, they can hope to gain a better understanding of how these viruses are affecting the planet. Viruses kill vast numbers of hosts. Some researchers have estimated that they kill up to 40 percent of all bacteria in the ocean every day. Paradoxically, though, this daily massacre could actually increase the biomass of the oceans. Mathematical models of ocean ecosystems suggest that by killing so many microbes, viruses could release carbon and other organic nutrients back into the environment, providing an easy source of nutrients for other organisms. Carbon that isn't consumed may drift down into the deep ocean, thereby causing vast supplies of carbon to fall to the seafloor rather than escape into the atmosphere.

Until now, scientists haven't known enough about ocean viruses to create precise models of these effects. So they haven't been able to say with confidence what the viruses are doing to our world. Duhaime said that the data coming from the Tara Oceans survey will go a long way toward pinning those models down. "We're very far from doing that," she said, "but the path is there."

Despite all this new data, Sullivan still considers the ecology of ocean viruses to be in its infancy. "The virus stuff isn't as mature as counting zebras," he said. "That's because it's easier to observe zebras and define a zebra species than it is for viruses." But Sullivan has built a pipeline they can now use to pump huge numbers of additional viruses. Animal ecologists have a head start that stretches hundreds of years, but according to Sullivan, "we may quickly be ahead."

Chapter 6 Genomes and Biodiversity

Genome sequencing for biodiversity analysis is at the forefront of innovation and discovery due to technological advances and the sequencing of whole genomes in the last 10 years. Information generated from biodiversity genomics will revolutionize our approach to taxonomy, phylogeny, conservation, ecological monitoring, wildlife management, agriculture, drug development, zoonotic disease forecasting and even aspects of national security.

Lesson 1
Genome 10K: a Proposal to Obtain Whole-Genome Sequence for 10 000 Vertebrate Species

The bold insight behind the success of the human genome project was that, although vast, the roughly 3 billion letters of digital information specifying the total genetic heritage of an individual is finite and might, with dedicated resolve, be brought within the reach of our technology. The number of living species is similarly vast, estimated to be between 10^6 and 10^8 for all metazoans and approximately 6×10^4 for Vertebrata, which includes our closest relatives. With the same unity of purpose shown for the Human Genome Project, we can now contemplate reading the genetic heritage of all species, beginning today with the vertebrates. The feasibility of a "Genome 10K" (G10K) project to catalog the genomic diversity of 10 000 vertebrate genomes, approximately one for each vertebrate genus, requires only one more order of magnitude reduction in the cost of DNA sequencing, after the 4 orders of magnitude reduction we have seen in the last 10 years. The approximate number of 10 000 is a compromise between reasonable expectations for the reach of new sequencing technology over the next few years and adequate coverage of vertebrate species diversity. It is time to prepare for this undertaking.

Living vertebrate species derive from a common ancestor that lived between 500 and 600 million years ago, before the time of the **Cambrian explosion** of animal life. Because a core repertoire of about 10 000 genes in a genome of about a billion bases is seen in multiple, deeply branching vertebrates and close **deuterostome** sister groups, we may surmise that the haploid genome (consisted of $10^8 \sim 10^9$ bases) of the common vertebrate ancestor was already highly sophisticated. In the descent of the living vertebrates, the roughly 10^8 bases in the DNA segments that specify these sophisticated features, along with more fundamental biological processes, recorded many billions of fixed changes, the outcome of innumerable natural evolutionary experiments. These and other genetic changes, including **rearrangements**, duplications, and losses, spawned the diversity of vertebrate forms that inhabit strikingly diverse environments of the planet today. A G10K project explicitly detailing these genetic changes will provide an essential reference resource for an emerging new synthesis of molecular, organismic, developmental, and evolutionary biology to explore the vertebrate forms of life, just as the human genome project has provided an essential reference resource for 21st century biomedicine (Fig. 6.1).

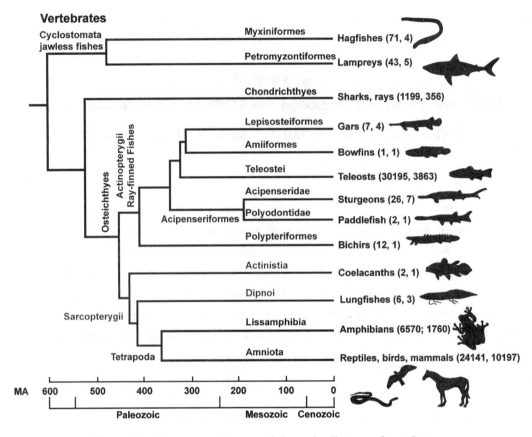

Figure 6.1　Consensus phylogeny of the major lineages of vertebrates

Beyond elaborations of ancient biochemical and developmental pathways, vertebrate evolution is characterized by stunning innovations, including adaptive immunity, **multichambered** hearts, **cartilage**, bones, and teeth, an internal skeleton, a variety of sensory modalities and specialized **endocrine** organs. At the cellular level, the **neural crest**, sometimes referred to as a fourth germ layer, is unique to vertebrates and gives rise to a great variety of structures. Integration of sophisticated vertebrate sensory, **neuroanatomical** and behavioral elaborations coupled with often dramatic anatomical and physiological changes allowed exploitation of oceanic, terrestrial, and aerial ecological niches. Anticipated details of expansions and losses of specific gene families revealed by the G10K project will provide new insights into the molecular mechanisms behind these extraordinary innovations.

Adaptive changes in noncoding regulatory DNA also play a fundamental role in vertebrate evolution and understanding these changes represents an even greater challenge for comparative genomics. Noncoding DNA segments represent the majority of the bases found to be under selection for the removal of deleterious alleles, and are likely to form the majority of the functional units in vertebrate genomes. They are also hypothesized to be the major source of evolutionary innovation within vertebrate subclades. The origins and evolutionary trajectory of the subset of noncoding functional elements under the strongest selection to remove deleterious alleles can be traced deep into the vertebrate tree, in many cases to its very root, whereas other noncoding functional elements have uniquely arisen at the base of a particular class, order or family of vertebrate species. This enables detailed studies of base-by-base evolutionary changes throughout the genome, in both coding and noncoding DNA. Thus, the G10K project will provide power to address critical hypotheses concerning the origin and evolution of functional noncoding DNA segments and their role in molding physiological and developmental definitions of living animal species.

Through comprehensive investigation of vertebrate evolution, the G10K project will also lay the foundation needed to understand the genetic basis of recent and rapid adaptive changes within species and between closely related species. Coupled with evolutionary studies of recently diversifying clades, it will help address an increasingly urgent need to predict species' responses to climate change, pollution, emerging diseases, and invasive competitors. It will enable studies of genomic phylogeography and population genetics that are crucial to assessment, monitoring, and management of biological diversity, especially of threatened and endangered species. Recent studies validate some of the potential contributions that the availability of genome sequences can provide to **endangered species** conservation efforts. Whole-genome sequence assemblies will be essential to facilitate genome-wide single nucleotide polymorphism discovery and to enable studies of historical **demography**, population structure, disease risk factors, and a variety of other conservation-related biological attributes. Such understanding could help curb the accelerating extinction crisis and slow the loss of biodiversity worldwide.

To this end, we propose to assemble a "virtual collection" of frozen or otherwise suitably preserved tissues or DNA samples representing on the order of 10 000 extant vertebrate species, including some recently extinct species that are amenable to genomic sequencing. The G10K species collection will include tissue/DNA specimens from 5 major organismal groups: mammals, birds, **amphibians**, nonavian **reptiles** and fishes. In addition to samples for DNA extraction, the collection will include 1006 **cryopreserved** fibroblast cell lines derived from 602 different vertebrate species, primarily mammals, but including representatives of 300 taxa comprising 42 families of nonmammalian **amniotes** and 1 amphibian species. These resources provide an additional window into the unique cell biology of these species. These cell cultures, along with cDNA derived from primary tissues, will provide direct access to gene expression and regulation data in the vertebrate species we catalog and provide a renewable experimental resource to complement the G10K genome sequences. For at least one species of each vertebrate order, we propose to assemble additional genomic resources (physical maps and a

BAC library, other cell lines, primary tissues for transcriptome analysis), to sequence multiple individuals to assess within-species diversity. A resource of this magnitude would help catalyze a much-needed extension of experimental molecular biology beyond the very limited set of model organisms it currently explores.

As the printing of the first book by Johannes Gutenberg altered the course of human history, so did the human genome project forever change the course of the life sciences with the publication of the first full vertebrate genome sequence. When Gutenberg's success was followed by the publication of other books, libraries naturally emerged to hold the fruits of this new technology for the benefit of all who sought to imbibe the vast knowledge made available by the new print medium. We must now follow the human genome project with a library of vertebrate genome sequences, a genomic ark for thriving and threatened species alike, and a permanent digital record of countless molecular triumphs and stumbles across some 600 million years of evolutionary episodes that forged the "endless forms most beautiful" that make up our living world.

Glossary

Cambrian explosion /ˈkæmbriən ɪkˈsploʊʒn/
寒武纪爆发
Cambrian explosion was the relatively short evolutionary event, beginning around 542 million years ago in the Cambrian Period, during which most major animal phyla appeared, as indicated by the fossil record. Lasting for about the next 20 ~ 25 million years, it resulted in the divergence of most modern metazoan phyla.

deuterostome /ˈdjuːtərəstoʊm/
后口动物
Deuterostome refers to any animal in which the initial pore formed during gastrulation becomes the anus, and the second pore becomes the mouth

rearrangement /ˌriːəˈreɪndʒmənt/
（染色体）重排
Chromosomal rearrangement is a type of chromosome abnormality involving a change in the structure of the native chromosome.

multichambered /məltɪtˈʃeɪmbəd/
多室的
Multichamber means having more than one chamber or rooms or caves.

cartilage /ˈkɑrtɪlɪdʒ/
软骨
Cartilage is a type of dense, non-vascular connective tissue, usually found at the end of joints, the rib cage, the ear, the nose, in the throat and between intervertebral disks.

endocrine /ˈendəkrɪn/
内分泌；激素；内分泌物
Endocrine means the secretion of an endocrine gland, producing internal secretions that are transported around the body by the blood.

neural crest /ˈnʊrəl krest/
神经嵴
Neural crest cells are a transient, multipotent（多能的）, migratory（游走的）cell population unique to vertebrates that gives rise to a diverse cell lineage including craniofacial cartilage and bone, smooth muscle, peripheral and enteric neurons and glia.

neuroanatomical /ˌnʊroʊəˈnætəmɪkəl/
神经解剖学的
Neuroanatomy is the study of the anatomy of the nervous systems.

endangered species /ɪnˈdeɪndʒəd ˈspiːʃiːz/
濒危物种
An endangered species is a species which has been categorized by the International Union for Conservation of Nature (IUCN) Red List as likely to become extinct.

demography /dɪˈmɑːɡrəfi/
人口统计学
Demography is the study of human populations, and how they change.

amphibian /æmˈfɪbiən/
两栖动物
Amphibians are ectothermic (变温的), tetrapod (四足的) vertebrates of the class Amphibia. They inhabit a wide variety of habitats with most species living within terrestrial, fossorial, arboreal or freshwater aquatic ecosystems. Amphibians typically start out as larvae living in water.

reptile /ˈreptaɪl/
爬行动物
Reptiles (class Reptilia) are an evolutionary grade of animals, comprising today's turtles, crocodilians, snakes, lizards and tuatara and some of the extinct ancestors of mammals.

cryopreserved /kraɪˈɒprɪzɜːvd/
冷藏保存的
Cryopreserved samples are often frozen and preserved in ultra-low temperature freezers or in liquid nitrogen.

amniote /ˈæmnɪoʊt/
羊膜动物
Amniotes are a clade of tetrapod vertebrates comprising the reptiles, birds and mammals which lay their eggs on land or retain the fertilized egg within the mother.

Notes to Difficult Sentences

(1) Whole-genome sequence assemblies will be essential to facilitate genome-wide single nucleotide polymorphism discovery and to enable studies of historical demography, population structure, disease risk factors, and a variety of other conservation-related biological attributes.

全基因组序列组装将推进基因组范围的单核苷酸多样性的发现，也使得历史人口学、人口结构学、探索疾病风险因素以及其他保护相关的生物特性等研究成为可能。

拓展：2013年"千人基因组计划"的研究成果发表在 *Nature* 上，研究的主要目标就是鉴定遍及不同人类种群间的罕见基因变异体。从基因层面上看，任何两个人都有超过99%的基因相似度。然而，尽管罕见的基因变异体出现频率极低（可能变异频率仅为1%），但它们仍被认为是引起罕见疾病乃至癌症、心脏病、糖尿病等常见疾病的罪魁祸首。药物治疗对某些病人不起作用，或出现恶心、呕吐、失眠以及一些心脏疾病甚至死亡等药物副作用，都有可能是基因发生罕见的变异在作祟。

(2) For at least one species of each vertebrate order, we propose to assemble additional genomic resources (physical maps and a BAC library, other cell lines, primary tissues for transcriptome analysis), to sequence multiple individuals to assess within-species diversity.

由于对于所有脊椎动物每一个目我们只采集一个物种的样本，因此我们努力收集尽可能多的基因资源（物理图谱，细菌人工染色体文库，细胞系，用于转录组研究的基本组织），并对（同一物种的）多个个体进行测序来评估种内多样性。

拓展：种内多样性一般所指的是种内个体之间或一个群体内不同个体的遗传变异总和，我们通常所说的遗传多样性也是指种内多样性（广义的遗传多样性是指地球上所有生物所携带的遗传信息的总和）。研究表明，种内多样性可以起到某些与种间多样性相同的作用。例如，植物种类较多的地区趋向于拥有更多种类的植食性昆虫，然而，有研究发现，仅靠单独一种植物内部的遗传变异（例如，发生变异的月见草花期不同吸引更多的昆虫），也能促进昆虫的多样性。

Lesson 2
Biodiversity, Genomes, and
DNA Sequence Databases

There are 1.4 million organisms that have been described and <10 000 of these (**terrestrial** vertebrates, some flowering plants, and invertebrates with pretty shells or wings) are popular enough to be well known. How many more species are still awaiting discovery? Nobody knows, but estimates for the grand total differ from 10^7 to 10^8 species.

The representation of the overall diversity of life at the molecular level is still relatively poor. At present, there are ~20 000 organisms represented with one or several sequences available at sequence databases; this means that of the ~1.4 million organisms that have been described **morphologically**, 98% ~ 99% have not yet been subjected to molecular scrutiny. Whereas a reasonable representation of this existing molecular diversity will remain a long-term goal, there will soon be a comprehensive catalogue of nucleotide sequences and genes for a number of model organisms; the human genome project and other large-scale sequencing projects are well underway and the genome analyses of *Sacchromyces cerevisiae* and three **prokaryotes** have been completed in 1996.

1. DNA databanks and sequence entries

There is no central repository for morphological data. Morphological information is scattered among the primary literature and monographs in periodicals, books, and increasingly also in electronic databases. In contrast, there are central repositories for sequence information. Data are exchanged daily between the three collaborating databases—DNA DataBank of Japan, European Bioinformatic Institute, and National Center for Biotechnology Information in the USA—ensuring that each database maintains a comprehensive set of all known and public molecular sequences.

At present, there are close on 900 000 nucleotide records available from the DNA databanks, the significance being that the databases have more than doubled in size within a year. It should not be overlooked, however, that most of this increase has come from the submission of partial cDNA sequences known as expressed sequence tags (ESTs) and ESTs now account for more than half of all records in the genetic databases. ESTs are derived from a very limited number of organisms, mostly humans and mice, and the number of non-EST nucleotide sequence entries in the genetic databases increases presently at the far slower rate of 50% per year.

2. The genomes

Large scale sequencing efforts have been directed at all elements of life on earth: viruses and **bacteriophages**, **organellar** (**mitochondrial/plastid**) genomes, **Eubacteria**, **Archaea**, and eukaryotes. For complete genomes, chromosomes, or other large contiguous pieces of DNA, GenBank has established the genomes database that features a clickable graphic interface that allows the user to zoom in on specific ORFs, or retrieve a particular sequence record—to name but a few options.

The large size of nuclear genomes ensures that sequencing efforts for eukaryotes do not proceed quickly. To date, the ascomycete **fungus** *Sacchromyces cerevisiae* is the only completely sequenced eukaryote. Other eukaryotes that are the subjects of major genomic or EST sequencing projects include the green plants *Oryza sativa* and *Arabidopsis thaliana*, and several **Metazoa**, the nematode *Caenorhabditis elegans*, the fruit fly *Drosophila melanogaster*, the puffer fish *Fugu rubripes*, mouse and human. When a **homologue** for a human gene is discovered in **yeast**, it is customary to make the point that the gene is found in a phylogenetically diverse array of organisms including the "lower" eukaryote yeast. This, however, is a serious misunderstanding as yeast by no means represents an early divergence on the eukaryotic "tree of life". Despite the obvious phenotypic differences between, say, humans, yeasts, and sunflowers, they do belong to a group of closely related taxa in the "crown" of the eukaryotic tree. Similarly, the genomic diversity of Metazoa is far smaller than what the rich variety of morphologically distinct "types" and species in this group might suggest. Therefore, although the genome projects have successfully accumulated a great amount of data, they have sampled only a tiny fraction of the molecular diversity of eukaryotes to date.

Given the smaller size of archaeal (1.9 ~ 4.2Mb) and eubacterial genomes, it is not surprising that prokaryotic genome sequencing efforts are further ahead than those of the metazoans. The genomes of *Mycoplasma genitalium* and *Haemophilus influenzae* have recently been completed and about as many as 20 prokaryotic genomes are expected to be sequenced completely within the next two years. What is surprising, then, is that—in contrast to the focus of the eukaryotic projects on the green plants, fungi, and Metazoa—the workers on the prokaryotic genome projects have made an (conscious?) attempt to sample organisms from all the major lineages. At present, there are genome projects underway for Crenarchaeota, several Euryarchaeota and quite a number of the eubacterial lineages.

A phylogenetically varied group of complete organellar genomes is also available. These include, among others, the mitochondrial genomes of the **protist** Acanthamoeba, the ciliate Paramecium, the "ancestral" unicellular chytridiomycete fungus Allomyces macrogynus, red algae and, of course, many metazoan mitochondria and **angiosperm** plastid genomes.

3. The growth of molecular biodiversity knowledge

Despite the focus on a few model organisms, the molecular dataset has also made recent progress with respect to the representation of the overall diversity of life. Within the period July 1995 to July 1996, the number of organisms that are represented has been growing by 78% overall, from ~13 000 to ~19 000. The strongest growth in representation has taken place in the fungi that have nearly doubled their representation in the genetic databases. A strong increase in the diversity of organisms that have been subjected to molecular scrutiny can also be observed in the green plants and the arthropods. The representation of mammals, bacteria and viruses at genetic databases has increased much slower and this can be attributed at least partially to the fact that a large number of these models have already been used in molecular studies; of the ~4200 mammals described, almost a quarter (~950) are already represented with one or several sequences in databases.

Although there is the indication that the representation of the diversity of life at the DNA databases is improving rapidly, it should not be overlooked that many of the newly accessed organisms are represented by only a single sequence. Recent publications that have employed **ribosomal** RNA sequence comparisons to focus on groups that are either phylogenetically diverse or little known include studies on trichomonads, the human pathogen Blastocystis hominis, lophophorates and other "minor" metazoan **phyla**, arthropod phylogeny and Antarctic bacteria, among others. Other molecules that are used fairly frequently as part of a "one-gene" approach to sample a part of the organismal diversity include elongation factor genes, rubisco in **photosynthetic** organisms, and heat-shock protein genes whereas studies that compare a variety of molecules along a diverse range of organisms are still a fairly rare commodity.

The studies that use one particular gene have been tremendously successful in elucidating the phylogenetic relationships of cellular life-forms but the genome projects, to date, have failed to utilize any information gained and to target a more diverse group of organisms, in particular those organisms found in the deepest branches of the eukaryotic "tree of life" where even basic processes such as transcription and translation initiation are poorly understood. This is about to change, however; projects to sequence two of the organisms that have diverged early in the tree, diplomonads and microsporidia, have been initiated (ML Sogin, personal communication).

4. Conclusions

To date, organismal morphological diversity is still far better studied than molecular diversity. In order to broaden our organismal knowledge and to improve our understanding of gene function and genome organization, we cannot limit ourselves to a few closely related model organisms. Although the potential immediate medical benefits justify the present focus on the genomes of humans and other organisms of close phylogenetic relation, it can only be hoped that funding for genome research will not diminish before there is the chance to study a more substantial representation of the eukaryotic diversity.

The study of taxa such as microsporidians, diplomonads, and trichomonads which diverge at the very base of the eukaryotic tree may be of particular interest because it should allow us to understand the minimum requirements for a functional eukaryotic genome. The genome of the diplomonad *Giardia* is ~12 Mb and Microsporidia range from 6~20 Mb. With sequencing costs decreasing slowly from ~50 cents per base in the U.S. at present, expenditures for one of these genomes could be in the five million dollar range.

The ultimate goal, although certainly not achievable in the near future, is to have a comprehensive molecular sample of genomic diversity that relates to the organismal range and depth of morphology acquired in evolution. It can be safely predicted that this will not happen as long as the cost of sequencing a single genome carries an enormous price tag but the scenario would change if a major technical breakthrough or a long string of incremental improvements could make the process as inexpensive and routine as, say, sequencing an 18S ribosomal DNA is today. Is that likely to happen? I don't think so—but, then again, I didn't believe there would be a completely sequenced eukaryotic genome by 1996 either.

(*This review article was written in 1996. We can get a general understanding of the scientists' perspectives towards genome sequencing and biodiversity in that period.*)

Glossary

terrestrial /təˈrestriəl/
陆地的；陆地生物
Terrestrial animals are animals that live predominantly or entirely on land, as compared with aquatic animals, which live predominantly or entirely in the water, or amphibians, which rely on a combination of aquatic and terrestrial habitats.

morphologically /mɔːfəˈlɒdʒɪklɪ/
形态学上地
Morphology (形态学) is a branch of biology dealing

with the study of the form and structure of organisms and their specific structural features.

prokaryote /ˌproʊˈkærɪɒt/
原核生物
A prokaryote is a single-celled organism that lacks a membrane-bound nucleus （核）, mitochondria, or any other membrane-bound organelles.

bacteriophage /bækˈtɪərəʃeɪdʒ/
噬菌体
Bacteriophage is a virus that infects and replicates within a bacterium.

organellar /ˌɔːɡeɪˈnelə/
细胞器的
An organelle is a specialized subunit within a cell that has a specific function. Individual organelles are usually separately enclosed within their own lipid bilayers.

mitochondrial /ˌmaɪtəʊˈkɒndriəl/
线粒体的
The mitochondrion is a membrane-bound organelle found in most eukaryotic cells often described as "the powerhouse of the cell", because it generates most of the cell's supply of ATP, used as a source of chemical energy.

plastid /ˈplæstɪd/
叶绿体
The plastid is a major double-membrane organelle found, among others, in the cells of plants and algae. Plastids possess a circular double-stranded DNA and are the site where photosynthesis happens.

Eubacteria /juːbækˈtɪəriə/
真细菌
Eubacteria = true bacteria

Archaea /ɑːˈkɪə/
古细菌
Archaea constitute a domain or kingdom of single-celled microorganisms. These microbes are prokaryotes, meaning that they have no cell nucleus or any other membrane-bound organelles in their cells.

fungus /ˈfʌŋɡəs/
真菌
A fungus is any member of a large group of eukaryote that includes microorganisms such as yeasts and molds, as well as mushrooms. These organisms are classified as a kingdom, Fungi, which is separate from plants, animals, protists and bacteria.

Metazoa /ˌmetəˈzoʊə/
后生动物
Metazoa refers to any animal that undergoes development from an embryo stage with three tissue layers, namely the ectoderm, mesoderm, and endoderm. The term applies to all animals except the sponges.

homologue /ˈhɒməˌlɒɡ/
同系物；同源物
Homologue genes are a group of similar DNA sequences that share a common ancestry.

yeast /jiːst/
酵母
Yeast is a single-celled fungus of a wide variety of taxonomic families.

protist /ˈproʊtɪst/
原生生物

angiosperm /ˌændʒɪəˌspɜːm/
被子植物
Angiosperms are seed-producing plants like the gymnosperms （裸子植物） and can be distinguished from the gymnosperms by characteristics including flowers, endosperm （胚乳） within the seeds, and the production of fruits that contain the seeds.

ribosomal /raɪbəˈsoʊməl/
核糖体的
The ribosome is a large and complex molecular machine, found within all living cells, that serves as the site of biological protein synthesis. Ribosomes link amino acids together in the order specified by messenger RNA (mRNA) molecules.

phyla /ˈfaɪlə/
门
Phyla is a taxonomic rank below kingdom （界） and above class （纲）.

photosynthetic /ˌfoʊtoʊsɪnˈθetɪk/
光合作用的
Photosynthesis is a process used by plants and other organisms to convert light energy, normally from the Sun, into chemical energy that can be later released to fuel the organisms' activities.

Notes to Difficult Sentences

Other molecules that are used fairly frequently as part of a "one-gene" approach to sample a part of the organismal diversity include elongation factor genes, rubisco in photosynthetic organisms, and heat-shock protein genes whereas studies that compare a variety of molecules along a diverse range of organisms are still a fairly rare commodity.

其他一些分子也常常用于"单基因"方式进行生物多样性研究的部分采样，例如延伸因子基因、光合生物中的二磷酸核酮糖羧化酶、热激蛋白基因等，对多种生物进行多个分子的比较研究相对较少。

拓展：20世纪末的多样性研究受到很多条件限制，一方面测序数据不多，另一方面计算机硬件和数据分析软件无法满足多基因多样本的比较分析，"单基因"方式在生物多样性研究上占据主导地位。随着测序技术和生物信息分析技术的发展和进步，现如今的多样性研究不再仅局限于单个基因，而是对多个基因或某些基因簇进行分析比对，让多样性分析更系统、更可靠。

Lesson 3
Examples of Genome & Transcriptome Projects

1. Fish-T1K (Transcriptomes of 1000 fishes)

With an estimated 32 000 species, ray-finned fishes represent over 50% of the global vertebrate biodiversity and encompass enormous variation in morphology, physiology, and ecology. Also, as the most abundant vertebrates and a primary source of protein for people worldwide, these fishes are an economically and ecologically significant group of animals. Despite their

Figure 6.2　Fish-T1K

importance, fishes are relatively underrepresented in the total number of sequenced vertebrate genomes and transcriptomes. Fish-T1K (Transcriptomes of 1000 fishes, http://www.fisht1k.org) project is officially launched by BGI-Shenzhen, with the aim of generating genome-wide transcriptome sequences for 1000 diverse species of fishes using next-generation RNA sequencing technology (Fig. 6.2). This resource will greatly advance the study of fish biology, eventually contributing towards global fish biodiversity conservation efforts and sustainable utilization of natural resources. In addition, the project will promote development of new technologies and software for transcriptome sequencing, data analysis, annotation, and storage.

2. 1KITE (1K Insect Transcriptome Evolution)

Insects are one of the most species-rich groups of metazoan organisms. They play a pivotal role in most non-marine ecosystems and many insect species are of enormous economical and medical importance. Unraveling the evolution of insects is essential for understanding how life in terrestrial and **limnic** environments evolved. The 1KITE (1K Insect Transcriptome Evolution, http://www.1kite.org/) project aims to study the transcriptomes (that is the entirety of expressed genes) of more than 1000 insect species encompassing all recognized insect orders (Fig. 6.3). For each species, so-called ESTs (Expressed Sequence Tags) will be produced using next generation

Figure 6.3　1KITE

sequencing (NGS) techniques. Sequencing and sequence assembly have been completed for more than 1200 species by the end of 2014. The expected data will allow inferring robust phylogenetic backbone trees of insects. Furthermore, the project includes the development of new software for data quality assessment and analysis.

3. 1KP (The 1000 Plant Transcriptomes)

The 1000 plants (1KP, http://www.onekp.com) project is an international **multidisciplinary** consortium that has now generated transcriptome data from over 1000 plant species (Fig. 6.4). One of the goals of our species selection process was to provide exemplars for all of the major lineages across the **Viridiplantae** (green plants), representing approximately one billion years of evolution, including flowering plants, **conifers**, **ferns**, mosses and streptophyte green algae. Whereas genomics

Figure 6.4 1KP

has long strived for completeness within species (e.g., every gene in the species), we were focused on completeness across an evolutionary clade-obviously not every species, but one representative species for everything at some phylogenetic level (e.g., one species per family, and perhaps more than one species when the family is especially large). Because many of our species had never been subjected to large-scale sequencing, 2 gigabases (Gb) of data per sample was sufficient to increase the number of plant genes by approximately 100-fold in comparison to the totality of the public databases.

4. i5k (5000 arthropod genomes initiative)

The 5000 arthropod genomes initiative (i5k, http://arthropod-genomes.org/wiki/i5k) community met formally in 2012 to discuss a roadmap for sequencing and analyzing 5000 high-priority arthropods and is continuing this effort via pilot projects (Fig. 6.5), the development of standard operating procedures, and training of students and career scientists. i5k is not a funding agency, nor does it have a single core group or institution that will tackle even a

Figure 6.5 i5k

modest subset of the 5000 targeted species for genomic analyses. Instead, this initiative seeks to have an impact through (I) prioritizing and promoting genome projects, (II) providing guidelines for designing and carrying out an arthropod genome project, (III) training scientists in the tools needed and standards expected for genome projects, (IV) fostering discussions that reduce redundant efforts and enhance the impacts of genome projects, and (V) presenting recommendations to fundholders for the support needed to provide new opportunities for arthropod genomics in addressing fundamental research questions.

5. Avian Phylogenomics Project

Birds are the most species-rich class of **tetrapod** vertebrates, with over 10 000 living species distributed in diverse niches all over the world. Birds are widely used as models for investigating evolutionary and ecological questions. Resolving phylogenetic relationships of Neoavian species and estimating divergence times have been a huge challenge for scientist. One for the challenge is that it has been proposed, but not proven, that to be that there was a "big bang" radiation for Neoavian birds, where many species are closely related at the dawn of the radiation. This radiation could theoretically be solved with whole genomes. However, by 2010, only three species (chicken, turkey and **zebra finch**) had whole genome sequences. Because of the lack of genomic data, many other avian-related questions could also not be addressed systematically.

Figure 6.6 Avian Phylogenomics Project

In this project we carefully selected other 45 avian species for whole genome sequencing and assembly (Fig. 6.6). The total of 48 birds sequenced represent all 32 **neognath** and two of the five **palaeognath** orders. With all 48 genomes, we performed large-scale phylogenomics analysis to investigate the bird family tree, and applied comparative genomics methods to address various questions such as avian genome evolution, sex chromosome evolution, molecular basis of flight, loss of teeth, vocal learning, and endangered birds. In addition, to address the technical problems encountered in this project (that is, large-scale tree estimation), we developed new bioinformatic methods and software tools. This project is the beginning of a project to sequence many living avian species.

6. MMETSP (Marine Microbial Eukaryote Transcriptome Sequencing Project)

The Marine Microbial Eukaryotic Transcriptome Sequencing Project (MMETSP, http://marinemicroeukaryotes.org/) aims to provide a significant foothold for integrating microbial eukaryotes into marine ecology by creating over 650 assembled, functionally annotated, and publicly available transcriptomes. These transcriptomes largely come from some of the more abundant and ecologically significant microbial eukaryotes in the oceans. The choice of species, strain, and physiological condition was based on a grassroots nomination process, where researchers working in the field nominated projects based on phylogeny, environmental and ecological importance, physiological impact, and other diverse criteria. The data have been assembled and annotated by **homology** with existing databases, providing baseline information on gene function. Because the majority of transcriptomes were sequenced from cultured species, they are also taxonomically well defined. Most organisms are available from public culture collections and, therefore, can be further investigated based on hypotheses derived from the transcriptome data. The project as a whole will go a substantial distance towards fulfilling the two criteria for relevant reference sequences noted above. This is not to say these data solve all our problems: new biases have been introduced, and Illumina-based transcriptomes can be challenging to assemble and work with. In addition, there is an apparently universal problem of low levels of contamination—some from other species living with the target organism in culture, others possibly from the process of library construction and sequencing. Importantly, however, the taxa from which these data are derived on aggregate conform much more closely to our understanding of marine eukaryotic diversity from sequence surveys than do the current reference databases, which are the result of ad hoc sequencing priorities that do not fit those of marine ecology. Indeed, digging deeper into the taxonomy of the more abundant and generally better-studied groups such as **prasinophytes** and **dinoflagellates** shows this to be true at multiple levels.

Glossary

limnic /ˈlɪmnɪk/
湖泊的；湖沼的；湖栖的
The term limnic means of or pertaining to fresh water.

multidisciplinary /ˌmʌltiˈdɪsəpləneri/
多学科的
A multidisciplinary approach involves drawing appropriately from multiple disciplines to redefine problems outside of normal boundaries and reach solutions based on a new understanding of complex situations.

viridiplantae /ˌvɪrɪdɪˈplæntɪ/
绿色植物界
Viridiplantae are a clade of eukaryotic organisms made up of the green algae, which are primarily aquatic, and the land plants (embryophytes), which evolved within them.

conifer /ˈkɑːnɪfər/
针叶树；松柏科植物
A conifer is a cone-bearing seed plant with vascular tissue, usually a tree.

fern /fɜːrn/
蕨；蕨类植物
A fern is a member of a group of roughly 12 000 species of vascular plants that reproduce via spores and have neither seeds nor flowers.

tetrapod /ˈtetrəˌpɒd/
四足动物
The superclass Tetrapoda comprises the first four-limbed vertebrates and their descendants, including the living and extinct amphibians, reptiles, mammals, and birds.

zebra finch /ˈzebrə fɪntʃ/
斑胸草雀
The zebra finch is the most common estrildid finch (梅花雀) of Central Australia and ranges over most of the continent, avoiding only the cool moist south and some areas of the tropical far north.

neognathae /ˌniːəɡˈneɪθiː/
新颚总目

palaeognathae /pælɪəˈɡnəθiː/
古颚总目

homology /hoʊˈmɒlədʒɪ/
同源
Homology is the existence of shared ancestry between a pair of structures, or genes, in different species.

prasinophyte /prəˈzɪnəfaɪt/
绿藻类
Prasinophyte refers to any of various flagellate, unicellular（单细胞的）green algae of class Prasinophyceae（绿藻纲）.

dinoflagellate /ˌdaɪnəˈflædʒəˌlɪt/
鞭毛虫类
Dinoflagellates are a large group of flagellate protists （有鞭毛的原生生物）.

Notes to Difficult Sentences

The choice of species, strain, and physiological condition was based on a grassroots nomination process, where researchers working in the field nominated projects based on phylogeny, environmental and ecological importance, physiological impact, and other diverse criteria.

选择什么物种、哪一品系、怎样的生理状态下的样品作为研究对象，都是基于一个民众提报流程，通过这个系统，研究者们根据系统发生、环境和生态多样性、生理影响及其他标准提出研究课题（和样本要求）。

拓展： 对于千种/万种动植物基因组/转录组这些大型项目来说，样本的选择是项目的难点之一，通常样本收集的理想状态是能够覆盖"生命之树"（across the tree of life），每个目或科采集1～2个物种。但由于样本分布广泛、采集困难等问题，往往这一标准很难实现。常用样本选择标准还有：关键进化节点物种、极端表型物种、濒危物种、经济物种以及满足各种子项目需求的（subprojects-based）其他物种。

Reading Material 1

Diark—the Database for Eukaryotic Genome and Transcriptome Assemblies in 2014

Eukaryotic genome research enormously benefits from the increasing number of sequenced organisms. Whereas in the time of Sanger-sequencing single-species analyses and small-scale comparative projects dominated, the throughput of the Illumina technology allowed initiating and conducting the sequencing of thousands of species. Examples are the Genome 10K project, the i5k project and the 959 Nematodes project intending to provide the genome sequences of a broad range of species, and the 1001 Arabidopsis project, the 1000 bull project and the 3000 rice project aiming to reveal phenotypic and genetic differences of breeds and varieties of economically important animals and plants. Usually, genome assemblies are generated for new species, whereas in population studies the sequencing reads are mapped against reference genomes without producing independent genome assemblies.

NCBI/ENA/DDBJ are the central repositories for sequence read archives (SRAs), the "raw data" for generating assemblies, but publishers and funding agencies often do not require assemblies to also be stored there. Thus, most large-scale sequencing centers like the Broad Institute of MIT and Harvard (Cambridge, MA, USA), the DOE Joint Genome Institute (Walnut Creek, CA, USA) and the Wellcome Trust Sanger Institute (Cambridge, UK) established own species-and taxa-dedicated databases such as Phytozome for plants and the Fungal Genome Initiative project pages. Powered by research community efforts, there are also excellent databases dedicated to single species such as FlyBase, WormBase and dictyBase, or repositories for species of certain taxonomic branches such as EuPathDB, VectorBase and FungiDB. Although these databases only comprise model species and related organisms, they are well known far beyond their research communities. In contrast, dedicated databases have been set up for many of the newly sequenced species that are only known to small communities. In addition, for many species it takes years from the first release of a draft assembly to the publication of the genome analysis (e.g. the *Babesia bigemina* genome is available since 2003 but was published in 2014; the *Callithrix jacchus* genome has been made available in 2007 but published in 2014). Therefore, it is necessary to have a database to identify and access all the available data.

The two major manually curated genome project databases are GOLD and diArk. Whereas GOLD is mainly focused on microbial genomes, we developed diArk as a central hub for all eukaryotes, for which large-scale transcriptome or genome assembly data have been produced and are available to the public. diArk provides measures and analyses of these assemblies, as well as links to the data generator repositories. Currently, diArk comprises 2577 eukaryotes and provides access to almost 6000 transcriptome and genome assemblies.

1. Current status of the database

diArk's growth reflects the exponentially increasing availability of sequenced eukaryotes, now (September 5, 2014) comprising 2577 species (806 in 2011, 415 in 2007) (Fig. 6.7). For 1999 of these species whole genome assembly data are available, and for 429 species transcriptome shotgun assemblies (TSAs), of which the first became available end of 2012. Assembly data for 2017 (78.3%) of the eukaryotes are available at NCBI/ENA/DDBJ meaning that data for 560 (21.7%) species can currently only be accessed at other resources. The data for these 560 species have not yet been or might never be submitted to NCBI/ENA/DDBJ.

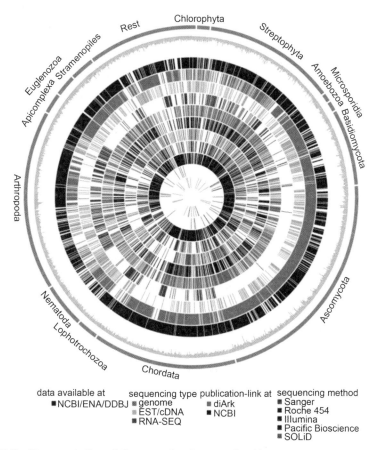

Figure 6.7 Representation of the nonredundant species (i.e., one strain per species) in diArk with their sequencing type and method

These species include, for example, the recently published fish *Electrophorus electricus* and the stick insect *Timema cristinae*, of which only the SRA data but not the genome assemblies have been deposited at NCBI/ENA/DDBJ, several species such as the snake *Boa constrictor constrictor*, whose genome assemblies are only available at (Giga)^{n}DB database, and species whose genome assemblies are only available at the sequencing centers such as 31 nematode and 22 Platyhelminth genomes recently finished by the Wellcome Trust Sanger Institute. These examples underline the unique value of diArk for the eukaryote sequencing and research community in providing a central hub integrating data available from single species repositories to large-scale sequencing centers. In the last 3 years, RNA-Seq based transcriptome assemblies have essentially replaced EST and cDNA sequencing efforts. Due to the lower costs and faster accessibility, TSAs have almost passed EST/cDNA data in diArk.

diArk links publications of sequence assemblies to species. At NCBI, there is a master record for each assembly to access the respective data, and to which respective publications are linked. Currently, these publication links (784 links) only comprise 79.6% of the publication links included in diArk (985 links). Examples for species, whose genomes have long been published but are still not linked to the NCBI genome entries. Instead, the genome assemblies of these 200 species are marked as "unpublished". Published and unpublished genomes are important resources for the community but it is also important that data generators get credits for their efforts. On the other hand, embargo rules for unpublished data should indefinitely not prohibit specific analyses. At diArk, researchers find the most complete list of references to genome assemblies for proper citation or for selection of appropriate subsets of published species to avoid data usage issues.

In the last years, most of the available genomes have been sequenced with Illumina machines. However, the Sanger method is still used to assist in scaffold and chromosome assembling. Roche's 454 sequencing method is currently the most widely used method for transcriptome shotgun sequencing. Other methods such as SOLiD, PacBio or IonTorrent are still rarely used to generate *de novo* genome or transcriptome assemblies.

2. New developments

diArk hosts and analyses whole-genome and transcriptome assemblies. Currently, the about 6000 assemblies comprise mitochondrial, chloroplast, apicoplast, nucleolar and nuclear genomic DNA and are made available to other services such as the gene reconstruction software WebScipio. The quality of genome assemblies can vary significantly. However, approaches resulting in excellent genomes for one species might not produce assemblies of similar quality in other cases. Therefore, diArk provides access to alternative assemblies and several measures for direct comparison such as number of contigs, genome size (larger = better), N50 value (higher = better), N50 length (higher = better), contig length distributions (A50 and N50 plots), sequencing coverage (higher = better), sequencing methods and used assembly software. Not only the number of alternative assemblies increased in the last years, but also the number of redundant species in terms of species diversity increased. Redundant species include, for example, different strains of the same fungal species, different breeds of animals, different varieties of plants and different isolates of protozoa. Within diArk, the respective genome and transcriptome assemblies can directly be compared and the most suitable for a certain research hypothesis be identified. diArk also provides chaos game representations, which are fingerprints of genomes, and frequency chaos game representations at different resolutions, which can be used, for example, for phylogenetic reconstructions.

Integration of RNA-Seq Data. The most noticeable innovation from v. 2 to v. 3 is diArk's integration of RNA-seq data. The first nonhuman transcriptome assemblies have been submitted to and released by NCBI in late 2012. Since then, not only the diversity of sequenced species has increased rapidly but also the number of species with transcriptome assemblies generated for different developmental stages and/or organs. Given the low costs of transcriptome compared to genome sequencing, the number of species with available transcriptome assemblies will pass the number of species with sequenced genomes in the near future. Several large-scale projects have already been announced and are expected to release their data this or next year, such as The 1000 plants (one KP or 1KP) initiative (https://sites.google.com/a/ualberta.ca/onekp/), the Marine Microbial Eukaryote Transcriptome Sequencing project and the Fish-T1K project (http://www.fisht1k.org/). Interestingly, there is not much overlap between species with transcriptome and genome assemblies. One reason is, that RNA-seq data is still rarely generated for species, for which genome assemblies have been produced, and if generated, the RNA-seq data had been used to assist in genome annotation or to generate expression profiles but not to produce independent transcriptome assemblies. In addition, many scientific questions can be answered sufficiently and faster with transcriptome data.

3. Conclusions

Herein, we present an updated version of diArk, which is a central hub for all sequenced eukaryotes, for which either genome or transcriptome assemblies, or large-scale EST/cDNA data are available. diArk is unique in providing direct access to most of the sequenced eukaryotes, whose number has more than tripled compared to the previous version. The number of analyzed genome and transcriptome assemblies now reaches 6000.

Reading Material 2

The Global Genome Biodiversity Network (GGBN) Data Portal

The Global Genome Biodiversity Network (GGBN) was formed in 2011 with the principal aim of making high-quality well-documented and vouchered collections that store DNA or tissue samples of biodiversity, discoverable for research through a networked community of biodiversity repositories (Fig. 6.8). This is achieved through the GGBN Data Portal (http://data.ggbn.org), which links globally distributed databases and bridges the gap between biodiversity repositories, sequence databases and research results. Advances in DNA extraction techniques combined with next-generation sequencing technologies provide new tools for genome sequencing. Many ambitious genome sequencing projects with the potential to revolutionize biodiversity research consider access to adequate samples to be a major bottleneck in their workflow. This is linked not only to accelerating biodiversity loss and demands to improve conservation efforts but also to a lack of standardized methods for providing access to genomic samples. Biodiversity biobank-holding institutions urgently need to set a standard of collaboration towards excellence in collections stewardship, information access and sharing and responsible and ethical use of such collections. GGBN meets these needs by enabling and supporting accessibility and the efficient coordinated expansion of biodiversity biobanks worldwide.

Figure 6.8 DNA Bank Netework Portal merged with GGBN Pages in 2012

Until now, no central platform existed that would globally aggregate biodiversity biobank data. While the need for data sharing and sample access increases, information on genomic samples is still as fragmented as the geographic distribution of the repositories that maintain them. Without a central data portal that aggregates genomic sample data, biodiversity genomics studies cannot reach their full potential. The German Research Foundation (DFG)—supported DNA Bank Network was established in 2007 as a first step towards this goal. The GGBN aims at closing this gap on a global scale by building on the DNA Bank Network's data model.

Chapter 6 Genomes and Biodiversity

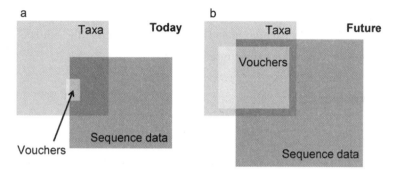

Figure 6.9 Schematic representation of data preserved now and future
a. The current state of play regarding the proportion of sequence data available in public repositories with proper voucher specimen information. **b.** What GGBN aims to facilitate in coming years, i.e. increase both the number of taxa sequenced and the proportion of taxa sequenced for which a voucher specimen information is readily available.

1. The network's mission

GGBN is an open network of currently 24 biodiversity repositories from across all continents that came together with the aim to endorse biodiversity biobank stewardship, information sharing and ethical use of collections in compliance with national and international conventions and regulations.

Key objectives of this global endeavor include establishing and adopting standards and best practices, accelerating access to specimens and data and enabling targeted collection. GGBN's most central mission is to promote access to information on the genomic samples maintained by its members. Goals include to:
(1) provide genome-quality DNA and tissue samples from across the tree of life for research and training;
(2) provide free access to a global Data Portal hosting the aggregated primary specimen and sample data as well as metadata of all member institutions;
(3) develop standards for sharing DNA and tissue information;
(4) develop best practices related to management and stewardship of genomic samples and their derivatives, including appropriate access and benefit-sharing;
(5) establish an infrastructure for deposition of genomic samples;
(6) promote targeted collection and preservation of genomic samples representing a synoptic sample of life on earth;
(7) provide a platform for biodiversity biobanking knowledge exchange;
(8) recruit partners with different regional and taxonomic foci, to preserve global genetic diversity in an efficient, planned and concerted effort.

Global biodiversity and collections initiatives around the world such as biodiversity observatories, genome projects, monitoring and barcoding campaigns will both contribute to and rely on GGBN resources for reaching their research goals.

2. GGBN data portal

GGBN's Data Portal (http://data.ggbn.org) bridges the gap between biodiversity repositories, sequence databases and research results by linking globally distributed biodiversity databases of genomic samples, representing the biodiversity of life on Earth to voucher specimens, sequence data and publications. At present, >70 000 DNA and tissue samples from almost 17 000 taxa are available. These have been collected in accordance with the Convention on Biological Diversity (CBD), the Convention on International Trade in Endangered Species (CITES) and in compliance with all relevant conventions with regard to the acquisition, maintenance and use of DNA and tissue material. The Data Portal enables scientists to:

(1) identify available resources held by GGBN members;

(2) query, request and obtain DNA and tissue material to conduct new studies or to extend and complement previous investigations;

(3) find collections for storing DNA and tissue samples under optimal conditions after project completion or data publication;

(4) verify geographic locations of taxa and links to sources of genomic verification;

(5) verify taxonomic identification through digital images;

(6) support good scientific practice as the deposition of DNA samples and related specimens facilitates the verification of published results.

The GGBN Data Portal provides a necessary service. Natural history collections, worldwide, use different specialized collection database systems. Some collection database systems have been extended to fulfill the needs of curating a biodiversity biobank. An open-source software for the management of a biodiversity biobank has been developed in the framework of the DNA Bank Network (DNA Module, http://wiki.bgbm.org/dnabankwiki/index.php/DNA_Module).

GBIF, BioCASe and the DNA Bank Network have established an infrastructure to link biodiversity data from such systems. This is achieved by direct data integration from multiple distributed databases through wrapper software packages implementing agreed exchange protocols such as the BioCASe protocol, or DiGIR (Distributed Information Retrieval) (http://www.digir.net), and through use of publishing tools such as the IPT (Integrated Publishing Toolkit) (http://www.gbif.org/ipt). BioCASe uses ABCD (Access to Biological Collection Data) and DiGIR uses Darwin Core as XML data schemas. The IPT also works with Darwin Core, but the data is packaged in a Darwin Core Archive, in a text-based tabular format with mappings to Darwin Core terms.

3. GGBN data access and sustainability

Login is only required for requesting DNA and tissue material. All members provide their data, based on the GBIF infrastructure, via web services (BioCASe) or Darwin Core Archive files (access points available via the registry at http://registry.ggbn.org). This enables third parties to retrieve data from our members. Furthermore, third parties are welcome to contact the Technical Manager of GGBN to get required data. To enable free access to genomic data via one central portal is a major goal of GGBN. The individual members may block individual samples from physical requests for certain reasons. The Botanic Garden and Botanical Museum Berlin-Dahlem (BGBM), Freie Universität Berlin is coordinating the DNA Bank Network (GGBN node with currently nine partners) and hosts the GGBN Data Portal as well as its precursor (data portal of the DNA Bank Network). The GGBN Data Portal is further developed, promoted and sustained in the framework of other projects and as a core activity of the BGBM's Biodiversity Informatics Research Group.

Chapter 7 Biobanking

A biobank is a type of biorepository that stores biological samples (usually human) for use in research. Since the late 1990s biobanks have become an important resource in medical research, supporting many types of contemporary research like genomics and personalized medicine. Biobanks give researchers access to data representing a large number of people. Samples in biobanks and the data derived from those samples can often be used by multiple researchers for cross purpose research studies. Biobanks have provoked questions on privacy, research ethics and medical ethics. While viewpoints on what constitutes appropriate biobank ethics diverge, consensus has been reached that operating biobanks without establishing carefully considered governing principles and policies could be detrimental to communities that participate in biobank programs.

Lesson 1
Current Status, Challenges, Policies & Bioethics of Biobanks

Biobanks provide important materials for many research realms, such as biomarker development for the early diagnoses of specific diseases, including cancer and genetic diseases, and for applying personalized drug therapies (Table 7.1). There is no consensus definition for a biobank, but it is considered a **biorepository** that stores biospecimens for use for diagnostic or research purposes. Also, a biobank is an institution that collects, stores, processes, and uses biological materials, genetic data, and associated epidemiological data from human beings or distributes them to researchers. The term "research biobank" means a collection of human biological material and data obtained directly by the analysis of this material, which is used or is to be used for research purposes. A repository is defined as an organization, place, room, or physical entity that may receive, process, store, maintain, and/or distribute specimens, their derivatives, and their associated data.

Table 7.1 Biobanks worldwide with sample sizes ≥ 200 000 (2012)

Name of Biobank	Size (age group)	Type of biobank	Year of start
UK Biobank	500 000 (40~69 y)	P-B & D-O biobank	2006
Estonian Genome Project	~1 million	P-B biobank	2001
Icelandic deCode Biobank	~250 000	P-B biobank	1996
Kadoorie Study of Chronic Diseases in China	500 000 (35~74 y)	P-B biobank	2004
Biobank Japan	300 000	D-O biobank	2002
Korea Biobank Project	500 000	P-B & D-O biobank	2008

P-B, population-based; D-O, disease-oriented.
Source: GBI Research, P3G data, KBN website, Biobank Japan website.

1. Types of biobank

The term "biobank" has been used in different ways but one way is to define it as "an organized collection of human biological material and associated information stored for one or more research purposes". Collections of plant, animal, microbe, and other nonhuman materials may also be described as biobanks but in some discussions the term is reserved for human specimens. Biobanks may be classified by purpose or design. Disease-oriented biobanks usually have a hospital affiliation through which they collect samples representing a variety of diseases, perhaps to look for biomarkers affiliated with disease. Population-based biobanks need no particular hospital affiliation because they take samples from large numbers of all kinds of people, perhaps to look for biomarkers for disease **susceptibility** in a general population.

2. Guidelines for management and quality assurance of biobanks

There are many guidelines for the management of biobanks, such as the International Society for Biological and Environmental Repositories (ISBER) guideline and Organization for Economic Cooperation and Development (OECD) guideline. ISBER is the largest international forum that addresses the technical, legal, ethical, and managerial issues relevant to repositories of biological and environmental specimens. ISBER has the "Best Practices for Repositories/ Collection, Storage and **Retrieval** of Human Biological Materials for Research." Also, ISBER has introduced standard PREanalytical Coding (SPREC) and can be used in the biobank. The OECD Best Practice Guidelines for Biological Resource Centers set out further complementary quality assurance and technical aspects for the acquisition, maintenance, and provision of high-quality biological materials in a secure manner.

3. Bioethics and safety in biobanks

Informed consent is getting a patient to sign a **written consent** form and is the process of communication between a patient and a medical doctor. In medical diagnosis and treatment, including invasive procedures, a doctor or a researcher must give sufficient information to the patient. Informed consent can be given based on a clear understanding of the process, implications, and consequences of an action. The consent process should include sufficient explanation about how individual information would be handled. The consent process includes the impact of research results on the lives of participants, their families, and their communities. Explanations should be on confidentiality, participants' rights of withdrawal, and specifications.

Due to the difficulties of securing specific informed consent, broad consent is a more general form of consent in which individuals agree to have their bio-samples and personal information collected and stored in the biobank and for future, unspecified research. Further issues have been discussed recently, such as privacy, confidentiality and data protection, controlling data access, accessibility to biospecimens, benefit sharing, commercialization, intellectual property rights, and genetic discrimination.

In order to ensure **bioethics** and bioethical safety in the life sciences and biotechnologies, each of the institutions should set up its own Institutional Review Board (IRB). When a genetic testing or research institution obtains written informed consent from a test subject concerning the use of specimens for research purposes, it may provide the specimens to either a person conducting research on genes or an institution licensed to open a biobank.

4. Distribution policy for biospecimens and data

Many biobanks have policies for the distribution of biospecimens and data. For example, there is a guideline to distribute biospecimens in the National Health and Nutrition Examination Survey (NHANES), which is a program of studies designed to assess the health and **nutritional** status of adults and children in the United States. All proposals for the use of NHANES samples are evaluated by a technical panel for scientific merit and by the NHANES Ethics Review Board (ERB). To determine if this limited resource should be used in the proposed projects, a technical panel will evaluate the public health significance and scientific merit of the proposed research. Distribution of a 0.5mL sample is available once, and after finishing the research, the remaining samples are abandoned, or remnants more than 0.3mL should be returned to NHANES; third-party biospecimen transfer is not permitted. Researchers who received specimens must submit the result of the analysis, such as quality control and analytical methods with documents, to the National Center for Health Statistics (NCHS). Surplus data without DNA analysis results would be opened in the website and given a period of 3 months for analysis.

The **Prostate**, Lung, **Colorectal**, and **Ovarian** Cancer Screening Trial (PLCO) biorepository in the United States has 2.9 million biological samples, including blood, and researchers can use samples and data through the process of peer review. Researchers can submit summarized proposals to the PLCO, and the chosen research is recommended for full research proposals and submissions are available twice in June/July or December/January annually. The review process takes 4 or 6 months. Researchers with approved proposals should submit IRB approval documents and contract the **Material Transfer Agreement** (**MTA**) mutually, and biospecimens are distributed to researchers when approved.

5. Future Plans for Biobanks

Due to the increased demands on qualified biospecimens for research, the number of biobanks has significantly increased recently. By virtue of the advancements in bioinformatics and biotechnology, storing biospecimens and data on a large scale requires that biobanks harmonize biobank processes and regulations.

Most biobanks did their best to secure more biospecimens at the inception of the foundation and comparably distribution rate for the researchers is low. According to a first survey of 456 biobank managers in the United States, nearly 70% of those questioned were concerned with underuse of the samples in their repositories. Therefore, many biobankers are trying to advertise their biospecimens to researchers in regional academic societies.

For maximizing the value of biospecimens, consistency in the methods by which they are retrieved, processed, stored, and transported is important. Ideally, this should involve the use of agreed SOPs (standard operating protocols) in general. The other issue in the next big step is automated biobanking, and today's biobanks demand and move toward automated sample management systems that meet the requirements for reliability, sample **integrity**, high capacity, and high throughput.

Horn, the former director of the Genetic Alliance, demonstrates that biobanks have to cooperate together to achieve their mission, and standardization is going to be important for researchers to get samples from different collections; we need catalogs that say where these samples exist. **Accreditation** processes can also be introduced to biobanks for harmonizing collections and encouraging use of biospecimens in the biobanks.

Glossary

biorepository /ˌbaɪoʊrɪˈpɑːzətɔːri/
生物样本库
A Biorepository is a biological materials repository that collects, processes, stores, and distributes biospecimens to support future scientific investigation.

susceptibility /səˌseptəˈbɪləti/
敏感性；易感性
Disease susceptibility is the possibility of getting a certain kind of disease.

retrieval /rɪˈtriːvl/
取回；恢复
Retrieval is the process of calling back the specimens which have been distributed before.

written consent /ˈrɪtn kənˈsent/
书面同意书；知情同意书
Written (informed) consent is an agreement or a permission given by a person who has a clear appreciation and understanding of the facts, implications, and future consequences of an action (such as donating his/her tissues for scientific research).

bioethics /ˌbaɪoʊˈeθɪks/
生物伦理学
Bioethics is the study of the typically controversial ethical issues emerging from new situations and possibilities brought about by advances in biology and medicine. It is also moral discernment as it relates to medical policy, practice, and research.

nutritional /njuˈtrɪʃənl/
营养的；滋养的
nutri—nutrition, nutrient, nutritious, nutritive, nutritionist
Nutrition（营养）is the process of nourishing or being nourished, especially the process by which a living organism assimilates food and uses it for growth. Nutritional status is the condition of the body in those respects influenced by the diet, or the levels of nutrients in the body and the ability of those levels to maintain normal metabolic integrity.

prostate /ˈprɑːsteɪt/
前列腺（的）
Prostate is a compound tubuloalveolar exocrine gland（管状外分泌腺）of the male reproductive system （生殖系统）in most mammals.

colorectal /ˌkoʊləˈrektəl/
结肠直肠的
Colon is the last part of the digestive system in vertebrates. Water is absorbed here and the remaining waste material is stored as feces before being removed by defecation.

ovarian /oʊˈveəriən/
卵巢的；子房的
Ovary is an ovum（卵）-producing reproductive organ, often found in pairs as part of the vertebrate female reproductive system.

Material Transfer Agreement（MTA）
材料转移协议
MTA is a contract that governs the transfer of tangible research materials between two organizations, when the recipient intends to use it for his or her own research purposes.

integrity /ɪnˈtegrəti/
完整性
Sample integrity refers to maintaining and assuring the high quality（the maintenance of the original status）and data-rich information of the collected sample.

accreditation /əˌkredɪˈteɪʃn/
评审；委派
Accreditation is the process in which certification of competency, authority, or credibility is presented.

Notes to Difficult Sentences

ISBER is the largest international forum that addresses the technical, legal, ethical, and managerial issues relevant to repositories of biological and environmental specimens.

　　ISBER 是最大的提供生物和环境样本库建设相关的技术、法律、伦理、管理解决办法的国际平台。

　　拓展：国际生物和环境样本库协会（ISBER，http://www.isber.org/）是美国研究病理学会下辖的一个分支机构。它试图通过建立规范和标准，利用培训等方式影响发展中国家的样本库建设，使其达到一定的质量和标准。目前，ISBER 下辖 6 个不同类型的生物样本库，分别是动物样本库、环境样本库、人体样本库、微生物样本库、博物馆样本库、植物/种子样本库。

Lesson 2
Building Better Biobank

The number of tissue samples in US banks alone was estimated at more than 300 million at the turn of the century and is increasing by 20 million a year. But many scientists still say they cannot obtain enough samples. A 2011 survey of more than 700 cancer researchers found that 47% had trouble finding samples of sufficient quality. Because of this, 81% have reported limiting the scope of their work, and 60% said they question the findings of their studies.

Whereas researchers would once have inspected biological specimens under a **microscope** or measured only a handful of **chemical constituents**, or **analytes**, now they want to profile hundreds of molecules, including DNA, RNA, proteins and **metabolites**. The popularity of genome-wide association studies, in which researchers scan the genome to look for genetic markers, has trained scientists to go on statistical hunts that require both more **quantitative** measurements and greater numbers of samples. "The manner in which biomedical researchers use biospecimens has changed substantially over the past 20 years," says Stephen Hewitt, a clinical investigator at the National Cancer Institute in Bethesda, Maryland, and an expert on sample quality. "Our knowledge of the factors that impact a biospecimen has not kept up, nor has the education of the users about how fragile a biospecimen is."

1. In the cold

Except for DNA, few biomolecules are preserved well at -20 ℃. Most samples can be stored at -80 ℃, but certain specimens, such as live cells, need to be kept at temperatures close to -200 ℃, at which point enzymes are thought not to be able to function at all. <u>Worse than having nothing to analyse are analytes that change in unpredictable ways.</u> One study showed that the **concentration** of two cancer biomarkers seemed to increase by around 15% from the time that the serum samples were collected and frozen to when they were thawed and measured again about 10 years later. In another experiment, some protein biomarkers seemed to be stable for decades even with multiple freeze-thaw cycles, while another one (**vascular endothelial growth factor**) was so unstable that the authors recommended that it should never be measured in samples that have been frozen. Not all biobanks document whether a sample has been thawed for analysis and then restocked, nor do they monitor freezer temperatures, says Daniel Simeon-

Dubach, a biobanking consultant based in Switzerland. Even short-term fluctuations in temperature can allow sample-damaging **ice crystals** to form.

2. On the shelf

Many of the larger biobanks are buying sophisticated freezers to maintain a **constant temperature**. Rather than opening freezer doors, researchers place sample tubes in a hatch, and a mechanical arm then moves them to interior shelves. The −80 ℃ freezer also records how many times each sample is removed from frozen storage and for how long.

To cut storage costs, most researchers study morphology by relying on a preservation technique that harks back more than a century. Tissue taken from a patient is soaked in the preservative **formalin**, and pieces of the 'fixed' tissue are then embedded in blocks of paraffin. The blocks allow a thin slice of tissue to be taken and **stained** for microscope slides, but biomolecules are not preserved as effectively. **Hypoxia** in the dying cells **degrades** RNA and alters proteins; formalin crosslinks protein and DNA into complexes, and causes nicks in RNA and DNA. When researchers go to recover biomolecules, removing the paraffin can cause more damage.

Although DNA and RNA have been extracted from paraffin-embedded samples, the quality varies and analysis is difficult. Scientists are working on techniques to slow hydrolysis and **oxidation** by removing water and reactive **oxygen**-containing molecules. If this technique works, it would allow researchers to study biomolecules but still maintain the morphology standards and staining protocols developed over decades of formalin fixation. Other approaches focus on removing formalin from the process to preserve biomolecules and to allow tissue specimens to be embedded in paraffin. This preservative method is starting to be used in place of deep freezing.

3. Quality collection

Some of the most intractable difficulties occur before preservation begins, says Carolyn Compton, the first director of the OBBR and chief executive of the Critical Path Institute. When cut off from a blood supply and exposed to abrupt changes in temperature, the cells' behavior becomes hard to predict. Gene expression and protein **phosphorylation** fluctuate wildly and cellular self-destruct pathways may be activated. Even if tissue is preserved well, it may not tell the full biological story.

Blood, urine and saliva samples from non-hospitalized volunteers can be collected during scheduled appointments. But solid-tissue samples are usually collected in hospitals as part of more urgent procedures. Medication, the **anaesthesia** regime and how blood is shunted from the tissue being removed all affect the sample. So does the length of time the sample stays at room temperature before it is frozen, the time and type of fixative, the rate at which it is frozen and the size and shape of the aliquots.

Medical staff will always be focused on the patient on the operating table, but a greater awareness of the impact that samples can have on medical research and patients' diagnoses is having an effect. Speed is also important for tissues collected post-mortem. Staff collecting tissues are expected to be ready around the clock so that they can begin work as soon as the team collecting donated organs has finished.

4. Assessing quality

Researchers need better biomarkers of sample quality both to prevent expensive experiments on inappropriate material and to reduce artefacts. Researchers need specific recommendations. They want markers that can say, "This is a bad sample. This is a good sample." Such a process is important not only for choosing samples to include in a particular study, but also for understanding how best to preserve them.

One difficulty with these efforts is that published guidelines are generally based on researchers' impressions and experience, not dedicated experiments that test for the best ways to preserve samples, says Vaught, whose office is now awarding grants for assessing and developing storage technology, and is maintaining a hand-curated database of relevant peer-reviewed literature. Biobank professionals often develop their own practices after a few pilot studies but do not publish them, he says. "There are no international standards based on solid research."

Indeed, resources for research and facilities for preserving biospecimen quality are in short supply. People want to allocate funds for the research project and analysis, not the infrastructure that supports it. Obtaining funds for ongoing expenses is also a challenge: academics are used to getting samples from their colleagues, rather than paying a repository for high-quality samples.

5. Preserving patient data

Ongoing health information about a donor is increasingly desired by researchers, along with information on the preservation of any particular class of biomolecule. This has already prompted considerable reanalysis of appropriate informed consent and data policies, as well as innovations in how data can be stored and mined.

The more information that is available about a specimen, the more valuable it becomes to other researchers (Fig. 7.1). Scientists studying the effects of a particular gene on a cancer pathway could save years of effort and thousands of dollars if they have ready access to a collection of tumour samples with mutations of interest. David Cox, a senior vice-president at drug-company Pfizer and a member of the BBMRI's scientific advisory board, believes that the way to get the most out of biological specimens is not prospectively banking samples but finding ways to reuse samples that researchers have already collected for their own questions.

Figure 7.1 **Bar-coded samples can be scanned and tracked from collection to analysis**

One problem is who pays for what, says Cox. "People are trying to make money off of these individual pieces instead of trying to get them all together." Government funding is tight; pharmaceutical companies are willing to fund studies that can lead to new products, and individuals are generally willing to donate specimens and data for the public good, but not for corporate profit. One idea is that research would be conducted for pharmaceutical companies within the biobanking infrastructure, but that companies would not retain the exclusive rights to the data; however, it is too early to say whether this would be viable. There needs to be a way to link infrastructure and information "in a precompetitive fashion, so we can understand the biology better, and we can make better medicines," says Cox. Perhaps the hardest problem of all will be establishing and maintaining investment.

Glossary

microscope /ˈmaɪkrəskoʊp/
显微镜
Microscope is an instrument used to see objects that are too small for the naked eye.

chemical constituent /ˈkemɪkl kənˈstɪtʃuənt/
化学组成

analyte /ˈænəˌlɪt/

分析物；被测物质

An analyte (or component) is a substance or chemical constituent that is of interest in an analytical procedure.

metabolite /meˈtæbəˌlaɪt/

代谢物

Metabolites are the intermediates and products (usually restricted to small molecules) of metabolism (the set of life-sustaining chemical transformations within the cells of living organisms).

quantitative /ˈkwɑːntəteɪtɪv/

量化的；定量的

concentration /ˌkɒnsenˈtreɪʃən/

浓度；浓缩

vascular /ˈvæskjələr/

血管的

The blood vessels are the part of the circulatory system that transports blood throughout the human body.

endothelial /ˌendəˈθiːliəl/

内皮的

The endothelium (内皮) is the thin layer of simple squamous cells (单层鳞状细胞) that lines the interior surface (内表面) of blood vessels and lymphatic vessels (淋巴管), forming an interface between circulating blood or lymph in the lumen and the rest of the vessel wall.

ice crystal /aɪs ˈkrɪstl/

冰晶

Ice crystals are solid ice exhibiting geometric atomic ordering. Ice crystals formed in cells because of low temperature will cause severe physical destruction to cells.

constant temperature /ˈkɑːnstənt ˈtemprətʃər/

恒温

formalin /ˈfɔːməlɪn/

福尔马林（甲醛溶液）

Formalin is widely used in sample processing and preservation as flexing agent.

stain /steɪn/

染色（剂）

Stain is chemical reagents used to highlight feature of tissue or cells, or the process of using these reagents.

hypoxia /haɪˈpɑːksiə/

低氧

Hypoxia a pathological condition in which the body or a region of the body is deprived of an adequate oxygen supply.

degrade /dɪˈɡreɪd/

降解

Degradation refers to the process of being broken down of living organisms or their tissues or cells.

oxidation /ˌɒksɪˈdeɪʃn/

氧化

Oxidation is the loss of electrons or an increase in oxidation state by a molecule, atom, or ion.

oxygen /ˈɑːksɪdʒən/

氧气

phosphorylation /fɒsfɒrɪˈleɪʃən/

磷酸化

Phosphorylation is the addition of a phosphate (PO_4^{3-}) group to a protein or other organic molecule. Phosphorylation turns many protein enzymes on and off, thereby altering their function and activity.

anaesthesia /ˌænəsˈθiːziə/

麻醉

Anaesthesia (anesthesia) is a temporary state consisting of unconsciousness, loss of memory, lack of pain, and muscle relaxation.

Notes to Difficult Sentences

Worse than having nothing to analyse are analytes that change in unpredictable ways.

与没有样本可供分析相比,更糟糕的是待分析的样本以不可预知的方式发生了改变。

拓展: 没有样本我们可以重新收集,但如果保存的样本发生了改变而研究者们并不知道的话,会导致研究结果不准确、不可信。这也是为什么现如今研究者们极其强调生物样本库的样本质量问题,样本质量是样本库的"灵魂",而要保证和维持样本的高质量就需要遵循一系列的 SOPs 和 best practices。

Lesson 3
Biobank Promises to Pinpoint the Cause of Disease

Figure 7.2 The logo of UK Biobank

UK Biobank (Fig. 7.2) is a major national health resource, and a registered charity in its own right, with the aim of improving the prevention, diagnosis and treatment of a wide range of serious and life-threatening illnesses—including cancer, heart diseases, **stroke**, diabetes, **arthritis**, **osteoporosis**, eye disorders, **depression** and forms of **dementia**. UK Biobank recruited 500 000 people aged between 40~69 years in 2006－2010 from across the country to take part in this project. <u>They have undergone measures, provided blood, **urine** and **saliva** samples for future analysis, detailed information about themselves and agreed to have their health followed.</u> Over many years this will build into a powerful resource to help scientists discover why some people develop particular diseases and others do not.

Figure 7.3 Samples ready for analysis
(By Christopher Furlong)

The UK Biobank is open for business. Medical, lifestyle and genetic information from 500 000 middle-aged British people is now available to medical researchers around the world to help in the hunt for the causes of and treatments for disease (Fig. 7.3).

"It's the biggest, most detailed collection of data that's ever been put in place," says Rory Collins, UK Biobank's founder. Its impact on dissecting the causes of disease, he says, will be as profound as the invention of the telescope was to astronomy, or the microscope to microbiology.

"If you're born, you will get sick and die, and there's no escape from that," says Barbara Collins, a 57-year-old Londoner who is a UK Biobank volunteer. "But if there's anything I can do to make a difference in someone else's life, I'm more than happy to do that. I hope what I'm doing will speed up research to find treatments for cancer, diabetes, heart disease and dozens of other illnesses."

Collins is one of the half-million Britons aged between 40 and 69 who have donated their DNA, medical history and details of their lifestyle to the UK Biobank. The volunteers will be followed for the next 30 years, and by comparing those who remain healthy with those who develop illnesses, researchers hope to be able to isolate the causes of disease.

In particular, UK Biobank will help measure the extent to which diseases have genetic or environmental causes. "For years, people have asked about nature versus nurture but now, with the data we have, we can tease out the contributions of what you're born with versus the environment you grow up in," says Wendy Ewart of the UK Medical Research Council, one of several backers of the project.

1. Public interest

First approved in 2006, UK Biobank officially launched on 30 March. Researchers applying for access to the Biobank must show that their work is in the interests of public health, and that its results will be published in peer-reviewed journals. Proposals will be assessed by UK Biobank's board.

The National Institutes of Health in Washington DC are apparently keen to use the UK Biobank—a resource that they considered too expensive and unwieldy to set up in the US, despite initial plans to do so.

"Francis Collins, the director of the NIH, would love to do what we've done, but came to the conclusion it would be too expensive, costing about $2 billion," says Rory Collins. "They can't afford it, and they don't have anything like the National Health Service which tracks everyone's medical records and details."

China has a similar database, called the China Kadoorie Biobank, which also contains the health details of 500 000 volunteers, but Rory Collins says that the UK version has more information on each volunteer. The two are complementary, and could be the focus for joint studies, he says.

The Chinese project hints at the kind of results the UK Biobank might turn up. It has found, for example, that thinner men are more at risk of developing chronic obstructive **pulmonary** disease in China, and that major risk factors for heart attacks include diabetes and **psychosocial stress.**

2. Future growth

There are more than 1000 categories of information for each of the UK participants, ranging from whether they use cellphones and how often they see friends and relatives to the usual spectrum of physiological measurements, including hand grip strength, bone density, blood pressure, lung function, body fat profile, and even scores on standard tests of cognitive ability.

Plans are afoot to add more, including fMRI scans of a fifth of the participants. Many will also be given accelerometers to wear on their wrists for a week, allowing physical activity to be measured accurately. Other ideas include ultrasound scans, and X-rays of bones and joints.

Around 20 000 volunteers will be completely retested every two to three years, and updates on the health of all UK Biobank participants will be automatically fed in from family doctors, hospital records and death registries.

Rory Collins says that all data given to researchers will be coded, so that no individuals can be identified. There will be no feedback to participants about changes in their health status, a condition to which all volunteers consented to at the outset.

Some of the participants already have illnesses, including 26 000 with diabetes, 50 000 with joint disorders and 11 000 who have had at least one heart attack. By 2022, some 40 000 are expected to have diabetes, and 28 000 to have had heart attacks. But Barbara Collins is undaunted by the prospect of ill health to come: "Even if I can't benefit from the results personally, I know my children, my children's children and perfect strangers will."

Glossary

stroke /stroʊk/
中风
Stroke, also known as cerebrovascular (脑血管) accident (CVA), cerebrovascular insult (CVI), or brain attack, is when poor blood flow to the brain results in cell death.

arthritis /ɑːrˈθraɪtɪs/
关节炎
Arthritis is a form of joint disorder that involves inflammation of one or more joints.

osteoporosis /ˌɑːstioʊpəˈroʊsɪs/
骨质疏松症
Osteoporosis is a disease where decreased bone strength increases the risk of a broken bone. It is the most common reason for a broken bone among people who are old.

depression /dɪˈpreʃn/

沮丧；抑郁症

Depression is a state of low mood and aversion to activity that can affect a person's thoughts, behavior, feelings and sense of well-being. Depressed mood is a feature of some psychiatric syndromes such as major depressive disorder, but it may also be a normal reaction to life events such as bereavement, a symptom of some bodily ailments or a side effect of some drugs and medical treatments.

dementia /dɪˈmenʃə/

痴呆

Dementia is a broad category of brain diseases that cause a long term and often gradual decrease in the ability to think and remember such that a person's daily functioning is affected.

urine /ˈjʊərən/

尿液

Urine is a liquid by-product of the body secreted by the kidneys through a process called urination（排尿）and excreted through the urethra（尿道）.

saliva /səˈlaɪvə/

唾液

Saliva is a watery substance located in the mouths of animals, secreted by the salivary glands.

pulmonary /ˈpʌlməneri/

肺部的；肺的

Chronic obstructive pulmonary disease（COPD，慢性阻塞性肺病）, also known as chronic obstructive lung disease（COLD）, and chronic obstructive airway disease（COAD）, among others, is a type of obstructive lung disease characterized by chronically poor airflow. It typically worsens over time. The main symptoms include shortness of breath, cough, and sputum production.

psychosocial stress /ˌsaɪkoʊˈsoʊʃəl stres/

心理社会应激

Psychosocial stress is the result of a cognitive appraisal of what is at stake and what can be done about it. More simply put, psychosocial stress results when we look at a perceived threat in our lives (real or even imagined), and discern that it may require resources we don't have. Examples of psychosocial stress include things like a threat to our social status, social esteem, respect, and/or acceptance within a group; threat to our self-worth.

Notes to Difficult Sentences

They have undergone measures, provided blood, urine and saliva samples for future analysis, detailed information about themselves and agreed to have their health followed.

他们接受体检，然后提供血液、尿液、唾液样品以便后期研究，同时提供他们自己的详细资料并同意（biobanks）跟进自己的健康状况。

拓展：目前 biobanks 只收集血液、尿液、唾液 3 种样本，但在大资源（big resources）背景下收集更多形式、不同时间段的样本将是整体趋势。由生物制药、生物样本库、生命科学研究等领域的自愿者共同维护的样本中心（Specimen Central, www.specimencentral.com）记录了来自美国、英国、中国、日本、德国等众多国家的上百家生物样本库信息，这些样本库中储存着极其丰富的样本资源，样本类型包括 blood, whole blood, buccal swab, DNA, RNA, protein, cell lines, marrow, plasma, serum, RBC, white cells, buffy coat, fluid, urine, stem cells, solid tissue such as tumor, and biopsy materials spanning all types of common and rare pathologies and indications including Alzheimer's, basal cell carcinoma, bladder cancer, bone cancer, brain cancer, breast cancer, cerebrospinal fluid, amniotic fluid, colorectal cancer, colon cancer, hodgkins and non-hodgkins lymphoma, kidney/renal cancer, leukemia, multiple sclerosis, liver cancer, lung cancer, melanoma, myeloma neuroblastoma, neurodegenerative diseases, ovarian cancer, pancreatic cancer, prostate cancer, synovial fuild, urinary cancer 等，对生物医学研究有重要价值。

Reading Material 1

Chinese Biobanks: Present and Future

In the early 1990s, researchers collected the biological specimens to meet their experimental requirements, and did not have the sense of bioresource sharing and information exchange. However, with the development of life science, researchers have realized that bioresource becomes a critical factor to specimen preservation, scientific research and clinic application etc. In China, the Immortalize Cell Bank of Different Chinese Ethnic Groups was set up in 1990s, while since 2000, the number of Chinese biobanks has increased rapidly, such as China Kadoorie Biobank, Guangzhou cohort biobank, Taizhou cohort biobank, Sun Yat-sen University Cancer Center affiliated tumour bank.

Chinese biobanks are scattered around China, and their organizational structure is not the same. In order to find their information, we conducted multiple search strategies by searching China Knowledge Resource Integrated Database (CNKI) and websites, as well as on-site investigating on hospital-affiliated biobanks. In total, 22 Chinese biobanks were surveyed. Human-oriented biobanks are classified into disease-oriented biobanks or population-based biobanks, depending on purpose or design; disease-oriented biobanks are usually affiliated with hospitals, such as tumour banks, which collect tumour tissue as well as blood and other specimens from a variety of diseases together with normal controls; population-based biobanks are generally situated outside hospitals.

1. Disease-oriented biobanks

In recent years, some disease-oriented biobanks have been established for disease research, which provided various valuable specimens for research needs. As early as 1996, the clinical tumour bank of the Clinical Oncology Institute in Beijing Cancer Hospital was established to collect, store and utilize human tumour tissues and blood specimens, and about 500 000 specimens were collected currently. One of the largest tumour banks in China was established based on the Sun Yat-sen University Cancer Center and the State Key Laboratory of Oncology in South China in 2001. Specimens were collected from tumour patients and healthy people, including blood, serum, plasma, blood cells, bone marrow cells, proteins, DNA, RNA and paraffin sections. The biobank stored 30 000 blood specimens from tumour patients, 6400 normal blood specimens and 6000 normal control tissues until 2008 and now the number of specimens is 1 million. Tianjin Medical University Cancer Institute & Hospital joint American

Cancer Research Foundation funded a tumour tissue bank in 2004 which had already collected 36 000 tissue specimens and 35 000 blood specimens with clinical data. The tumour bank of Zhejiang Cancer Hospital was established in 2007 and has the capacity to store nearly 140 000 specimens from 4700 patients.

2. Population-based biobanks

Population-based biobanks mainly collect specimens from normal volunteers. For example, the China Marrow Donor Program (CMDP) owns 31 provincial sub-banks with 1.65 million specimens by the end of 2012. China Kadoorie Biobank had started to be built since 2003, aiming to collect blood specimens and various lifestyle and medical data from more than 510 000 middle-aged adults from ten geographic areas of China, to investigate the genetic and environmental causes of common chronic diseases in the Chinese population. The Key Laboratory of Xinjiang Endemic and Ethnic Disease has set up a biobank for Xinjiang ethnic diseases research. The biobank stored 20 000 blood specimens from nationalities of Uygur, Kazak and Han from 2004 to 2009. In 2007, Taizhou (Fudan University) Institute of Health Sciences established a biobank based on a population health-tracking research project, which had collected 100 000 DNA samples. The Institutional Specimen Bank was set up by the Fifth People's Hospital of Shanghai in 2010, and collects over 100 000 blood and urine specimens for chronic diseases research.

Cell is the basic unit of the structure and function in organisms and plays an important role in scientific research. There are several cell banks which have been established in China. For example, the Immortalize Cell Bank of Different Chinese Ethnic Groups, the largest immortalized cell lines bank in China, has been established in 1994. The immortalized cell bank stored 3982 immortalized cell lines and 7210 DNA from 70 ethnic groups until 2008. The first (also the largest) Chinese human sperm bank was created in Hunan province. In total, 17 human sperm banks had been set up in 17 provinces respectively by January 2013.

China National Genebank (CNGB) was established in 2011 and located in Shenzhen (Fig. 7.4). CNGB is committed to constructing an integrated national institute which is composed of a standardized Biological Bank, Bioinformation Bank and the resource sharing Consortium. The biobank in CNGB collects, preserves and comprehensively utilizes various kinds of human-related specimens including blood, urine, tissues, cells etc. The number of specimens has already reached 1.8 million. Standard specifications are strictly implemented in its practical operation, and first-class facilities and professional staff are employed to support massive storage, processing and application of specimens.

Figure 7.4 Conceptual layout of China National Genebank

3. Preservation tendency

3.1 Specimen types

With large population and great variety of clinical illnesses, Chinese biobanks have special advantages to collect all kinds of disease-related specimens. On the other hand, researchers realize the importance of the human specimens, and different organizations collect and preserve more and more types of specimens from blood, urine and tumour tissues to hairs, faeces, saliva, umbilical cord, ascites, stem cells and somatic cell. Integrating all kinds of specimens and comprehensively studying the diseases like cardiovascular disease, diabetes and cancer, can make it possible to predict, prevent, intervene and control the diseases, eventually reduce risks and offer effective solutions for the diseases.

3.2 Micro-specimens

Long fragment read (LFR) allows genome sequencing and haplotyping at a clinically relevant cost, quality and scale and provides new insights into small amount of specimens preservation. Trace amount of DNA extracted from small amount of specimens could meet the requirement of whole-genome sequencing; the method offers facilities for the specimen collection and storage with the goal of sequencing. It is possible to detect and analyse the proteins and metabolites using trace amount of specimens with technological advancements. The amount of specimen collection moves towards micro-quantity, which could save an enormous amount of human labor, material resources and financial resources. How to control the quantity and quality to fulfill the application demands and decrease the consumption of the original specimens will be a big challenge for micro-specimens collection and preservation.

3.3 Novel storage technologies

For now, most specimens use cold chains or are deep-frozen in the transportation and preservation process, but the emergence of novel storage reagents and technologies allows preservation of specimens at room temperature. For example, as an aqueous, non-toxic tissue storage reagent, RNAlater can rapidly permeate tissue to stabilize and protect cellular RNA *in situ* in unfrozen specimens, and eliminate the need to immediately process tissue specimens or to freeze specimens in liquid nitrogen for later processing; this is convenient for simplified specimen handling and shipping. There are well-documented high-quality nucleic acids preservation solutions such as GenTegra (IntegenX), RNAstable (Biomatrica) and RNAshell (Imagene); all of these commercial matrices could preserve DNA/RNA at room temperature for long-term and reduce energy costs. All of these new types of preservation reagents and technologies, which are technologically feasible and economically reasonable both in quality and cost, provide new directions for specimen preservation at ambient temperature.

3.4 Trans-OMICS

Next-generation sequencing technologies and mass spectrometry etc. has brought revolutionary impacts on life science research. Massive omics data would be generated relying on high-throughput sequencing platforms and mass spectrometers. Systematic study can be carried out including genomics, transcriptomics, proteomics and metabolomics and discover their internal relation by analysing these big data. At the same time, it is possible to make the most of the all kinds of specimens. To reveal the occurrence and development of diseases and to clarify the inherited susceptibility of certain diseases and complexity of genome could help to improve the diagnosis and treatment. Three elements, involving high-quality and sufficient amount of specimens and related comprehensive information, as well as research-generated big data supported by high-performance storage and computing platform, will be the vital foundation for and stimulate the development of future translational medical research and personalized medicine. Integration and application of resources and big data by extensive collaborations will accelerate transition from science to technology, and to industry.

Reading Material 2

A Poop Bank in Massachusetts Will Pay You $40 Every Day

Are you under 50 years old, willing to make daily trips to Medford, and have regular bowel movements? You, my friend, could be earning $40 a day—just for pooping.

All you have to do is visit OpenBiome, launched in 2012 as the only independent nonprofit stool bank in the country. The brainchild of MIT postdoctoral associate Mark Smith, OpenBiome collects, tests, and provides fecal samples to 122 hospitals in 33 states for one of the most interesting medical treatment innovations today: fecal microbiota transplantation.

Figure 7.5　Mark Smith packages the samples for shipment on dry ice with a colleague Laura Burns

(By Carolyn Edelstein)

"Think of us as a blood bank, but for poop," said Smith, who developed OpenBiome when he saw the gap in the medical structure to provide many patients with the life-saving fecal samples. "You shouldn't have to fly across the country to get poop."

Smith works with a team of full-time and part-time researchers, graduate students, gastroenterologists, and business minds to ensure that fecal samples are in every city and town and within a two-hour radius for every person who needs them (Fig. 7.5). Smith said that they've hit the four-hour radius so far.

1. Wait, who wants someone else's poop?

To keep your digestive and immune systems functioning properly, your body needs to maintain a natural balance of bacteria in your gut. But antibiotics taken to treat infections kill both "good" and "bad" bacteria indiscriminately. They kill it all, upsetting the balance and making the gastrointestinal tract susceptible to C. difficile, a "bad" bacteria. The resulting infection, according to the Centers for Disease Control and Prevention, affects more than 500 000 Americans per year, causing fever, nausea, abdominal pain, and serious diarrhea—and kills 14 000 Americans per year, especially in hospitals and long-term care facilities. There are antibiotics that treat difficile, but as many as 20 percent of the infections return.

Our poop, it turns out, is a plentiful source of this good bacteria, and how do you get one person's good-bacteria-filled poop into an ailing person? A fecal transplant.

"From the cost perspective, it's a really efficient treatment for patients who aren't responding to antibiotics," said Smith. Including the donor screening costs, research has shown that fecal transplants save on average $17 000 per patient compared to treatment with antibiotics.

While large hospitals and health systems have their own stool banks, many independent physicians and hospitals often do not. This is where OpenBiome comes in, selling them poop at $250 per sample. That's one price point for a 250 mL sample of fecal microbiota prepared for a lower transplant delivery (yep, that low) or a 30 mL sample for an upper transplant delivery (nose) (Fig. 7.6).

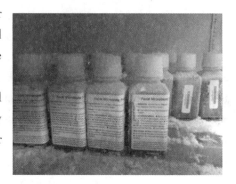

Figure 7.6 Here's what a sample of fecal microbiota looks like

(By Carolyn Edelstein)

While health insurance companies cover some of the cost, Smith said the price tag is key to paying for the processing and distribution of the samples, finding and screening the donors, while still keeping it affordable for patients paying out of pocket.

"The real challenge is that right now it's still categorized as an explorational drug by the FDA. Until that changes it's really not going to find universal adoption because there's still challenges with how insurance companies reimburse it," said Smith.

Unfortunately, the fecal transplantation process tends to be very uncomfortable and invasive. Physicians traditionally transplant the stool samples through a colonoscopy, enema, or a nasogastric tube that runs from the nose into the digestive tract.

Soon, however, poop may come in the form of a pill. The latest research by doctors at Massachusetts General Hospital, and published in JAMA Internal Medicine in October 2014 has shown frozen capsules of fecal material to be 90 percent effective in treating the C. diff infections. OpenBiome has collaborated with many hospitals across the country in developing and manufacturing these capsule-size samples for treatment.

2. Where do I sign up to donate?

To become a paid donor to OpenBiome, you have to undergo thorough screenings, from a 120-question health history with a physician to a travel history analysis and, of course, recent use of antibiotics. Once a donor's sample dump is reviewed by the lab for any infectious agents and the health of the bacteria, the donor's blood is tested for standard blood borne diseases as well as hepatitis A, B, C, syphilis, and HIV/AIDS. All of these screening costs (which total more than $1000 per donor) are covered by OpenBiome, so the markup on the poop donations seems pretty reasonable (Fig. 7.7).

Figure 7.7　Vladimir Pootin icon, a nickname for one of OpenBiome's anonymous donors

(By Carolyn Edelstein)

OpenBiome targets younger adults, since they tend to be a lot healthier, with the average donor's age ranging from late 20s to early 30s. The company has also focused its recruitment efforts on nearby Tufts University's student population.

Once a donor's sample passes the medical exam, he or she is enrolled and scheduled to visit the Medford facility every day. Each visit takes 30 minutes, during which the donor produces a sample into a hat-shaped bowl that rests over an ordinary toilet. Then the donor walks out with $40.

The cold, hard cash is not, however, the only reward. To further encourage new donors to sign up, and current donors to donate more often, OpenBiome is turning pooping into a game, awarding Super Pooper nicknames—such as Vladimir Pootin, King of Poop, and Winnie the Poo—to those donors with the most samples. (These heroes remain anonymous.) The more doo you donate, the higher your Super Pooper character will climb in the rankings. So eat your fiber!

"These donors may seem very mild-mannered and think going to the bathroom is a humble thing," said Smith, "but each sample they bring in can treat four or five patients."

Chapter 8　Big Resources in Biobanks

Organizations now collect and preserve more and more types of specimens from blood, urine and tumor tissues to hairs, faces, saliva, umbilical cord, ascites, stem cells and somatic cells. Conserved sample types include not only tissues exclusively but also DNA, RNA, proteins, metabolin and corresponding sequences or relative information. Integrating all kinds of specimens and comprehensively studying the diseases like cardiovascular disease, diabetes and cancer, can make it possible to predict, prevent, intervene and control the diseases, eventually reduce risks and offer effective solutions for the diseases.

Chapter 8　Big Resources in Biobanks

Lesson 1
Specimen Types for DNA Net Earth

1. About DNA Net Earth

Human activity has dramatically accelerated the **extinction of species**. Man-made **habitat alteration** has been the leading cause, in combination with direct exploitation. Now climate change threatens to increase extinction rates even more. Preservation in the wild—*in situ*—is the top priority, but it is clear that many more species will disappear and we will lose access to the genetic information they contain unless their DNA is also kept *ex situ*—in captivity, cultivation, or preserved storage.

A global network of facilities should be organized to preserve DNA for every known species and for new species as they are described. This "DNA Net Earth" will be a safety net for biodiversity that can provide genetic libraries for research and commerce, be used to recover species that are endangered, and offer the potential to selectively restore species that have gone extinct.

2. What should be kept?

An initial question is whether any biological material should be preserved, or whether the DNA of specimens should be initially sequenced and only the data stored. It is unproven, however, whether raw DNA can be used to produce a eukaryotic organism, or how much it would cost (estimates predict in the millions). Also, DNA is not the only information in organisms and cells, which have epigenetic factors and countless chemicals and structures whose link to DNA is equivocal or difficult to discern. In addition, although the cost of DNA sequencing has dropped dramatically, the current cost of sequencing an individual organism's genome is still much higher than freezing it, and frozen DNA can be sequenced in the future, almost certainly at a lower cost. Sequencing DNA is an important objective, but not as an alternative to its preservation.

3. Live organisms and frozen viable seeds and cells

Living organisms are the gold standard for DNA Net Earth. Most botanic gardens, zoos and aquariums are attuned to the value of species diversity in holdings of living organisms. Mostly these institutions are limited in what they can hold by space and money. Live animals, especially, are expensive to keep.

Frozen **viable seeds** and cells of plants and animals are the silver standard for DNA Net Earth and provide the greatest opportunity for progress. Seeds are often abundant, typically compact, comparatively easy to freeze and store, and self-packaged for germination. Plant tissue cuttings for many species can be used fresh or after being frozen to **propagate** new whole plants. Viable animal sperm and eggs can also be kept frozen and combined later to produce **fertilized eggs.**

Cloning animals from such viable cells, however, is a far less developed and practiced technology than for plants, although with promising beginnings. Cloning by nuclear insertion or induction of differentiated cells has to date been difficult and limited, and no one can predict with certainty how the technology will develop in the future. That said, if the future is measured by a century and more, it seems likely that there will be more widely available and less expensive technologies.

Additionally, frozen viable collections should, whenever possible, represent multiple individuals of a species. In essence, they are frozen populations just as living populations exist in the wild, and captive and cultivated populations live in zoos and botanical gardens. On average, the Frozen Zoo® currently maintains 20 samples for every species that it holds. This is important because frozen populations—like the living—provide genetic diversity for adaptive traits, and larger populations pose less risk that **deleterious** genes will be expressed in **offspring**. Small population size and **inbreeding** is a bane for endangered species, which zoos and frozen cell cultures can counter by augmenting genetic diversity.

Live organisms and frozen viable seeds and cells should be treated as preferred but nonexclusive items in a portfolio of preservation options, and the relatively costly maintenance of live animals and viable animal cell cultures should be focused on priorities such as endangered species conservation and representation of higher taxonomic groups such as families or genera. Nevertheless, collection and frozen storage of viable animal cells for any species not adequately represented should be considered in all-species "grassroots" initiatives, and a current lack of funds or technology for establishing cultures does not mean viable cells should not be preserved for potential culturing in the future. In the case of small animals, such as insects, this can be whole animals in a vial.

4. Dead cells with sequenceable DNA

The value of viable cell cultures notwithstanding, many frozen and room-temperature collections include specimens of non-viable cells. The Smithsonian Institution's new **cryogenic** biorepository is primarily expanding its limited current collection with frozen tissue kept by its curators and collections managers in their own labs. Some of these tissues will have viable cells but most will not.

Freezing dead cells is not a bad idea. It is more convenient and cheaper for collectors in remote places to kill animals like fish, frogs or ants and bring specimens back at room temperature than it is to freeze them on the spot and keep them frozen all the way home. Also, collection is often done without preservation of viable cells in mind or by local collectors without reagents or equipment for freezing. The DNA of dead cells may remain largely intact depending on time and conditions before freezing. Indeed, under favorable ambient conditions, the cells of a just departed animal may remain alive for days or even a few weeks. Freezing dead whole organisms or cells with still intact DNA is the bronze standard for preservation, not the best but still a winner. With time, money and new sequencing technology that can evaluate partially degraded DNA, it has even been possible to reconstruct the genomes of extinct species from animals found in circumstances favorable to preservation where they died long ago. This has been done for the mammoth and Neanderthal. If the DNA of these can be sequenced, so might the DNA from at least some species in the vast dried and otherwise preserved collections of natural history museums, side-stepping the need for recollection of fresh specimens insofar as DNA sequence information is the objective. Furthermore, cloning is only one objective. Indeed, it is unlikely that more than a small fraction of known species will be cloned in the future even though the potential for cloning any species as needs are identified is a central purpose of DNA Net Earth. Once DNA is sequenced its genes can be identified and studied and the products of gene expression examined for values. One gene may turn out to be just what a related endangered species needs to survive or research may determine that another gene upon insertion will alleviate a disease in man.

However, time and money cut both ways in deciding whether to preserve viable or dead animal cells. Culturing and cloning from viable cells is now straight-forward for some species and the cost is measured in thousands of dollars, rather than the millions along with technical uncertainties and time that would be required to clone a species such as the Asian **gaur** using DNA from dead tissue. Cloning from dead cells would require sequencing their DNA, **synthesizing** matching DNA and then situating the new DNA in a **nucleus** within an egg or other **undifferentiated** cell in such a way that cellular mechanisms for gene expression work, and the cell divides and develops. This has been done for the bacterium *Mycoplasma mycoides*, but it lacks a nucleus and has a tiny genome. Furthermore, an individual of each sex would be required for "natural" reproduction to follow in species that have sex, and inbreeding in the progeny of such a pair would challenge population fitness and growth. Genetic engineering, breeding strategy and supportive, compensating environmental regimes might fix adaptive frailties, but would be difficult.

5. Extracted sequenceable DNA

DNA can be extracted from cells, stored, and replicated without diminishing the source. The extracted DNA can be frozen, and efforts are being made to establish conditions for room temperature storage that provide long-term stability that matches freezing, with hoped for lower cost and ease of handling. Yet, DNA is not the only information about a species in the whole organism, its tissues, or its cells, albeit the most important. DNA Net Earth should encompass a full portfolio of preservation choices including living organisms, frozen viable seeds and cells, dead cells with sequenceable DNA, and extracted DNA.

Glossary

extinction of species
物种灭绝
The moment of extinction is generally considered to be the death of the last individual of the species, although the capacity to breed and recover may have been lost before this point.

habitat alteration /ˈhæbɪtæt ˌɔːltəˈreɪʃn/
生境交替
Habitat alteration is a change in land use or land cover that has an impact on local ecosystems.

viable seeds /ˈvaɪəbl siːdz/
可育的种子
Viable seeds are seeds that are available to reproduce new organisms.

propagate /ˈprɑːpəgeɪt/
繁殖
Propagation is the production of more individuals.

fertilized eggs /ˈfɜːrtɪlaɪzd egz/
受精卵
Fertilized egg (zygote) is a eukaryotic cell formed by a fertilization event between two gametes. The zygote's genome is a combination of the DNA in each gamete, and contains all of the genetic information necessary to form a new individual.

deleterious /ˌdeləˈtɪriəs/
有害的
A deleterious gene is one that virtually all reasonable individuals would judge consistently to cause very premature death or serious health problems that drastically compromise the capacity of afflicted individuals to carry out normal or near-normal life plans.

offspring /ˈɔːfsprɪŋ/
子孙后代
Offspring is the product of reproduction of a new organism produced by one or more parents.

inbreeding /ˈɪnbriːdɪŋ/

近亲繁殖

Inbreeding is the production of offspring from the mating or breeding of individuals or organisms that are closely related genetically, in contrast to outcrossing, which refers to mating unrelated individuals.

cryogenic /ˌkraɪəˈdʒenɪk/

冷冻的

"Cryogenic" means being or relating to very low temperature. Cryogenic samples are often frozen in liquid nitrogen or ultral-low temperature freezers to protect their molecular from degradation.

gaur /gaʊə/

（印度）野牛

Gaur also called Indian bison, is the largest extant bovine and is native to South Asia and Southeast Asia.

synthesize /ˈsɪnθəsaɪz/

合成

Synthesize means the creation of an organic compound in a living organism, usually aided by enzymes. This process could also happen *in vitro* artificially.

nucleus /ˈnuːkliəs/

细胞核

The (cell) nucleus is a membrane-enclosed organelle found in eukaryotic cells.

undifferentiated /ˌʌndɪfəˈrenʃieɪtɪd/

未分化的

Cellular differentiation is the process by which a cell changes from one cell type to another. Usually this is because a less specialized type becomes a more specialized type, such as during cell growth. Undifferentiated cells are cells that have not yet acquired a special structure and function.

Notes to Difficult Sentences

Preservation in the wild—*in situ*—is the top priority, but it is clear that many more species will disappear and we will lose access to the genetic information they contain unless their DNA is also kept *ex situ*—in captivity, cultivation, or preserved storage.

野外保护，也称就地保护，当为首选，但显然仍会有物种不断灭绝，除非我们使用迁地保护的方法圈养它们、养殖它们、仓库存储它们从而保存它们的DNA，不然我们就会（永远）失去它们的遗传信息。

拓展： 就地保护是指以各种类型的自然保护区方式，对有价值的自然生态系统和野生生物及其栖息地予以保护，以保持生态系统内生物的繁衍与进化，维持系统内的物质能量流动与生态过程。迁地保护，又叫做易地保护。迁地保护指为了保护生物多样性，把因生存条件不复存在，物种数量极少或难以找到配偶等原因，生存和繁衍受到严重威胁的物种迁出原地，移入动物园、植物园、水族馆和濒危动物繁殖中心，进行特殊的保护和管理，是对就地保护的补充。

Lesson 2
Specimen Collections in U. S. Biobanks: Results from a National Survey

In 2012, we conducted the first national survey of biobanks in the U. S., collecting information on their origins, specimen collections, organizational structures, and market contexts and sustainability. From a list of 636 biobanks assembled through a multi-faceted search strategy, representatives from 456 U. S. biobanks were successfully recruited for a 30-minute online survey (72% response rate). Both closed and open-ended responses were analyzed using descriptive statistics.

1. Number of specimens in storage

The number of specimens currently in storage by the responding biobanks ranged from tens to over 50 million. The distribution is shown in Table 8.1. Due to a small number of very large banks, the mean number of specimens reported was 461 396; the median was 8000. As can be seen from Table 8.1, it is difficult to discern a "typical" sized collection; rather, biobank collections in the U. S. cover a wide **spectrum** of very small to very large. It should be noted that the survey question asked how many specimens the bank currently stored, which may not be the best measure of size for some banks. Some respondents provided comments at the end of the survey indicating that the number of specimens they have in storage at any given time varies greatly.

The number of specimens in storage can reflect duplicate contributions and processed **derivatives** of contributed samples, so we also asked respondents approximately how many individual contributors were represented among their specimens in storage. Responses ranged from just a few to 10 million. To get an idea of the number of contributors typically represented in biobanks relative to the number of specimens, we calculated the ratio of specimens to contributors for each biobank. The values ranged from 1 (one specimen per contributor) to 277. The mean number was 12.6; however the distribution was skewed by a small number of banks with large numbers of specimens per contributor. Thus, the modal response was 1 and the median was 3.2 even though the mean was 12.6. Most biobanks (65%) had a ratio of 5 or fewer specimens to contributors. Thus, it appears that most biobanks contain only a small number of specimens from each contributor.

Table 8.1 Number of specimens in storage

Number of specimens	n	%
Less than 500	63	15
500 to 999	28	7
1000 to 1999	31	7
2000 to 4999	54	13
5000 to 9999	44	10
10 000 to 49 999	70	16
50 000 to 99 999	38	9
100 000 to 499 999	65	15
500 000 +	33	8
Total	426	100

Mean: 461 396; standard deviation: 3 324 096; median: 8000; interquartile range: 1200 to 76 000; skewness: 12.76; kurtosis: 181.

2. Types of specimen in storage

We asked respondents which type(s) of biological specimen(s) their bank stores. As shown in Table 8.2, serum or plasma are the specimens most commonly stored (77% of biobanks have them) with solid tissues following close behind (69%). Fifty-five percent of biobanks store whole blood, and 49% store **peripheral** blood cells or bone marrow. Though cord blood or cord derivatives were the least common among the categories we specifically asked about (11%), by coding the "other, please specify" responses, we determined that 7% of biobanks store pathological body fluids (such as the **peritoneal** fluid that accumulates in ascites) and 3% store hair or toenails—two categories we had not anticipated to be this common.

Table 8.2 Types of specimens in storage

Types of specimens	n	%
Serum or plasma	349	77
Solid tissue specimens, including paraffin-embedded, frozen, or other	315	69
Whole blood	251	55
Peripheral blood cells or bone marrow	222	49
Cell lines	162	36
Saliva or **buccal** cells	155	34
Urine or stool	138	30
Cerebral spinal fluid	85	19
Cord blood or cord blood derivatives	51	11
Other biological specimens	40	9
Pathological body fluids	30	7
Hair/toenails	14	3

3. Number of types of specimens in storage

As shown in Table 8.3, most biobanks (87%) store more than one type of specimen; 8% store eight or more types. The most frequent combination of types was whole blood, plasma, and solid tissues. Banks with only one type of specimen are most likely to be those which only store solid tissue.

Table 8.3 Number of types of specimens in storage

Number of types of specimens	n	%
1	58	13
2	59	13
3	81	18
4	62	14
5	66	15
6	50	11
7	38	8
8 +	36	8
Total	453	100

We asked respondents to identify the main biomolecule their bank **isolates** from specimens, if any. Nearly 50% said "DNA," 11% said "RNA," and 7% said "Protein." Twenty-four percent of respondents indicated "None". The 9% who chose "Other" provided open-ended responses to explain. Virtually all indicated that they were unable to choose just one biomolecule because the biobank isolates more than one in equal proportions (most frequently DNA and others). The large percentage of respondents who indicated their banks were isolating DNA (and RNA) suggests that the majority of biobanks are engaging in genetic research of one sort or another.

4. Acquisition of specimens

We wanted to determine biobanks' sources for acquiring specimens. As shown in Table 8.4, the two largest sources of specimens are direct contribution by individuals (75%) and residual specimens from hospitals and other clinical settings (57%). In fact, many (41%) include specimens from both these sources, and only 8% do not report either individuals or clinical settings as sources of specimens. The third largest source of specimens is research studies (13%). Other sources reported by a small number of biobanks include vendors, organ or body donation organizations, other repositories, or that they acquired "orphaned" collections (those which were presumably abandoned by their original owners).

Table 8.4 Acquisition of specimens

Percentage of biobanks which get specimens from...	n	%
Direct from individuals donating them	343	75
Residual specimens acquired from clinical care in hospitals, clinical laboratories, or pathology departments	261	57
Research	60	13
Residual specimens from public health departments or programs	19	4
Vendors	8	2
Organ/body donation organization	7	2
Other repositories	7	2
Other	6	1
Orphaned collections	4	1

Respondents were asked whether specimens in their collection represent any particular group of individuals. Forty-four percent of biobanks store specimens from children under the age of 18, though only 2% house exclusively **pediatric** specimens. In 36% of biobanks, the collection includes specimens collected **postmortem**, including 9% which store exclusively postmortem specimens, most of which are brain banks.

5. Conclusion

Biobanks are not a new phenomenon. However, the steep rate of increase in establishment in the last decade is a sign of rapid change, and likely also contributes to the organizational diversity we document. Undoubtedly, some of this increase may be attributed to advances in genomics and bioinformatics and increased emphasis on translational research, all of which stimulate the demand for stored specimens and associated data. In fact, our survey results indicate that the majority of biobanks are storing specimens that can be used for genetic or genomic research, which raises particular concerns regarding privacy and identifiability. Our prior work on genetic researchers' perspectives documents their reluctance to discard samples, and preliminary data analysis from our case studies and open-ended comments from our survey confirm this belief in the tremendous value of research specimens.

Findings that document highly diverse numbers, types, and sources of specimen collections raise questions regarding how biobanks should be managed and governed. For example, while the large number of banks that collect and retain residual clinical specimens is unsurprising, it is nevertheless important because of recent controversies regarding whether and how consent for such specimens should be obtained. Perhaps more surprising is our finding that such a large number of biobanks contain pediatric and postmortem specimens in their collections, along with specimens from other sources. While biobanks with exclusively pediatric or postmortem specimens (9% and 2% of our surveyed biobanks, respectively) typically adopt particular guidelines for human subjects protections, it is less clear how these specimens might impact governance in mixed-source collections.

Glossary

spectrum /ˈspektrəm/
谱
Wide spectrum（广谱）refers to a wide range of something.

derivative /dɪˈrɪvətɪv/
派生物；衍生物
Derivatives are compounds which are products from that of other chemicals.

peripheral /pəˈrifərəl/
外周的；外围的；（神经）末梢区域的
Peripheral blood cell are the cellular components of blood, consisting of red and white blood cells, and platelets, which are found within the circulating pool of blood and not sequestered within the lymphatic system, spleen, liver, or bone marrow.

peritoneal /perɪtəˈhiːəl/
腹腔的

Peritoneal fluid is a liquid that is made in the abdominal cavity to lubricate the surface of the tissue that lines the abdominal wall and pelvic cavity and covers most of the organs in the abdomen. An increased volume of peritoneal fluid is called ascites.

buccal /ˈbʌkəl/

口腔的

Buccal cells are cells in mouth.

cerebral /səˈriːbrəl/

大脑的；脑的

cerebrum = brain

spinal /ˈspaɪnl/

脊髓的

Cerebral spinal fluid (CSF) is a clear, colorless bodily fluid found in the brain and spine. It acts as a cushion or buffer for the brain's cortex, providing basic mechanical and immunological protection to the brain inside the skull, and it serves a vital function in cerebral autoregulation of cerebral blood flow.

isolate /ˈaɪsəleɪt/

分离，提取

Isolates are chemicals resulting from certain kind of purification process from a mixture. Isolates are often a single type of molecules like DNA, RNA, proteins, etc.

pediatric /ˌpiːdiˈætrɪk/

儿科的；小儿的

Pediatric medicine deals with the medical care of infants, children, and adolescents, and the age limit usually ranges from birth up to 18 years of age.

postmortem /ˌpoʊstˈmɔːtəm/

验尸；尸检；死后的

Postmortem is a highly specialized surgical procedure that consists of a thorough examination of a corpse to determine the cause and manner of death and to evaluate any disease or injury that may be present.

Notes to Difficult Sentences

Undoubtedly, some of this increase may be attributed to advances in genomics and bioinformatics and increased emphasis on translational research, all of which stimulate the demand for stored specimens and associated data.

毫无疑问，这一增长可能是由于基因组学和生物信息学的进步，以及对转化研究的加倍重视，因为这些学科的进步和研究的发展均刺激了样本和相关数据的存储需求。

拓展：转化研究（通常指转化医学）旨在将基础研究的成果"转化"为实际患者的疾病预防、诊断和治疗及预后评估。其基本特征是多学科交叉合作，针对临床提出的问题，深入开展基础研究，研究成果得到快速应用，实现从"实验室到床边"的转化（bench to bedside translation），又从临床应用中提出新的问题回到实验室（bedside to bench），为实验室研究提出新的研究思路。

Lesson 3
Examples of Aquatic Biobanks Worldwide

1. China National Infrastructure of Fishery Germplasm Resources

China National **Infrastructure** of **Fishery Germplasm** Resources (http://zzzy.fishinfo.cn/ShowMain.asp, Fig. 8.1) aims to collect and preserve economically important and academically valuable aquatic living organisms, vouchers and germplasm. Furthermore, this platform also provide detailed digital information of conserved resources' characteristics and features, such as taxonomic status, morphological characteristics, ecological habit, genetic information, conserving status and so on. Now there are 37 participants inputting 6661 records representing 2844 species including:

(1) Living organisms: 757 species, 1133 records;
(2) Cells and cell lines: 42 species, 66 records;
(3) Sperms: 145 species, 204 records;
(4) Vouchers: 2300 species, 4022 records;
(5) DNA: 512 species, 799 records;
(6) Pathogenic bacteria: 170 species, 182 records.

Figure 8.1 National Infrastructure of Fishery Germplasm Resources

2. The Division of Fishes-Smithsonian National Museum of Natural History

Ichthyology is the study of fishes. Research by staff and associates in the Division covers a broad spectrum of the great diversity of fishes, generally relying on the vast resources of the national fish collection. The fish collection, at the National Museum of Natural History (http://vertebrates.si.edu/fishes/, Fig. 8.2), is the largest in the world, with approximately 540 000 lots (a lot consists of all specimens of a species collected at the same time and place) and about 4 million specimens.

Figure 8.2 National Museum of Natural History

3. Marbank

Marbank (http://www.imr.no/marbank/en, Fig. 8.3) is a national marine biobank coordinating a network of marine collections in Norway. The mission of Marbank and the network is to provide national and international academia and industry with easy access to marine biodiversity, its associated data and extractable products. There is a special focus on samples for marine **bioprospecting** i.e. the systematic search for interesting and unique genes, molecules and organisms from the marine environment with features that could be useful to society and/or have potential for commercial development.

Figure 8.3 Marbank

Contents of the Marbank collection at present:
(1) Taxonomic vouchers from approximately 1000 invertebrate/vertebrate species;
(2) Genetic samples from 265 invertebrate/vertebrate species;
(3) Extracts from roughly 400 invertebrate/vertebrate species;
(4) Approximately 3000 isolates of marine bacteria;
(5) Approximately 50 strains of marine micro algae;
(6) Approximately 800 isolates of marine fungi.

4. Canada's National Aquatic Biological Specimen Bank and Database (NABSB)

NABSB (http://www.ec.gc.ca/inre-nwri/default.asp?lang=En&n=D488F7DE-1) houses more than 83 025 frozen biological samples from 22 855 specimens of top **predator** fish and **forage** fish over 30+ years. Each specimen is homogenized and divided into 5 to 15 subsamples of ~20 g. All samples are stored at −80 ℃ in a dedicated climate-controlled building with continuous monitoring of security and storage conditions. In the event of mechanical failure in any of the freezer units, temperature sensors will trigger the release of liquid CO_2 to maintain freezing temperatures until the specimens can be manually transferred to another freezer.

5. Marine Environmental Specimen (BankMarine ESB)

The Marine Environmental Specimen Bank (Marine ESB, http://www.nist.gov/mml/csd/esb/marineesb.cfm), established by NIST in 2001 at the Hollings Marine Laboratory (HML) in Charleston, South Carolina, cryogenically banks well-documented environmental specimens collected as part of other agency marine research and monitoring programs. Specimens include marine mammal tissues, **mussels** and oysters, fish tissues, seabird eggs, and **peregrine falcon** eggs and feathers. The bank emphasizes cryogenic storage using ultra-cold (−80 ℃) electric freezers and liquid nitrogen vapor (−150 ℃) freezers. Many of these specimens are being analyzed retrospectively to determine time trends in emerging contaminants of concern in the environment and as part of a multi-agency effort to determine health trends in marine animals.

6. The Ocean Genome Legacy

Ocean Genome Legacy (http://www.northeastern.edu/marinescience/ogl/) is a non-profit organization dedicated to creating a global biobank housing the DNA blueprints (genomes) of a broad cross-section of the endangered organisms of the sea. Our aim is to preserve and provide access to this global genomic legacy, and so to support understanding and protection of our planets greatest ecosystem. More than 35 500 frozen biological samples archived in the Ocean Genome Resource biorepository. Materials in the collection are stored at ultra-cold temperatures in −80 ℃ freezers or −180 ℃ liquid nitrogen dewars. The Ocean Genome Resource is a central repository for genomic materials, including tissue, DNA, RNA, DNA libraries and amplified DNA products.

Glossary

infrastructure /ˈɪnfrəstrʌktʃər/
基础设施
Infrastructure refers to the fundamental facilities and systems serving a country, city, or area, including the services and facilities necessary for its economy to function.

fishery /ˈfɪʃəri/
渔业；渔场
A fishery is an entity engaged in raising or harvesting fish which is determined by some authority to be a fishery.

germplasm /ˈdʒɜːmplæzm/
种质资源
Germplasm is the living genetic resources such as seeds or tissue that is maintained for the purpose of breeding, preservation, and other research uses. These resources may take the form of seed collections stored in seed banks, trees growing in nurseries,

animal breeding lines maintained in animal breeding programs or gene banks, etc.

ichthyology /ˌɪkθɪˈɒlədʒɪ/

鱼类学

Ichthyology is the branch of biology devoted to the study of fish.

bioprospecting /baɪɒpˈrɒspektɪŋ/

生物勘探

Bioprospecting is the process of discovery and commercialization of new products based on biological resources. Despite being intuitively helpful, bioprospecting has only recently begun to incorporate indigenous knowledge in focusing screening efforts for bioactive compounds.

predator /ˈpredətər/

捕食者；肉食动物

Predator fish（捕食鱼）are fish that predate upon other fish or animals. Some predatory fish include perch, muskie (muskellunge), pike, walleye, and salmon.

forage /ˈfɔːrɪdʒ/

饵料

Forage fish（饵料鱼）are small pelagic fish which are preyed on by larger predators for food.

mussel /ˈmʌsl/

贻贝

Mussel is the common name used for members of several families of clams（蛤蚌）or bivalve mollusks（双壳软体动物）, from saltwater and freshwater habitats.

peregrine falcon /ˈperɪɡrɪn ˈfælkən/

游隼

Peregrine falcon is a widespread bird of prey in the family Falconidae（隼科）.

Notes to Difficult Sentences

In the event of mechanical failure in any of the freezer units, temperature sensors will trigger the release of liquid CO_2 to maintain freezing temperatures until the specimens can be manually transferred to another freezer.

万一低温冰箱发生机器故障，温度感应器就会触发液态二氧化碳的释放以维持低温状态直到样本被手动转移到其他冰箱中。

拓展：一方面，低温冷冻技术的快速发展让样本保存更便捷和安全，温度感应器、液态二氧化碳储备装置、停电时的备用发电机或储蓄电池等设备，都能更好地对低温样本进行管理。另一方面，一些新兴的不需低温、常温即可起到保护作用的保护剂如RNALater、Gentegra等在样品保存特别是运输过程中展现出越来越显著的优势，是对低温保存方法的有效补充。

Reading Material 1

Defining Characteristics of Biobanks Containing Clinical Specimens

In 2012, we conducted a survey of U. S. biobanks—which we define as "organizations that acquire and store human specimens and associated data for future research use." We identified 636 eligible biobanks and 456 (72%) responded to our survey. In this paper we present simple response frequencies, with percentages where appropriate. Where percentages do not add to 100, it is due to rounding. Analyses were conducted in SAS version 9.2 (SAS Institute Inc., Cary, NC, USA).

In identifying biobanks for our study, we tried to eliminate organizations that serve solely as storage facilities for individual researchers—ones in which a researcher deposits specimens until they are needed, with no possibility that the specimens could be shared with others. We did not place any requirement on how the biobank acquires its specimens in order to be eligible for our study. Within the survey, we asked whether any of the specimens in the biobank's collection come from each of the following sources:
(1) Hospitals, clinical laboratories, or pathology departments providing residual specimens from clinical care;
(2) Public health departments or programs providing residual specimens;
(3) Individuals providing specimens directly to the biobank;
(4) Any other sources.

For this paper, we focus only on the 261 biobank managers who said "yes" to the first source. As shown in Table 8.5, forty-three respondents (16%) reported that their biobank acquires specimens only from hospitals, clinical laboratories, or pathology departments. One hundred thirty-eight banks (53%) acquire specimens from clinical settings and from individuals providing specimens directly. Thirty-nine (15%) acquire them from clinical settings, from individuals directly, and from "other" sources; twenty-seven (10%) acquire specimens from clinical and other sources. Only 7 biobanks (3%) acquire specimens from all four sources, and the remaining 7 biobanks (3%) acquire from clinical and public health settings, with or without collecting from individuals as well. Since we did not ask the respondent to indicate the number of specimens acquired from clinical settings relative to others in their collection, we do not know, for the 218 biobanks with mixed sources, whether the clinical specimens form only a small portion of their collection, nearly the entirety of it, or something in between.

Table 8.5　Sources for acquisition of specimens

Sources	n	%
Clinical and direct contributions	138	53
Clinical only	43	16
Clinical, direct contributions and "other"	39	15
Clinical and "other"	27	10
Clinical and public health dept/program	7	3
Clinical, public health dept/program, and "other"	5	2
Clinical, public health dept/program, direct contributions, and "other"	2	1
Total	261	100

Clinical: hospitals, clinical laboratories, or pathology departments providing residual specimens from clinical care.

Public health dept/program: public health departments or programs providing residual specimens.

Direct contributions: individuals providing specimens directly to the biobank.

"Other": any other sources.

Table 8.6 shows the number and percentage of biobanks storing various types of biological specimens. Solid tissue and serum/plasma are the most common. Twenty-four biobanks reported "other biological specimens," meaning they store something not listed on our survey. Nineteen of these wrote in a description of the "other" specimens, which are detailed in Table 8.7. Most biobanks (88%) store more than one type of specimen. As shown in Table 8.8, biobanks reported as many as 10 different types of specimens in their collections. The size of the specimen collection (number of specimens currently in storage) ranged from only 20 specimens to 54 million. Table 8.9 provides more detail on the number of specimens in storage. The range most frequently reported by the surveyed biobanks (19%) was that of 10 000 ~ 49 999 specimens. Due to a few very large banks, the mean number of specimens is 610 245 but the median is 7650.

Table 8.6 Types of specimens in storage

Percentage of biobanks storing specimens of this type	n	%
Solid tissue specimens, including paraffin embedded, frozen, or other	231	86
Serum or plasma	203	79
Whole blood	147	56
Peripheral blood cells or bone marrow	138	53
Cell lines	95	36
Saliva or buccal cells	85	33
Urine or stool	83	32
Cerebral spinal fluid	59	23
Cord blood or cord blood derivatives	30	11
Pathological body fluids	27	10
Other biological specimens	24	9
Hair/toenails	6	2

Table 8.7 Other types of biological specimens

(Each type below was reported by only one biobank)
Amniotic fluid
Bronchoalveolar lavage
Monoclonal antibodies, biological research reagents
Muscle, hair, pituitary
Over 200 human, animal and environmental material types
Seminal plasma
Animal and human specimens of all kinds
Bacterial plasmids
Body fluids, tissue scrapings, aspirates, swabs, cultures, extracted DNA or RNA
Bone
Breast milk
Breast milk, meconium, dust, placenta, buffy coats, dried blood spot cards
Cell pellets
Cells cultured from biopsy samples collected from patients
Cervicovaginal lavage
Mucus
Prostatic fluid
Seminal vesicle, prostatic fluid, fresh tissue
Sperm, oocytes, embryos & semen

Table 8.8 Number of types of specimens

	n	%
1	31	12
2	32	12
3	38	15
4	45	17
5	35	13
6	34	13
7	17	7
8	12	5
9	12	5
10	3	1
Total	260	100

Table 8.9 Number of specimens in storage

	n	%
Less than 500	30	12
500 ~ 999	19	8
1000 ~ 1999	23	9
2000 ~ 4999	34	14
5000 ~ 9999	24	10
10 000 ~ 49 999	48	19
50 000 ~ 99 999	24	10
100 000 ~ 499 999	30	12
500 000 +	17	7
Total	260	100

Mean: 610 245 Std deviation: 4 280 855.

Median: 7650. Range: 20 ~ 54 000 000.

Also of interest in describing a biobank's collection is whether pediatric and/or post mortem specimens are included. In our survey, six biobanks (2%) house exclusively pediatric specimens, and an additional 44% include some pediatric specimens. Seven percent of biobanks report collections composed entirely of specimens that were collected post mortem; an additional 37% contain some post mortem specimens. Thus we found tremendous variation in the size and nature of specimen collections among these biobanks housing clinical specimens.

As we document, the world of this sub-set of 261 biobanks is highly variable in the types and numbers of specimens maintained and the policies that govern them. This uncertain and heterogeneous landscape demands careful consideration and planning by biobank managers to maintain high quality practices in acquisition, storage, and release of specimens all the while striving to protect the rights of subjects.

Reading Material 2

Biobank Managers Bemoan Underuse of the Collected Samples

Hundreds of thousands of individuals have freely donated bits of their bodies to biological repositories, proffering a vial of blood or a slice of skin in exchange for the promise of advancing medical research. But contrary to donor intentions, many of those specimens are sitting unused in lab freezers, suggesting that the biobanking system is not as efficient or effective as it could be (Fig. 8.4).

According to a first-of-its-kind survey of 456 biobank managers in the US, nearly 70% of those questioned expressed concern that the samples in their repositories are underused. "Biobankers really worry," says Gail Henderson, a medical sociologist at the University of North Carolina-Chapel Hill who led the study published in late January. "They have an imperative to collect, but they really want to make sure the specimens are used, and they worry about how to make that happen."

It's not just a problem unique to US institutions either. "There are so many samples and data connected to these samples, but nobody is using them," says Loreana Norlin, a project manager at the BioBanking and Molecular Resource Infrastructure of Sweden, a national biobanking facility and network based at the Karolinska Institute in Stockholm. "They're lying around in a freezer."

Figure 8.4 Specimens are lying around in a freezer
(By Pacific Science)

Numerous causes for this underuse have been proposed, including the supply of samples outstripping demand, restrictive policies that allow only researchers affiliated with particular institutions or projects to access certain biobanks, and poor marketing. To encourage more researchers to use biobank wares, Liz Horn, former director of the Genetic Alliance BioBank, a Washington, DC-based repository operated by five patient advocacy organizations, recommends that biobanks advertise their collections at institutional events and external conferences. "You can't just collect," she says.

Without fail

The Mayo Clinic Biobank (http://www.mayoclinic.org/, Fig. 8.5), for example, regularly publicizes its collection during grand rounds at the Rochester, Minnesota-based hospital, enticing researchers with results gleaned from past studies done with the biobank's samples. "Our feeling is if people don't use the samples, then it's a failure," says James Cerhan, principal investigator of the Mayo biobank.

Figure 8.5 The Mayo Clinic Biobank has a goal of enrolling 50 000 Mayo Clinic patients by 2015

In addition to homegrown advertising, biobanks may need to work together to fulfill their mission, notes Horn. "Standardization is going to be important for researchers to get samples from different collections," she says, "and we need catalogs that say where these samples exist."

A national registry, like that currently being built in Sweden, could show researchers comparable types and quantities of samples within biobanks around a country. Meanwhile, accreditation could provide further incentives for biobanks to harmonize collections and encourage use (Fig. 8.6). Two years ago, the College of American Pathologists introduced a Biorepository Accreditation Program, and already 18 banks have been certified and an additional 15 are in the process.

"It's expensive," says Henderson, "but it might be a first step toward making biobanks into a harmonized system."

Biorepository Accreditation

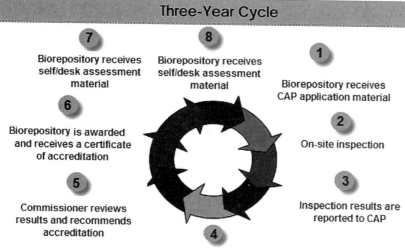

Figure 8.6 Biorepository accreditation program
(By College of American pathologists)

Glossary

A

abnormality /ˌæbnɔːrˈmæləti/
畸形

accreditation /əˌkredɪˈteɪʃn/
评审；委派

acylcarnitine /əsɪlkɑːnɪˈtaɪn/
酰基肉碱

adaptability /əˌdæptəˈbɪləti/
适应性

adaptor /əˈdæptə/
接头

agrigenomic /æɡrɪdʒəˈnɒmɪk/
农业基因组学的

agronomic /æɡrəˈnɒmɪk/
农事的；农艺学的

algae /ˈældʒiː/
藻类

alkaline /ˈælkəlaɪn/
碱性的；碱的

allergy /ˈælədʒi/
过敏症

amniote /ˈæmnɪoʊt/
羊膜动物

amphibian /æmˈfɪbɪən/
两栖动物

amplicon /ˈæmplɪkɒn/
扩增子

anaesthesia /ˌænəsˈθiːziə/
麻醉

analyte /ˈænəˈlɪt/
分析物，被测物质

angiosperm /ˈændʒɪəˌspɜːm/
被子植物

annotated /ˈænəteɪtɪd/
（基因）注释

annotation /ˌænəˈteɪʃn/
注释

antibiotics /ˌæntɪbaɪˈɒtɪks/
抗生素

antigen /ˈæntɪdʒən/
抗原

apyrase /əˈpaɪreɪs/
三磷酸腺苷双磷酸酶

Archaea /ɑːˈkɪə/
古细菌

architecture /ˈɑːrkɪtektʃər/
建筑学；建筑风格；建筑式样

artemisinin /ɑːtɪmɪˈsaɪnɪn/
青蒿素

arthritis /ɑːrˈθraɪtɪs/
关节炎

arthropod /ˈɑːrθrəpɑːd/
节肢动物门

assimilate /əˈsɪməleɪt/
吸收；使同化

asthma /ˈæzmə/
哮喘

autism /ˈɔːtɪzəm/
自闭症；孤独症

B

back-up /ˈbækˈʌp/
备份；为…做备份
bacteriophage /bækˈtɪərəʃeɪdʒ/
噬菌体
barren /ˈbærən/
不育的；贫瘠的
base-call
碱基识别
bee colonies /biː ˈkɔːlənɪz/
蜂群
beetle /ˈbiːtl/
甲虫
bioethics /ˌbaɪoʊˈeθɪks/
生物伦理学
biogeographic /biːəʊdʒiəˈɡræfɪk/
生物地理的
bioinformatics /biːəʊɪnˈfɔːmətɪks/
生物信息学
bioprospecting /baɪɒpˈrɒspektɪŋ/
生物勘探

biopsy /ˈbaɪɑːpsi/
活组织检查；活组织切片检查
biorepository /ˌbaɪoʊrɪˈpɑːzətɔːri/
生物样本库
biospecimen /ˈbaɪəʊˈspesɪmən/
生物样本；生物标本
biotype /ˈbaɪoʊtaɪp/
生物型；同型小种
birth canal /bɜːrθ kəˈnæl/
生殖道；产道
branched-chain amino acids
支链氨基酸
breeding /ˈbriːdɪŋ/
繁殖；育种
bridge amplification /ˌæmplɪfɪˈkeɪʃn/
桥式扩增
buccal /ˈbʌkəl/
口腔的

C

Cambrian explosion
/ˈkæmbriən ɪkˈsploʊʒn/
寒武纪爆发
capillary /ˈkæpəleri/
毛细管；毛细管的
cartilage /ˈkɑrtɪlɪdʒ/
软骨
cavity /ˈkævəti/
（体）腔
celiac /ˈsiːlɪˌæk/
腹腔的

centrifugation /sentrɪfjʊˈɡeɪʃən/
离心分离
cerebral /səˈriːbrəl/
大脑的；脑的
cesarean section
剖腹产术
cetacean /sɪˈteɪʃn/
鲸类动物
chemical constituent
/ˈkemɪkl kənˈstɪtʃuənt/
化学组成

chemotherapy /ˌkiːmoʊˈθerəpi/
化学疗法
chimp /tʃɪmp/
（非洲）黑猩猩
ChIP-Seq
染色质免疫共沉淀测序
cholera /ˈkɑːlərə/
霍乱
chromosome /ˈkroʊməsoʊm/
染色体
clade /kleɪd/
进化枝；分化枝
clinical /ˈklɪnɪkl/
临床的
clonal /ˈkloʊnəl/
无性（繁殖）系的；无性（繁殖）系般的
cloud or utinity computing
云或效用计算
colorectal /ˌkoʊləˈrektəl/
结肠直肠的
complexion /kəmˈplekʃn/
肤色
computing cluster /kəmˈpjuːtɪŋ ˈklʌstər/
计算机集群

concentration /ˌkɒnsenˈtreɪʃən/
浓度；浓缩
confounding variables /kənˈfaʊndɪŋ ˈveəriəblz/
混杂变量
conifer /ˈkɑːnɪfər/
针叶树；松柏科植物
constant temperature /ˈkɑːnstənt ˈtemprətʃər/
恒温
contraindicate /ˌkɒntrəˈɪndəˌkeɪt/
禁忌（某种疗法或药物）
coronary /ˈkɔːrəneri/
冠状动脉或静脉的
crossbreeding /ˈkrɒsbriːdɪŋ/
杂交育种
cryogenic /ˌkraɪəˈdʒenɪk/
冷冻的
cryopreserved /ˌkraɪɒprɪzɜːvd/
冷藏保存的
cultivar /ˈkʌltɪvɑːr/
栽培品种；栽培品系
cystic fibrosis /ˈsɪstɪk faɪˈbroʊsɪs/
囊泡性纤维症

D

degrade /dɪˈɡreɪd/
降解
deleterious /ˌdeləˈtɪriəs/
有害的
dementia /dɪˈmenʃə/
痴呆
demography /dɪˈmɑːɡrəfi/
人口统计学

depression /dɪˈpreʃn/
沮丧；抑郁症
derivative /dɪˈrɪvətɪv/
派生物；衍生物
deuterostome /ˈdjuːtərəstoʊm/
后口动物
diabetes /ˌdaɪəˈbiːtiːz/
糖尿病

diagnose /ˌdaɪəɡˈnoʊs/
诊断
diagnostic /ˌdaɪəɡˈnɑːstɪk/
诊断的；特征的
dinoflagellate /ˌdaɪnəˈflædʒəˌlɪt/
鞭毛虫类
diploid /ˈdɪplɔɪd/
二倍体
discrimination /dɪˌskrɪmɪˈneɪʃn/
歧视；区别，辨别；识别力

divestiture /dəˈvestətʃə/
剥夺
domestication /dəˌmestɪˈkeɪʃn/
驯养；教化
drug-resistant /ˈdrʌɡrɪzˈɪstənt/
耐药的；抗药的
dynamics /daɪˈnæmɪks/
动力学

E

ecological fallacy /ˌiːkəˈlɑːdʒɪkl ˈfæləsi/
生态谬误；生态学谬论
eczema /ɪɡˈziːmə/
湿疹
embryo /ˈembrioʊ/
胚胎
emission spectra
发射光谱
emulsion PCR /ɪˈmʌlʃn/
乳液 PCR
endangered species
/ɪnˈdeɪndʒəd ˈspiːʃiːz/
濒危物种
endocrine /ˈendəkrɪn/
内分泌；激素；内分泌物
endothelial /ˌendəˈθiːlɪəl/
内皮的
enzymatically /ˌenzaɪˈmætɪklɪ/
酶促地
enzyme /ˈenzaɪm/
酶
epidemiology /ˌepɪˌdiːmiˈɑːlədʒi/
流行病学；传染病学

epidemiology /ˌepɪˌdiːmiˈɑːlədʒi/
流行病学；传染病学
epigenetic /ˌepədʒəˈnetɪk/
后生的；表观的
epigenome /ˈepaɪdʒənəm/
表观基因组
epigenomics /ˌepaɪdʒəˈnɒmɪks/
表观基因组学
ethical /ˈeθɪkl/
伦理的；道德的
Eubacteria /juːbækˈtɪərɪə/
真细菌
eukaryotic /uːkeəriˈɒtɪk/
真核的；真核生物的
exponentially /ˌekspəˈnenʃəli/
以指数方式
expressed sequence tags（EST）
表达序列标签
extinction of species
物种灭绝
extract /ˈekstrækt/
（DNA/RNA/蛋白）提取

F

fatalism /ˈfeɪtəlɪzəm/
宿命论
feces /ˈfiːsiːz/
粪便
femtoliter /ˈfemtoʊlɪtə/
飞升
fern /fɜːrn/
蕨；蕨类植物
fertilized eggs /ˈfɜːrtɪlaɪzd egz/
受精卵
fetus /ˈfiːtəs/
胎；胎儿
fibre-optic cable
纤维光缆
fishery /ˈfɪʃəri/
渔业；渔场

flora /ˈflɔːrə/
植物群；真菌/细菌群
flowcell /flaʊˈsel/
流动池
fluorescently labeled
荧光标记的
forage /ˈfɔːrɪdʒ/
饵料
forensic /fəˈrensɪks/
鉴证；辩论术；辩论练习
formalin /ˈfɔːməlɪn/
福尔马林（甲醛溶液）
fraternal /frəˈtɜːrnl/
兄弟姐妹的
fungus /ˈfʌŋɡəs/
真菌

G

gaur /ɡaʊə/
（印度）野牛
generalizability /dʒenərəlaɪzəˈbɪlɪtɪ/
普遍性；概括性
genetic mapping /dʒəˈnetɪk mæpɪŋ/
遗传作图
genital tract /ˈdʒenɪtl trækt/
生殖道；产道
genotyping /dʒenəʊˈtaɪpɪŋ/
基因分型
geographic /ˌdʒiːəˈɡræfɪk/
地理的；地理学的

germplasm /ˈdʒɜːmplæzm/
种质资源
ghrelin /rəˈlɪn/
饥饿素；生长素
Global Positioning System（GPS）
全球定位系统
glucose /ˈɡluːkoʊs/
葡萄糖
grid computing /ɡrɪd kəmˈpjuːtɪŋ/
网格计算
gut /ɡʌt/
肠道

H

habitat alteration /ˈhæbɪtæt ˌɔːltəˈreɪʃn/
生境交替

haplotype /ˈhæploʊtaɪp/
单体型

health surveillance /helθ sɜːrˈveɪləns/
健康监护

herbivorous /hɜːˈbɪvərəs/
食草的

heterogeneity /ˌhetərədʒəˈniːəti/
异质性

heterogeneous /ˌhetərəˈdʒiːniəs/
多相的；异种的；不均匀的

high-definition /ˈhaɪˌdefɪˈnɪʃn/
非常鲜明的；高清晰度

Homo sapiens /ˌhoʊmoʊˈseɪpienz/
人；智人

homologue /ˈhɒməˌlɒg/
同系物；同源物

homology /hoʊˈmɒlədʒɪ/
同源

homozygote /ˌhɑːməˈzaɪgoʊt/
纯合子；纯合体；同质接合体；均质接合体

hormone /ˈhɔːrmoʊn/
荷尔蒙；激素

hybrid /ˈhaɪbrɪd/
杂种

hybridization /ˌhaɪbrɪdaɪˈzeʃn/
杂交；配种

hygienic /haɪˈdʒenɪk/
卫生的；保健的

hypothesis /haɪˈpɑːθəsɪs/
（科学）假说

hypoxia /haɪˈpɑːksiə/
低氧

I

ice crystal /aɪs ˈkrɪstl/
冰晶

ichthyology /ˌɪkθɪˈɒlədʒɪ/
鱼类学

immunological /ˌɪmjunəˈlɒdʒɪkl/
免疫学的

immunoprecipitation /ˈɪmjʊnoʊprɪsɪpɪˈteɪʃən/
（IP）免疫沉淀反应

implantation /ˌɪmplɑːnˈteɪʃn/
移植

in situ /ɪnˈsaɪtuː/
原位；在原地

in vitro /ɪnˈvɪtroʊ/
体外；离体

inbreeding /ˈɪnbriːdɪŋ/
近亲繁殖

infection /ɪnˈfekʃn/
传染；传染病

influenza /ˌɪnfluˈenzə/
流行性感冒；家畜流行性感冒

infrastructure /ˈɪnfrəstrʌktʃər/
基础设施

inherited disease /ɪnˈherɪtɪd dɪˈziːz/
遗传疾病

iniparib /ɪnɪˈpærɪb/
一种抗癌药物
integrity /ɪnˈtegrəti/
完整性
interoperability /ˌɪntərɒpərəˈbɪləti/
互操作性；互用性
intervention studies /ˌɪntəˈvenʃn ˈstʌdiz/
干预性研究
intestine /ɪnˈtestɪn/
肠道
intratumor /ˌɪntrɑːtˈjuːmər/
瘤内的
intrauterine insemination
/ˌɪntrəˈjuːtəraɪn ɪnˌsemɪˈneʃn/
子宫内受精；人工授精
isolate /ˈaɪsəleɪt/
分离；提取
iterative process /ˈɪtəˌreɪtɪv ˈprəʊses/
迭代过程
IVF /ˌaɪviːˈef/
试管受精

J

jumping library
跨步文库

L

late-onset /ˈleɪtˈɒnset/
晚发性的；迟发性的
leukemia /luːˈkiːmɪə/
白血病
leukocyte /ˈluːkəˌsaɪt/
白细胞
library /ˈlaɪbreri/
文库
ligase /ˈlaɪˌgeɪs/
连接酶
ligation /laɪˈgeɪʃn/
（核酸分子末端）连接
limnic /ˈlɪmnɪk/
湖泊的；湖沼的；湖栖的
linearization /lɪnɪəraɪˈzeɪʃən/
线性化
luciferase /luːˈsɪfəˌreɪs/
荧光素酶

M

macroscopic /ˌmækrəˈskɒpɪk/
宏观的；肉眼可见的
make-up /ˈmeɪkˌʌp/
构造；排版；化妆品；补考

malaria /məˈleriə/
疟疾

marijuana /ˌmærəˈwɑːnə/
大麻

marsupial /mɑːrˈsuːpiəl/
有袋动物

Material Transfer Agreement（MTA）
材料转移协议

metabolite /meˈtæbəˌlaɪt/
代谢物

metagenomics /metədʒəˈnɒmɪks/
宏基因组学

metastasis /məˈtæstəsɪs/
（远端）转移

metazoa /ˌmetəˈzoʊə/
后生动物

methylation /meθɪˈleɪʃn/
甲基化

microarray /ˌmaɪkroʊəˈreɪ/
微矩阵

microbe /ˈmaɪkroʊb/
细菌

microbiome /ˈmaɪkroʊˈbaɪoʊm/
微生物组

microliter /ˈmaɪkroʊlɪtə/
微升

microscope /ˈmaɪkrəskoʊp/
显微镜

miscarry /ˌmɪsˈkæri/
流产

mitochondrial /ˌmaɪtəʊˈkɒndriəl/
线粒体的

molecular clocks
分子钟

mollusk /ˈmɒləsk/
软体动物

morphologically /mɔːfəˈlɒdʒɪklɪ/
形态学上地

multichambered /məltɪtˈʃeɪmbəd/
多室的

multidisciplinary /ˌmʌltiˈdɪsəpləneri/
多学科的

mussel /ˈmʌsl/
贻贝

mutation /mjuːˈteɪʃn/
突变

N

nanoarray /ˈnænoʊˌəˈreɪ/
纳米阵列

nematode /ˈnemətoʊd/
线虫类

neoadjuvant /niːəʊədʒˈjʊvənt/
新辅助疗法

neognathae /niːəɡˈneɪθiː/
新颚总目

network bandwidth /ˈnetwɜːk ˈbændˌwɪdθ/
网络带宽

neural crest /ˈnʊrəl krest/
神经嵴

neuroanatomical /ˌnʊroʊəˈnætəmɪkəl/
神经解剖学的

nucleotide /ˈnjuːklɪəˌtaɪd/
核苷酸

nucleus /ˈnuːkliəs/
细胞核

nutritional /njuˈtrɪʃənl/
营养的；滋养的

O

obesity /əʊˈbiːsəti/
肥胖的
oculocutaneous albinism
/ˌɒkjʊlɒkʌˈteɪniəs ˈælbɪnɪzəm/
眼皮肤白化病
offspring /ˈɔːfsprɪŋ/
子孙后代
oncogene addiction /ˈɒŋkəˌdʒiːn əˈdɪkʃn/
癌基因成瘾性
orangutan /oʊˈræŋuːˌtæn/
猩猩
organellar /ɔːɡeɪˈnelə/
细胞器的
organism /ˈɔːrɡənɪzəm/
有机体；生物体
osteoporosis /ˌɑːstioʊpəˈroʊsɪs/
骨质疏松症
ovarian /əʊˈveəriən/
卵巢的；子房的
ovulation /ˌɒvjuˈleɪʃn/
排卵
oxidation /ˌɒksɪˈdeɪʃn/
氧化
oxygen /ˈɑːksɪdʒən/
氧气

P

palaeognathae /pælɪəˈɡnəθiː/
古颚总目
paradoxically /ˌpærəˈdɒksɪkli/
自相矛盾地；似非而是地；反常地
parapatric /pærəˈpeɪtrɪk/
邻接群体的
parasite /ˈpærəsaɪt/
寄生虫
particle-collision /ˈpɑːrtɪkl kəˈlɪʒn/
粒子碰撞
pathogen /ˈpæθədʒən/
病原体
pathogenesis /ˌpæθəˈdʒenɪsɪs/
发病机制；致病原因
pathogenic /ˈpæθəˈdʒenɪk/
致病的；病原的；发病的
pathway /ˈpæθweɪ/
通路；路径
pediatric /ˌpiːdiˈætrɪk/
儿科的；小儿的
penetrance /ˈpenətrəns/
外显率
penis /ˈpiːnɪs/
阴茎；阳物
peregrine falcon /ˈperɪɡrɪn ˈfælkən/
游隼
peripheral /pəˈrɪfərəl/
外周的；外围的；（神经）末梢区域的
peritoneal /perɪtəˈhiːəl/
腹腔的
pharmaceutical /ˌfɑːrməˈsuːtɪkl/
药物；制药（学）
phenotypic /ˈfiːnətɪpɪk/
表型的
phosphorylation /fɒsfɒrɪˈleɪʃn/
磷酸化

photosynthetic /ˌfoʊtoʊsɪnˈθetɪk/
光合作用的
phyla /ˈfaɪlə/
门
phylogenetic /ˌfaɪloʊdʒəˈnetɪk/
系统发生的；动植物演化史的；动植物种类史的
physician /fɪˈzɪʃn/
内科医生
picoliter /ˌpɪkəˈlaɪtə/
皮升
placental /pləˈsentl/
有胎盘哺乳动物
plague /pleɪɡ/
瘟疫；灾祸
Plasmodium falciparum
镰状疟原虫
plastid /ˈplæstɪd/
叶绿体
platyfish /ˈplætiːˌfɪʃ/
新月鱼；阔尾鱼
pollutant /pəˈluːtənt/
污染物
polyandry /ˌpɑːliˈændri/
一妻多夫制；一雌多雄配合
polymerase /ˈpɒləməˌreɪs/
聚合酶
polymorphism /ˌpɒlɪˈmɪfzəm/
多态性
postmortem /ˌpoʊstˈmɔːtəm/
验尸；尸检；死后的
prasinophyte /prəˈzɪnəfaɪt/
绿藻类
precipitation /prɪˌsɪpɪˈteɪʃn/
沉淀
preclinical /prɪˈklɪnɪkəl/
临床前的；潜伏期的

predator /ˈpredətər/
捕食者；肉食动物
predisposition /ˌpriːdɪspəˈzɪʃn/
倾向；癖性；（易患病的）体质
pregnancy /ˈpreɡnənsi/
怀孕；妊娠
presymptomatic /ˌprɪsɪmptəˈmætɪk/
症状发生前的
primate /ˈpraɪmeɪt/
灵长类动物
primer /ˈpraɪmər/
引物
probe /proʊb/
探针
probiotic /ˌproʊbaɪˈɑːtɪk/
益生素的；益生菌的
prognostic /prɒɡˈnɒstɪk/
预兆；预言；预后症状
prokaryote /ˌproʊˈkærɪɒt/
原核生物
propagate /ˈprɑːpəɡeɪt/
繁殖
prostate /ˈprɑːsteɪt/
前列腺（的）
protist /ˈproʊtɪst/
原生生物
psychological /ˌsaɪkəˈlɑːdʒɪkl/
心理的；精神上的
psychosocial stress /ˌsaɪkoʊˈsoʊʃəl stres/
心理社会应激
pulmonary /ˈpʌlməneri/
肺部的；肺的
pulp /pʌlp/
果肉
pyrosequencing /pəˈɪərəʊzkwənsɪŋ/
焦磷酸测序

Q

quantitative /ˈkwɑːntəteɪtɪv/
量化的；定量的

R

randomized clinical trials
随机临床试验
rearrangement /ˌriːəˈreɪndʒmənt/
（染色体）重排
recessive /rɪˈsesɪv/
隐性的
repository /rɪˈpɑzətɔːri/
贮藏室，仓库；知识库；智囊团
reproductive /ˌriːprəˈdʌktɪv/
生殖的
reptile /ˈreptaɪl/
爬行动物
resequencing /reˈzekwənsɪŋ/
重测序

restriction endonuclease
/rɪˈstrɪkʃn ˌendoʊˈnjuːkliːˌeɪs/
限制性（核酸）内切酶
retrieval /rɪˈtriːvl/
取回；恢复
ribosomal /ˌraɪbəˈsoʊməl/
核糖体的
rodent /ˈroʊdnt/
啮齿动物
rudimentary /ˌruːdɪˈmentri/
基本的；初步的；退化的；未发展的
rumen /ˈruːmen/
瘤胃

S

saliva /səˈlaɪvə/
唾液
scientific discipline /ˌsaɪənˈtɪfɪk ˈdɪsɪplɪn/
科学学科
serial analysis of gene expression（SAGE）
基因表达序列分析
side effect /saɪd ɪˈfekt/
副作用
single-nucleotide polymorphisms
单核苷酸多态性
somatic /soʊˈmætɪk/
躯体的；肉体的；体壁的

sonication /ˌsɒnəˈkeɪʃən/
声波降解法
speciation /ˌspiːsiːˈeɪʃən/
物种形成
spectrum /ˈspektrəm/
谱
sperm /spɜːrm/
精子
spinal /ˈspaɪnl/
脊髓的
spurious /ˈspjʊriəs/
假的；伪造的；欺骗的

stain /steɪn/
染色（剂）
stool /stuːl/
粪便
stroke /stroʊk/
中风
susceptibility /səˌseptəˈbɪləti/
敏感性；易感性

swordtail /ˈsɔːrdˌteɪl/
剑尾鱼
symbiotic /ˌsɪmbaɪˈɒtɪk/
共生的
sympatric /sɪmˈpætrɪk/
同域的
synthesize /ˈsɪnθəsaɪz/
合成

T

tendril /ˈtendrəl/
卷须；蔓；卷须状物
terrestrial /təˈrestriəl/
陆地的；陆地生物
tetrapod /ˈtetrəˌpɒd/
四足动物
therapy /ˈθerəpi/
疗法；治疗

transcriptome /trænskˈrɪptɒm/
转录组
tsunami /tsuːˈnɑːmi/
海啸
tumor suppressor gene
肿瘤抑制基因

U

ultraviolet radiation
/ˌʌltrəˈvaɪələt ˌreɪdiˈeɪʃn/
紫外线
underpinning /ˌʌndərˈpɪnɪŋ/
基础；基础材料
undifferentiated /ˌʌndɪfəˈrenʃieɪtɪd/
未分化的

urchin /ˈɜːrtʃɪn/
海胆
urine /ˈjʊərən/
尿液
uterus /ˈjuːtərəs/
子宫

V

variant /ˈveriənt/
变体；变异型

vascular /ˈvæskjələr/
血管的

vascular system /ˈvæskjələr ˈsɪstəm/
维管系
vertebrate /ˈvɜːrtɪbrət/
脊椎动物
viable seeds /ˈvaɪəbl siːdz/
可育的种子

Vibrio /ˈvɪbrɪˌoʊ/
弧菌属
viridiplantae /ˌvɪrɪdɪˈplæntɪ/
绿色植物界

W

warfarin /ˈwɔːrfərɪn/
杀鼠灵；华法令阻凝剂
womb /wuːm/
子宫

wrangle /ˈræŋgl/
争论；争吵；辩驳
written consent /ˈrɪtn kənˈsent/
书面同意书，知情同意书

Y

yeast /jiːst/
酵母

Z

zebra finch /ˈzebrə fɪntʃ/
斑胸草雀

References

[1] 1K insect transcriptome evolution [EB/OL]. http://www.1kite.org.

[2] Avian phylogenomics project [EB/OL]. http://avian.genomics.cn/en/index.html.

[3] Baker M. Building better biobank [J]. Nature, 2012, 486: 141-146.

[4] Barabási A L, Oltvai Z N. Network biology: understanding the cell's functional organization [J]. Nat Rev Genet, 2004, 5(2): 101-113.

[5] BGI Americas [EB/OL]. http://bgiamericas.com/applications/animal-plant/.

[6] BGI [EB/OL]. http://www.genomics.cn/en/index.

[7] Brown W Y. DNA net earth, Global Economy of Develop ment at Brookings, 2013.

[8] Canada's National Aquatic Biological Specimen Bank and Database [EB/OL]. http://www.ec.gc.ca/inre-nwri/default.asp lang=En&n=D488F7DE-1.

[9] Carl Zimmer. Scientists Map 5000 New Ocean Viruses [EB/OL]. https://www.quantamagazine.org/20150521-ocean-viruses/2015-05-21.

[10] Chan I S, Ginsburg G S. Personalized medicine: progress and promise [J]. Annu Rev Genomics Hum Genet, 2011, 12:217-244.

[11] Cheng L, Shi C, Wang X, et al. Chinese biobanks: present and future [J]. Genet Res (Camb), 2013, 95(6): 157-164.

[12] China National Infrastructure of Fishery Germplasm Resources [EB/OL]. http://zzzy.fishinfo.cn/ShowMain.asp.

[13] Coghlan A. Biobank promises to pinpoint the cause of disease [J]. New Scientist, 2012.

[14] Dickenson D. "Me" medicine could undermine public health measures [J]. New Scientist, 2013.

[15] Drmanac R. The advent of personal genome sequencing [J]. Genet Med, 2011, 13(3): 188-190.

[16] Droege G, Barker K, Astrin J J, et al. The Global Genome Biodiversity Network (GGBN) Data Portal [J]. Nucleic Acids Res, 2014, 42(Database issue): D607-612.

[17] Edwards T, Cadigan R J, Evans J P, et al. Biobanks containing clinical specimens: defining characteristics, policies, and practices [J]. Clin Biochem, 2014, 47(4-5):245-251.

[18] Geddes L. First baby born after full genetic screening of embryos [J]. New Scientist, 2013:8-9.

[19] Genome 10K Community of Scientists, Genome 10K: a proposal to obtain whole-genome sequence for 10 000 vertebrate species [J]. J Hered, 2009, 100(6): 659-674.

[20] Grada A, Weinbrecht K. Next-generation sequencing: methodology and application [J].

J Invest Dermatol, 2013, 133(8): e11.

[21] Hamzelou J. Too much information: better health from big data [J]. New Scientist, 2014.

[22] Henderson G E, Cadigan R J, Edwards T P, et al. Characterizing biobank organizations in the U. S. : results from a national survey [J]. Genome Med, 2013, 5(1):3.

[23] Hofer U. Environmental microbiology: Exploring diversity with single-cell genomics [J]. Nat Rev Microbiol, 2013, 11(9): 598.

[24] Illumina. Plant and animal sequencing [EB/OL]. http://www.illumina.com/applications/agriculture/plant-animal-sequencing.html.

[25] IRRS. Rice breeding course: Molecular breeding [EB/OL]. 2006. http://www.knowledgebank.irri.org/ricebreedingcourse/bodydefault.htm.

[26] Joly D, Faure D. Next-generation sequencing propels environmental genomics to the front line of research [J]. Heredity (Edinb), 2015, 114(5):429-430.

[27] Kang B, Park J, Cho S, et al. Current status, challenges, policies, and bioethics of biobanks [J]. Genomics Inform, 2013, 11(4): 211-217.

[28] Khan N, Yoqoob I, Hashem I A, et al. Big data: survey, technologies, opportunities, and challenges [J]. ScientificWorld Journal, 2014.

[29] Khoury M J and Ioannidis J P. Medicine. Big data meets public health. Science, 2014, 346(6213):1054-1055.

[30] Shelswell K J. Metagenomics: the science of biological diversity [EB/OL]. 2006. http://www.scq.ubc.ca/metagenomics-the-science-of-biological-diversity/.

[31] Koboldt D. New challenges of next-gen sequencing [EB/OL]. 2014. http://massgenomics.org/2014/07/new-ngs-challenges.html.

[32] Kollmar M, Kollmar L, Hammesfathr B, et al. diArk—the database for eukaryotic genome and transcriptome assemblies in 2014 [J]. Nucleic Acids Res, 2015, 43(Database issue): D1107-1112.

[33] Lam T T, Zhou B, Wang J, et al. Dissemination, divergence and establishment of H7N9 influenza viruses in China [J]. Nature, 2015.

[34] Lasken R S. Genomic sequencing of uncultured microorganisms from single cells [J]. Nat Rev Microbiol, 2012, 10(9): 631-640.

[35] Leipe D D. Biodiversity, genomes, and DNA sequence databases [J]. Curr Opin Genet Dev, 1996, 6(6).

[36] Liu L, Li Y, Li S, et al. Comparison of next-generation sequencing systems [J]. J Biomed Biotechnol, 2012.

[37] Marbank [EB/OL]. http://www.imr.no/marbank/en.

[38] Marine Environmental Specimen [EB/OL]. http://www.nist.gov/mml/csd/esb/marineesb.cfm.

[39] Marx V. Biology: The big challenges of big data [J]. Nature, 2013, 498:255-260.

[40] May M. Big biological impacts from big data [J]. Science, 2014, 13.

[41] McGuire A L, Cho M K, McGuire S E, et al. Medicine. The future of personal genomics [J]. Science, 2007, 317(5845): 1687.

[42] Microbiology: Focus on Metagenomics [EB/OL]. http://www. nature. com/nrmicro/focus/metagenomics/index. html.

[43] O'Driscoll A, Daugelaite J, Sleator R D. "Big data", Hadoop and cloud computing in genomics [J]. J Biomed Inform, 2013, 46(5):774-781.

[44] Pollack A. DNA sequencing: caught in the deluge of data[N]. New York Times, 2011.

[45] Rice C. A poop bank in Massachusetts will pay you $40 every day [EB/OL]. 2014. http://www. boston. com/health/2014/10/15/poop-bank-massachusetts-will-pay-you-per-dump/FMMhBXMKyFNTRXKoThmnpM/story. html.

[46] Rinke C, Schwientek P, Sczyrba A, et al. Insights into the phylogeny and coding potential of microbial dark matter [J]. Nature, 2013, 499(7459):431-437.

[47] Scudellari M. Biobank managers bemoan underuse of collected samples [J]. Nat Med, 2013, 19(3):253.

[48] Shendure J and Ji H. Next-generation DNA sequencing [J]. Nat Biotechnol, 2008, 26(10):1135-1145.

[49] Swan B K, Tupper B, Sczyrba A, et al. Prevalent genome streamlining and latitudinal divergence of planktonic bacteria in the surface ocean [J]. Proc Natl Acad Sci, 2013, 110(28): 11463-11468.

[50] The 1000 plants [EB/OL]. http://www. onekp. com.

[51] The 5000 arthropod genomes initiative [EB/OL]. http://arthropodgenomes. org/wiki/i5k.

[52] The Division of Fishes-Smithsonian National Museum of Natural History [EB/OL]. http://vertebrates. si. edu/fishes/.

[53] The marine microbial eukaryotic transcriptome sequencing project [EB/OL]. http://marinemicroeukaryotes. org/.

[54] The Ocean Genome Legacy [EB/OL]. http://www. northeastern. edu/marinescience/ogl/.

[55] Transcriptomes of 1000 fishes [EB/OL]. http://www. fisht1k. org.

[56] UK Biobank [EB/OL]. http://www. ukbiobank. ac. uk/about-biobank-uk/.

[57] Wallis C. How gut bacteria help make us fat and thin [J]. Scientific American, 2014.

[58] Wang W, Krishnan E. Big data and clinicians: a review on the state of the science [J]. JMIR Med Inform, 2014, 2(1):1.

[59] Welsh J. Our favorite genome sequence studies [EB/OL]. 2012. http://www. livescience. com/20647-favorite-genome-sequence-studies. html.

[60] Whitcomb D C. What is personalized medicine and what should it replace? [J]. Nat Rev Gastroenterol Hepatol, 2012, 9(7): 418-424.

[61] Yue G H. Recent advances of genome mapping and marker-assisted selection in aquaculture [J]. Fish and Fisheries, 2013, 15(3):376-396.

[62] Zardavas D, Pugliano L, Piccart M. Personalized therapy for breast cancer: a dream or a reality? [J]. Future Oncol, 2013, 9(8): 1105-1119.